DATE DUE

AP 5'99			
AG 5'99			
AG 8'02			
DE 9'03			
MY 1 2 '08			

VIETNAM: DAWN OF A NEW MARKET

By the same author

THE RAMPANT DRAGON
SYNERGY: JAPANESE COMPANIES IN BRITAIN
CHINA: THE LAST GREAT MARKET
SINGAPORE: THE GLOBAL CITY STATE

About the author

GEOFFREY MURRAY has spent over 25 years in the Far East as a business consultant/journalist/analyst, including 16 years in Japan and five years in Singapore. More recently, he has spend several years in China pursuing both research and writing. He is an associate and visiting lecturer at the Centre for Pacific Rim Studies, John Moores University, Liverpool, and is author of *China: The Last Great Market* (1994) and *Singapore: The Global City State* (1996). He is also a contributor to *Business, Trade and Economic Development in Pacific Asia*.

VIETNAM: DAWN OF A NEW MARKET

Geoffrey Murray

ST. MARTIN'S PRESS
NEW YORK

VIETNAM: DAWN OF A NEW MARKET

First published in the United States of America in 1997

Printed in England

ISBN: 0-312-17390-3 (Cloth)
ISBN: 0-312-17392-X (Paper)

Library of Congress Cataloguing-in-Publication Data

Murray, Geoffrey, 1942—
    Vietnam : dawn of a new market/ Geoffrey Murray.
        p.   cm.
    Includes bibliographical references and index.
    ISBN 0-312-17390-3 (cloth). — ISBN: 0-312-17392-X (pbk.)
    1. Vietnam—Economic conditions. 2. Vietnam—Economic policy.
    3. Investments. Foreign—Vietnam.   I. Title.
    HC444.M87 1997
    3318.9597—DC21

97–23013
CIP

Contents

Foreword

It TOOK me almost 30 years to make a return visit to Vietnam, where I began my career in Asia as a foreign correspondent for Reuters News Agency in 1966. But in that time-frame what history and what changes had taken place! To name a few of the key events: the Vietnam War finally brought to a close with the fall of Saigon in 1975; four years later, in 1979, Vietnam's invasion of Cambodia led to its isolation from the international community while the severe economic hardships that existed were exacerbated by lack of access to international aid and extensive foreign trade; then there was the remarkable political U-turn in the mid-1980s from a strict Socialist centrally-planned economy to an era of economic reform in which market forces would be allowed reasonably full play; and, finally, total reconciliation with the international community, culminating in membership of the Association of Southeast Asia States (ASEAN) and the establishment of diplomatic relations with the United States. Vietnam is once more open to trade and investment and many foreign businessmen have already taken full advantage of the opportunities on offer. All these events will be dealt with in some detail in the ensuing pages of this work.

This, it should be stressed, is a business book, not the nostalgia-tinged reminiscences of a former war correspondent. Nevertheless, a few personal impressions can be mentioned here as a preliminary to the discussions to follow. In researching this book, I flew first to Ho Chi Minh City, formerly Saigon, capital of the old South Vietnam, which had been my base in the mid-1960s. To me, the most remarkable aspect was the discovery that 'Saigon', the old Saigon of the war years, was still very much alive and well. Admittedly, the gaudy bars packed with GIs that were such a blight on central Tu Do Street (now Dong Khoi) and surrounding areas, had disappeared, but other landmarks remain remarkably untouched.

The Continental Hotel, made famous in Graeme Green's *The Quiet American*, was almost the same — although the famous old verandah bar open to the street had been glazed in; the Caravelle Hotel across the street, where I had lived for a year, looked exactly as I had known it three decades earlier. The nearby US military information office, site of the famous 'five o'clock follies' — daily 5pm briefings for the world press corp — had been absorbed into the Rex Hotel next door and become the 'Paradise' coffee shop. Meanwhile, the old US Embassy on Le Duan Boulevard is a gaunt, empty building awaiting renovation — still sporting the famous rooftop helicopter pad where the final American evacuation took place in April 1975. These are superficial changes, however. Along with all the bustle of commercial life spilling out across the pavements, the ingenuity of people trying to make a dollar any way they can, and the incessant roar of traffic, mainly motorcycles, from dawn to late night on the streets, the war veteran returning today could easily wonder whether he had ever been away.

Equally significant is the fact that there are no signs of bitterness, no hint of recriminations. The war is history, it is time to move on. Responding to polite questions about whether the visitor has been to Vietnam before with a wry admission that, yes, he was here 30 years ago, the Vietnamese interlocutor inevitably smiles and passes on — or asks with genuine interest what are one's impressions of the country today.

Visiting Hanoi, one is impressed with a thriving city of colour and excitement, with few reminders of the terrific pounding it took from American bombers in the 1960s and early 1970s. The only evident symbol of the past is the outer wall of the 'Hanoi Hilton', where downed American pilots were imprisoned during the war, but this only hides a construction site where a 22-storey hotel, service apartment and office block is being erected. At the Revolutionary Museum, one can see a record of 100 years of struggle for national independence that include some of the horrific images of the Vietnam War with which people of my generation are so familiar. But even here, the final few rooms of the almost-deserted museum are devoted to more hopeful aspects — the reunited nation's renewal and drive for prosperity. And attitudes here as well, although somewhat stricter than the south, are becoming more relaxed as time goes by.

So the past is the past. The emphasis in all conversations now is on today, and tomorrow; the drive for economic development, the problems to be overcome, the need for foreign help, the determination to overcome any obstacle.

In 1966–7, when I was last in Vietnam, there was hope on the 'allied' side that the war was being won; but it proved to be a false hope. In 1996, there is hope again, this time on the Vietnamese side, which I believe is not only genuine but can be fulfilled. The prime purpose of this book, therefore, is to look at the evidence that justifies this hope, and see how realistic it is. It will cover the road to economic reform the Vietnamese suddenly took a mere 10 years ago and the vast distance that has been covered since. It will record the many frustrations, and in some cases shattered hopes, of those foreign businessmen who decided to enter this unknown market as soon as the door opened. But while detailing the very real grievances that some investors have, it will also seek to provide balance by looking at the question each time from the Vietnamese as well as the foreign side — if there are problems, are they being recognized and is something being done about them? And, ultimately, it will seek to come to some conclusions as to Vietnam's chances of achieving its ambitious goals, and the prospects for the potential foreign investor now wondering whether this is the right time to take the plunge.

This is the third in a series on key economies in Pacific–Asia, begun in 1994 with *China: The Last Great Market* and followed in 1995 with *Singapore: The Global City State*, and adopts the same format in blending the past, present and the future. It can be read either as a connected socio-economic study or as a practical textbook where the reader can dip in and out as specific interests dictate regarding day-to-day business negotiations and operations in Vietnam.

Each chapter begins with a list of key points to help the reader locate areas of specific interest — supported by a detailed contents list — which can usually be found in the text under indicative cross-heads. The aim throughout is to provide a comprehensive overview. More specific detail on key areas is contained in various appearances for those who require it.

The target audience for each one of these books is fairly broad. It is naturally aimed at giving the businessman and potential investor information that will help determine whether Vietnam is really where he or she should be. But the structure also allows for consideration of broader socio-economic issues which will be of interest to both the academic and student, and even the general reader who simply wishes to become better informed about one of the world's most economically dynamic regions.

In conclusion, I would like to make a few brief acknowledgements to those who have given me much valued assistance with this book. First, my thanks to the Vietnamese Ministry of Foreign Affairs Foreign Press Centre, which arranged such an excellent programme of interviews for my visit in April and May 1996. Especially, I wish to acknowledge the contribution of Mr Nguyen Thanh Tam, my guide and interpreter, who provided me with many valuable insights into Vietnamese thinking. The many people who gave me so much of their time in the various interviews are mentioned in the text, and so I will not repeat their names here but will only express my gratitude for their frankness and patience in answering my questions. Apart from that, I would like to thank Audrey Perera, my co-author on the Singapore book, who tracked down valuable information on the Vietnamese economy published in the republic which was of considerable help.

Geoffrey Murray
Beijing,
December 1996

1 A Fresh Start

NEW ERA BEGINS

AT 5 P.M. on 28 July, 1995, an army brass band blared out *Tien Quan Ca* (Soldiers of Vietnam, March Forward), and the flag of the Socialist Republic of Vietnam — gold star on red background — was raised outside a conference hall in the Brunei capital of Bandar Seri Begawan. Vietnam had become the seventh member of the Association of Southeast Asian Nations (ASEAN), joining Brunei, Indonesia, Malaysia, the Philippines, Singapore and Thailand to form an economic bloc of 420 million people. 'You are just across the water from us, [but] for too long we have been distant strangers,' declared Brunei's Foreign Minister Prince Mohamed Molkiah.

Also in 1995, after years of argument over the 'missing in action' issue, the United States agreed to normalize its relations with Vietnam. The latter also concluded a substantial agreement with the European Union, paving the way for an extension of trading

1

relations, and began serious attempts to warm up relations with its giant neighbour, but traditional enemy, China.

In all these developments, there is a real sense of a fresh start after 125 years of turmoil and bloodshed that virtually sapped Vietnam dry. The flag-raising ceremony in Bandar Seri Begawan was a symbolic moment tinged with some irony — ASEAN having been founded a quarter of a century ago partly as an anti-Communist bulwark against a seemingly expansionist North Vietnamese war machine.

Vietnam's membership of the regional grouping — which will eventually include Burma, Cambodia and Laos — is, in the short term, a political exercise; mutual economic benefits are a long way off given the gap in economic development. Illustrative of the chasm: Vietnam has a per capita gnp of $220.[1] just a quarter of the $880 for the Philippines. Singapore, meanwhile, has reached a level of over $22,000. Even with a population 25 times that of Singapore, Vietnam has an overall economy just one quarter of its size.[2]

More important, in the short term, is that after years of virtual diplomatic and economic isolation Hanoi has joined the mainstream. Alone, it would have struggled to have its voice heard on the world stage. As an ASEAN member it will have considerably more clout in international affairs. Expect to hear a lot more from and about Vietnam in the years ahead.

As one Asian diplomat in Hanoi observed: 'The Vietnamese realize that [the ASEAN connection] will strengthen their bargaining power at international level. They'd rather pin their hopes of a multilateral setting than a bilateral one in which they may be at a disadvantage,' particularly in dealing with China over territorial issues such as the disputed ownership of the Spratley Islands in the South China Sea. At the same time, however, ASEAN needed to include Vietnam in order to have any hope of achieving its ultimate goal of peace, stability and prosperity in Southeast Asia.

There is a growing sense within the region now that an important step has been taken forward in creating a multi-polar structure for promoting the idea of Pacific Asia taking the lead in promoting global economic well-being in the twenty-first century. Inter-regional cooperation is already apparent through the emergence of such arrangements as the Singapore-Indonesia-Malaysia Growth Triangle, the Greater Mekong Area Sub-Regional Cooperation, the ASEAN Free Trade Zone, and the broader Asia-Pacific Economic

Cooperation (APEC), some of which are bound to overlap and eventually be merged.

Those with vision see a three-centre Asia emerging with a delicate balance between Japan, the current Asian economic power, China, the emerging giant, and a restructured ASEAN sharing the responsibility for building and maintaining the momentum of growth and creating a stability long lacking from the area.

In the long term, Vietnam will play its full role in this. For the moment, looking at ASEAN membership in purely economic terms, the road ahead looks difficult. Concerns that lower tariffs and a more open economy will leave them exposed to formidable rivals among Asia's competitive tigers have already been expressed by Vietnamese businessmen. 'Many businesses are very worried about surviving or being competitive even in the domestic market,' says Pham Chi Lan, Secretary General of the Vietnam Chamber of Commerce and Industry (VCCI).

Vietnam produces similar commodities and manufactured goods as other ASEAN countries at a time when it is facing more than enough strains in trying to shift from a command economy to a market system. 'Businesses are still not ready for this event,' says Thai Van Hung, vice director of the Shoe and Leather Association. 'Besides lack of capital, technology and infrastructure, we don't have capable management who know international laws and trading rules. Unless we prepare well it will only be the Vietnamese firms who suffer.'

But others see closer relations with Vietnam's more developed neighbours as a dose of medicine that may shake up moribund sectors of the economy and put the country on the path to global export competitiveness. Diplomats believe pressure from ASEAN could help prise open the Vietnamese economy, where, as will be discussed in due course, businesses have to navigate a maze of regulations and tariffs which tend to protect weak state industries often at the expense of undermining the growth potential of the private sector.

State industries, with massive infusions of government capital, may have given some of the neighbouring economies a jump start, but most have long since moved on to a far greater reliance on private business initiative. If Vietnam continues to hang on to heavy reliance on its state-owned enterprises, this could prove a barrier to achieving smooth integration in the future.

Economist Do Dc Dinh draws up a list of advantages and disadvantages for ASEAN membership. What seems to emerge is that disadvantages today may become advantages tomorrow, and vice versa. But overall the balance is towards the good.

On the credit side, Vietnam is coming out of its shell into what has become an extremely dynamic region epitomized by the example of the 'Four Tigers' — the Newly Industrialized Economies (NIEs) of South Korea, Taiwan, Hong Kong and Singapore — and now 'mini-Tigers' such as Malaysia and Thailand. Economic policy-makers can learn from the successes and failures of these countries to cut some corners to accelerate the catch-up process. However, these other countries began their economic expansion at a time when the big markets of the United States and Europe were open to them.

Vietnam will not for the moment enjoy these same privileges,[3] and, in addition, there is very limited access to the Japanese market. To compensate, however, there is the new guaranteed access to ASEAN. Alone, none of the regional economies offer a market to compare with Japan or the United States, but together they offer a potential 400 million customers — in pure numbers at least, more than the European Union. Eighty per cent of Vietnam's exports now go to its neighbours — a fortunate arrangement compensating for the loss of exactly the same percentage previously shipped to the former Soviet Union [see below].

There is a potential for long-term economic synergies within ASEAN, as more advanced members of the club such as Malaysia, Singapore and Thailand can relocate their labour-intensive manufacturing in Vietnam, which has a large work force and is endowed with natural resources — as two other Asian 'tigers', Taiwan and South Korea, have already done in becoming among the leading investors in Vietnam today.[4]

But Do Duc Dinh says this is less significant than it might have been a few years ago. 'When the emerging economies of Asia began their advance 30 years ago, cheap labour was definitely the big advantage. But the percentage of labour in any product today is much less than it was before.'

ASEAN membership has probably come earlier than either Vietnam or the regional group expected, pushed ahead by political forces and a desire to keep the momentum going. In recognition of this, Vietnam has been granted an important concession allowing it to lag behind other members by three to five years in reaching a target of drastic import tariff reductions — down to an average level of five per cent — under the Common Effective Preferential Tariff scheme which is part of an ASEAN Free Trade Agreement (AFTA) by 2003.

ASEAN diplomats admit they are taking a risk in allowing the Vietnamese to move at their own speed, but see the group's strength in its flexibility — an attribute that will be tested even more when Cambodia, Laos and Myanmar join later, creating the danger of a two-tier organization such as threatens to emerge in the EU.

WHAT IS VIETNAM? WHO ARE THE VIETNAMESE?

There are two questions that might be asked at this stage in the discussion: what is Vietnam and who are the Vietnamese? The answers are complex. It is a country with a fragile economy, but with a battle-hardened people ready to endure great hardships. It is a country whose government has epitomized for years ideological hardness, but has also demonstrated the most remarkable pragmatism. It is a country built on fierce national pride, but demonstrating a ready openness to accept new, foreign ideas. It is a country that can change fast — witness, for example, the transformation from 1986 when the rice harvest was so poor parts of the country faced near famine, climaxing decades of food deficiency at least in the north, and the fact that the country was the world's third largest rice exporter in 1989.

History tends to show that no country can achieve economic development in isolation. Superior economic performance normally has been achieved by those countries which have been more open to external relations as opposed to those which have been inward-looking and isolated.

In a short space of time Vietnam has emerged from neo-isolation into the full glare of international attention. Much of the isolation was imposed on it by political developments — isolation from the United States, its potential largest market and most generous aid-giver, by post-war bitterness, exacerbated by the US-led embargo by Western countries due to Vietnam's 1979 invasion of Cambodia [only ended with the 1991 signing of a UN-sponsored peace accord]. Even given the ideological rhetoric from Hanoi, it is doubtful the Vietnamese would have chosen self-imposed isolation in the post-1975 period.

But economic development cannot be the result of external economic relations alone. It has to do first and foremost with internal willingness to find the right path towards economic development. And the fact is that the economic progress achieved by Vietnam since the mid-1980s reforms have been carried out largely 'without external funding and assistance and implemented even while major fundamental changes in external economic relations were taking place.'[5]

Until the collapse of the Soviet Union and its East European allies in the late 1980s, these members of the Council for Mutual Economic Assistance (CMEA)[6] had accounted for over half of Vietnam's total exports and three-quarters of its imports, often through barter or on subsidized credit terms. All this came to an abrupt end. 'Credits were stopped, old loans demanded settlement and trade took place on a hard currency basis.'[7] Allied with an already existing lack of foreign aid and investment due to the Western embargo, this was a heavy blow.

Drastic steps were needed, and were taken. They will be discussed in detail in the next chapter. Here, it will only be necessary to note some of the results. Vietnam's economic planners can claim some genuine success, even if many problems still remain, and many of the impressive numerical gains are due to starting from a very low base. Inflation that was running at levels up to 500 per cent in the mid-1980s has largely been tamed (down to 12.7 per cent in 1995, and with the government determined to try and bring it down to a single digit as soon as possible)

Before 1998, Vietnam was importing about half a million tonnes of food to make up for domestic deficiencies. In that year it became self-sufficient and began exporting in 1990 – reaching a total of two million tonnes in 1995. The gross domestic product has been growing at an annual rate nudging 10 per cent, while industrial growth has averaged 14 per cent. For many years there was a three to one imbalance in imports over exports and trade was negligible – as recently as 1988 it was only $800 million (although it was mostly in roubles). In 1995, exports grew 28 per cent to $5.5 billion, while imports rose 20 per cent to $7.5 billion. In 1996, the expectation was that both figures would grow by a further $1 billion.[8]

Only in 1993 has there been a trade surplus – a modest $68 million – but that was before a big surge in foreign direct investment, which is benefiting the country as a whole, but ensures that the trade imbalance continues for the foreseeable future as the growing number of foreign-invested joint ventures are forced to import much of the machinery and materials needed for their operations due to lack of availability within Vietnam or because of quality problems.

Foreign direct investment has grown from $300 million in 1988, when the door was first thrown open, to $7 billion in 1995,[9] with a similar amount expected in 1996. There are now some 1,500 foreign-invested projects underway or planned involving commitments totalling around $20 billion.[10]

In the late 1980s, the economy was still dominated by state-owned enterprises, whose poor performance in general held back the country's advancement. These have now been reduced by half to some 6,000 firms — although still far too many — while the private sector has grown from some 3,000 companies to 27,000. By the year 2000, estimates Hoang Van Dung, Deputy Director General of the Chamber of Commerce and Industry in Hanoi, there will be some 200,000 private companies, accounting for 60 per cent of employment and making the major contribution to industrial output — 58 per cent to the state sector's 42 per cent.[11]

But, at the same time, as I will explain shortly, every effort will be made by the government to ensure that the state sector continues to play a key role. For, as the Chinese have insisted, without that what is there left that genuinely can be called socialism?

But it would be wrong to place too much stress on ideology, which might suggest rigidity and refusal to change. There is certainly a problem with bureaucratic obtuseness that can make life miserable for the Vietnamese businessman as much as the foreign one. But Do Duc Dinh argues that this should not obscure what he calls the 'great change in the thinking of the people. We've had great success in food production, curbing inflation, achieving high industrial growth and large gains in the annual gdp. But one success is moving all these things: the radical changes in thinking at all levels. Nobody sticks with an idea if it is not working.

'The good thing is that we are moving forward. It's one step at a time and sometimes we stumble, but the movement continues. There are choices between moving fast or slow. If we find a positive element in one of our experiments we move fast. If we find something that seems negative, we slow down again to reconsider. But we're always moving forward.'

Le Dang Doanh, President of the Central Institute for Economic

Management in Hanoi, is even more blunt. 'There will be continuous economic reform, bold administrative reform and a strong determination to succeed. We have no use for self-adulation. The Vietnamese people are too proud and too intelligent to follow any suicidal policy no matter what name it is given.'

THE WAY FORWARD

The great need in the next five years is to build on these gains as rapidly as possible. The government estimates it needs to spend $50 billion in that period to develop its economic programme and create the necessary infrastructure that will bring in more foreign investors. At least $20 billion of this will have to come from foreign direct investment, with additional large injections of capital from international donors such as the World Bank and Asian Development Bank.

But if all goes well, state economists are predicting that the gdp will continue to grow at annual rates of between nine and 10 per cent, industrial growth will maintain a steady momentum of around 15 per cent and exports will expand at about 24 to 28 per cent a year – although it is doubtful if will further narrow the trade gap in view of the continued strong need. Strenuous efforts, meanwhile, will be made to bring inflation down to a single digit and stabilize it there.

In the draft political report to the National Congress of the Communist Party of Vietnam[12] by the Central Committee, the economic policies for the period to the end of the century were described as concentrating resources on 'developing the state sector [to continue playing the leading role as the foundation of economic development] in such key areas as social and economic infrastructures, financial, banking and insurance systems, important production, trade and service establishments and a number of enterprises undertaking tasks related to national defence and security. State enterprises in general shall be medium or large sized, equipped with advanced technology, run with efficiency and able to generate large budget revenue [for reinvestment in basic infrastructure development]'.

Economist Le Dang Doanh explains that what this means is that all the government's efforts will be concentrated on supporting a few hundred of the biggest state-owned enterprises in areas where the private sector is considered too weak to be able to offer a proper service. This will include the development of about 100 multi-sectoral 'conglomerates'. Small and medium-sized state companies, if they are to survive at all, will be 'equitized' in order to raise investment capital in place of the old government subsidies.

Even more significant, at the time of being interviewed, Mr Doanh was working on changes to the company law which would allow foreign investors to buy shares in the equitized public companies rather than be totally dependent on joint ventures or wholly-owned operations for gaining a niche in Vietnam. Foreign stakes of up to 30 per cent would probably be permissible.

But he for one is sure that a lot more has to be done to liberate the potential of the private sector. And even the Central Committee document acknowledged that in the long run the 'individual and small owner economy has an important position. Assistance should be given to it to [. . .] guide and motivate individuals and small owners to step by step join in cooperatives voluntarily, or to work as satellites for state enterprises or [state] cooperatives.' It is the Party's policy to 'encourage a private capitalist economy to invest and operate long-term businesses, protecting ownership rights and legitimate interests.'

In a separate document on political policy, it is also stated that 'application of the market mechanism requires enhancement of the managerial capability of the State and, at the same time, fully-fledged autonomy of economic units, with a view to promoting the great and positive impact of the market while preventing, restraining and overcoming its negative aspects. The State controls the market with laws, plans, policy mechanisms, economic leverages and the physical strength of the State economic sector.'

In concrete terms, the documents stress greater priority will be given to the manufacturing sector, particularly the processing of staple and non-staple foods, production of consumer goods, as well as 'engineering, electronics and informatics.' Key targets in the year 2000 are production of one million tonnes of sugar, 500 million metres of fabrics, 300,000 tonnes of paper, 16 million tonnes of crude oil, 3.7 billion cubic metres of natural gas, 30 billion kWh of electricity, 10 million tonnes of coal, 16–20 million tonnes of cement, two million tonnes of steel, 1.2 million tonnes of phosphate, and 950,000 tonnes of urea.

Given present worries about social instability caused by rising unemployment, the initial emphasis will be on labour-intensive industries, where Vietnam can utilize its current significant cost advantage. At the time of writing, the unemployment rate in the cities was up to seven per cent — about 2.6 million people — but nearly 40 per cent, or some six million people, in the countryside. What the Vietnamese want to avoid at all costs is the situation facing China, where millions of jobless peasants are roaming the country in search of work and creating great strains of the social fabric of the big cities towards which they naturally gravitate.

The nation's current work-force numbers 29.5 million in the countryside and 9.2 million in the cities, and is growing steadily. And addition, the amount of land available for agriculture and improved methods of cultivation, actually mean that a rural work-force of only about 19 million labourers are actually needed. What to do with the rest?

Unemployment is unlikely to come down unless something drastic happens to the economy. The Ministry of Planning and Investment is coordinating a joint effort involving a wide range of government ministries and agencies, the national Job Provision Programme, which aimed to create 6.5 million new jobs between 1996 and 2000. Of this, foreign aid and foreign direct investment will probably contribute at most around one million jobs.[13]

But if Vietnam is to follow the example of the other developing economies of Asia, labour-intensive industries are only a temporary phase. It will gradually be looking for ways to increase mechanization and move towards a high-technology-based economy at some stage around 2020. But long before then, it is hoped, Vietnam will have followed the lead of Japan, and then South Korea, in developing a strong shipbuilding industry, taking advantage of the country's long coast and a number of superb natural harbours, along with a major petrochemical industry to take advantage of recent offshore oil and natural gas discoveries, which through exports could fund a great deal more economic development.

INVESTMENT SHOPPING LIST

The Central Committee, says the ultimate goal, in which foreign investment will play an increasingly important role, is to create a modern industrial-technical base, a society with high standards of material and intellectual well-being so that within 25 years Vietnam will have become an industrially advanced country with per capita gdp eight to 10 times the present level.

In Chapter 3, I will examine the role of foreign investment in some detail. At this stage, however, I would merely like to outline what the Vietnamese are expecting from FDI. According to the official plan, this will focus on several key sectors:

- **Oil and gas** is expected to take about a quarter of all investment in an effort to develop commercial offshore fields to raise the country's total oil output to 20–25 million tonnes, and pave the way for the development of petrochemicals, lpg and fertilizer,
- **Industrial zones and high-tech industrial parks**: 11 of these are planned, scattered around the country with an initial budget of some $2 billion. The high-tech parks will mainly concentrate on consumer goods production at the beginning. The emphasis will be on exports, although investors will have access to the growing domestic market.
- **Infrastructure**: this sector is expected to attract around $5 billion, divided between road and rail building and upgrading, port development, energy and telecommunications.
- **Construction materials**: related to the preceding item, another $1.2 billion is needed to build up more plants to produce cement, glass, fire bricks etc.
- **Heavy industry**: the sector wants to attract around $7.6 billion in registered capital in the next five years, mainly for investment in mining, steel, fertilizer, vehicle and motorcycle assembly, electrical generators, electronics, shipbuilding and ship repair.
- **Light industry**: around $2 billion is required for upgrading existing factories and building new ones.
- **Agriculture**: No figures have been given, but the sector wants to attract investment in sugar, forestry products, banana, rubber and coffee plantations, silk production, and meat processing.

Vietnam wants to expand its exports to $10 billion by the end of the century, compared to $1.97 billion at the start of the decade.[14] Exports, however, are hobbled because the country does not process much of what it produces, being forced to export the raw materials that other countries turn into value-added products. It has a great variety of agricultural commodities that many countries do not have, but these are mostly exported as raw materials and other countries then process them.

Hoang Tich Phuc, head of the Import-Export Department of the Ministry of Trade, says the government's main tasks are:

1 Re-organize exporters. 'For example, until recently, there were too many rice exporters competing so fiercely for business that prices fell dramatically. Vietnam's exports were being sold at rock bottom prices as a result.'
2 Substitute raw material exports with increased exports of processed commodities. 'That means we need to make a list of important commodities like crude oil, seafood, leather garments, rice and invest in new processing technology.'
3 Prepare a comprehensive trade law.
4 Regularly 'correct' exchange rate policies, export credits and the tax system.
5 Improve procedures regarding the granting of licences and quotas.

When set against the massive amounts of foreign investment pouring into China, for example, Vietnamese needs seem somewhat modest, and the money once spread around will look a bit thin. But it is probably about the limit of what the country can digest at this time. As will be discussed in Chapter 3, there are a number of problems associated with gaining foreign investor confidence, including the continued lack of a proper legal and regulatory structure that is fully transparent, corruption and inefficiency at certain levels of the bureaucracy, and lack of sufficient investment incentives.

Government officials promise that all these areas are being worked on. The Law on Foreign Direct Investment, the Company Law, the taxation system, are all being overhauled and new policies being developed covering key issues such as capital contribution, land rights, investor protection, and investment incentives, especially for capital moving into currently disadvantaged areas. The Ministry of Agriculture and Rural Development, for example, is working on plans to offer tax reductions for foreigners willing to put their money into under-developed areas of the countryside.

The amended Law on Foreign Investment was approved by the National Assembly in October 1996. A key element in this was that issuance of the necessary operating licences will continue to be centralized in the Ministry of Planning and Investment (MPI) in Hanoi. This ignores the pleas of many local authorities for at least partial decentralization to speed things up.

But according to one source, 'decentralizing the licensing authority would lead to inequitable competition harmful to the national interest'. Not to mention removing a potential source of bribery! The time period for granting licences, a source of great distress to many investors up to now, will be reduced so that in some cases in can be weeks, even days, rather than months.

Also on the horizon is a possible move to allow foreign-invested enterprises to move from being limited liability companies, prevented from raising capital by issuing shares, to gain this right through becoming joint stock companies. If nothing else, this will be an important step forward in overcoming the present deficiencies in the Vietnamese financial environment and bring the country more into line with international practice.

It is too early to say whether these measures, assuming they are all adopted, will be sufficient, but the will is certainly there at the highest level to make the changes work to the advantage of both Vietnam *and* the foreign investor.

CONCLUSION

The main thrust of this book will be to look at this issue of foreign investment — where it comes from, how it is being used and where it needs to go in the future. There will also be an examination of whether the goals the Vietnamese have set themselves are feasible, as well as looking at the challenges that they face in integrating with the rest of the world economy.

Before moving on to review these topics in detail, however, I believe it will be helpful to go back briefly and sketch in Vietnam's history from the late nineteenth century up to the current decade of the 1990s.

Readers interested only in practical tips about how to do business in Vietnam may feel this is a chapter that can be skipped. But it is important in understanding what has moulded Vietnamese thinking today, as well as demonstrating the toughness, pragmatism and willingness to change direction quickly in order to achieve strategic goals that has epitomized the Vietnamese ever since they began their struggle for national independence.

NOTES

1. Although, as will be discussed later, there are great discrepancies between the poor countryside and the richer cities which hold the average back. In 1995, for example, the per capita gdp of the capital Hanoi was $650. Communist Party officials in the city say this will reach $1,100 by the turn of the century. In Ho Chi Minh City (Saigon) meanwhile, the growth will be even more spectacular – to $1,500. [Figures from the Vietnam News Agency and the *Saigon Times Daily*, 8 May 1996].

2. World Bank estimates, 1995.

3. There was hope that a trade agreement with the US could be negotiated by the end of 1996, despite some lingering political opposition within Congress, leading perhaps in a year or two to the granting of Most Favoured Nation (MFN) treatment which would really open up the American market to Vietnamese goods.

4. See the appendices for a breakdown of current foreign investment on a country-by-country basis.

5. Thant, M and Vokes, R. 'Vietnam and ASEAN: Near Term Prospects for Economic Cooperation', in *Vietnam's Dilemmas and Options*, Than, M and Tan, J. (eds.), 1993, Singapore, Institute of Southeast Asian Studies, p241.

6. Formerly COMECON.

7. Thant and Vokes (op.cit. pp241–2).

8. Figure provided by Hoang Ngoc Cu, Deputy General Director of the Foreign Investment Department, Ministry of Trade.

9. This was 84 per cent more than the previous year.

10. Only about half of this amount has actually been disbursed so far.

11. Although in Chapter 2, I will discuss the reservations that some analysts have about the government's willingness to allow the private sector to take such a dominant economic role.

12. Released in April for public discussion in advance of the meeting in June. An English translation was transmitted by the official Vietnam News Agency in two parts on 10 and 11 April.

13. *Vietnam Investment Review*, 8–14 April 1996.

14. Compared to other countries in the region, Vietnam has a long way to go. In 1993, the population was 70 million and export turnover was $3 billion. Comparative figures for other countries: Thailand: 57 million and $33.2 billion; South Korea: 43 million and $79 billion; Taiwan: 20 million and $86.5 billion; Malaysia: 18 million and $43.5 billion. (Figures supplied by the Ministry of Planning and Investment).

2 From War to *Doi Moi*

HISTORY OF RESISTANCE

VIETNAM as we know it today first began to emerge when land-hungry Viets spilled out of the crowded Red River valley around Hanoi before the fifteenth century, going on to defeat the Cham people on the central coast and colonizing the south in the seventeenth and eighteenth centuries. A Vietnamese sense of identity has been honed by resistance to French rule from the late nineteenth Century to 1954, and to subsequent American support for the government of South Vietnam, as well as China's ever-present attentions and interference, friendly or unfriendly — a highlight of the Historical Museum in Hanoi being a record down the centuries of Vietnamese triumphs over invading Chinese armies.

China also shaped Vietnam peacefully, imparting attitudes the Vietnamese were classically taught to prize. These included Confucian values like respect for hierarchy, order and rules, a taste for

15

learning, a sense of decorum and a regard for sincerity, courage and perseverance; and, for balance, Buddhist ones such as compassion, flexibility and equality. Whether this ethical cocktail was suited to independence and national renewal was much debated by Vietnamese intellectuals a century ago, wondering why Vietnam had fallen under French control. Some blamed their country's decline on outmoded Confucian–Buddhist values, some on modern Western ones.

On 31 August 1850, a French naval squadron came and attacked Da Nang, on the central coast of Vietnam, unleashing a war of colonial conquest which raged on and off from 1858 to 1884, until the total annexation of the country was complete. The French were attacking a decaying feudal monarchy. The Nguyen dynasty, which had mounted the throne after having repressed a large-scale uprising, restored a feudal regime in its most backward forms, with an administrative apparatus essentially composed of a body of mandarins trained in a very conservative and ritualistic Confucian ideology, and supported in the villages by the landlord class. Peasant revolts continued unabated, and with its rudimentary technical means, the royal court could not rule effectively over a territory stretching more than 2000 kilometres.

It was in the south that the French made their initial incursions, first conquering and setting fire to Da Nang, before turning their attention to Saigon, which they eventually took along with the surrounding provinces. From there they began a piecemeal takeover of the country gradually moving north to the strategic Red River delta and Hanoi. The French Indochina empire eventually comprised five elements – Cochin China, Tonkin and Annam (now all part of Vietnam), Cambodia (a kingdom which had once controlled a good part of southern Vietnam) and Laos.

For a quarter of a century after the French invasion, there was a fierce struggle to control the unruly local inhabitants. Incipient guerrilla wars were waged – poorly-armed local protagonists often winning tributes from their French opponents for their bravery and tenacity unto death – as a forerunner to the much bloodier and more determined campaigns that eventually led to the US-backed South Vietnam being forcibly reunited with the North in 1975.

The French sucked the colonies dry. Vast rubber, coffee and sugar plantations were established by colonist traders for export. Indigenous industries were ruthlessly crushed in favour of imports from

France. Crushing taxes and land requisition for the colonial administration's favourites created a vast army of landless peasants for
eventual conscription into French-run mines and factories both in
Vietnam and in France itself – but also creating in the process a fruit-
ful breeding ground for the new Communist dogma that swept out
of Russia with the October Revolution of 1917 and seized on by a
young Vietnamese revolutionary Nguyen Ai Quoc (Ho Chi Minh).

France certainly occupied and had administrative control of Vietnam, but it never, in the phrase much beloved of American
propagandists in the 1960s, managed to 'win the hearts and minds'
of the vast majority of the people. There was, at best, sullen acquies-
cence, interspersed with sporadic uprisings put down with great
loss of life and helping to swell the jail population in such hellholes
as the island of Poulo Condore.[1] The only Vietnamese who actively
cooperated with the colonial administration were, by the frank
admission of French officials, nothing but 'intriguers and rascals,'
and 'a bunch of low-class ruffians'.[2]

Another layer of misery was added in the Second World War, when
the Japanese moved south from their attempt to conquer China to
develop a joint administration of Vietnam with the French Vichy regime.
What that meant in practice was Vietnam contributing food, cash
and other resources to the Japanese war effort. With the military collapse of Japan, Ho Chi Minh saw an opportunity to declare Vietnam's
independence.[3] It was short-lived. Under an arrangement with the victorious allies, Vietnam was briefly divided at the 16th parallel, with
Nationalist Chinese troops given the task of disarming the defeated
Japanese north of this line, and the British doing the same in the south,
as a prelude to the return of the French colonial administration.

Fighting soon broke out, and with France pouring in troops in a
determined effort to regain its colony, Ho Chi Minh was forced back
into the jungle to continue the guerrilla war. With the advent of the
cold war, and ever hardening anti-Communist attitudes in Washington with the fall of China to the Communist armies of Mao Zedong
and the outbreak of the Korean War in which the Chinese partici-
pated on the North Korean side, the United States now slowly
began to be sucked into the Vietnamese abyss.

At first it was military equipment to aid the French in their struggle to
put down the growing insurrection; then, with the stunning defeat at
Dien Bien Phu in 1954 that forced France to abdicate all further
responsibility for its erstwhile colony – now temporarily divided at

the 17th parallel, with Ho Chi Minh triumphant in the north – the Americans found themselves propping up an 'anti-Communist' regime in the south. There is little need to discuss what happened next, for the Vietnam War – or Second Indochina War as the North Vietnamese call it – is ingrained in the memories of a whole generation.

All that needs to be said, as it impinges on this story of Vietnam's attempts to promote economic development, is that by the time the country was forcibly reunited with the entry of the North Vietnamese army into Saigon on 30 April 1975, Vietnam was devastated. An estimated 14 million tonnes of bombs and shells had torn apart the land (20 million bomb craters in the south alone); much of the foliage had been stripped away by napalm and chemical defoliants, with the threat of long-term genetic damage caused by the latter. There were one million military war dead and another 1.5 million civilian dead. Sixty per cent of southern villages were destroyed; in the north every major town and provincial capital, along with main roads, railway lines, bridges, ports and industrial facilities had been repeatedly bombed. Fifteen million people were rendered homeless throughout the country.[4]

But the end of the Vietnam War was not the end of the killing. Within the next four years, Vietnam found instead embroiled in battles with two of its Communist neighbours. Border disputes with the Pol Pot regime in Cambodia eventually led to the Vietnamese invading that country and installing a friendly government in Phnom Penh. This led to deteriorating relations with China, which eventually decided that Hanoi needed to be taught a lesson – PLA forces spilling across the border in the far north of Vietnam in 1979, but quickly being forced to retreat with heavy losses as the battle-hardened Vietnamese army showed its mettle.[5]

The Vietnamese are a proud people who do little to puncture the notion that they are special. They like to play up the 'David and Goliath' mystique to outsiders and perhaps half-believe it themselves. How else would they have dared to take on France, America and China?

'Perhaps it is living next to China that has led the Vietnamese, like younger brothers everywhere, to prefer negative attention to none. Whatever the reason, Vietnam has more stage presence that you would guess from the size of its population (75 million), its wealth (annual income $200 per head), and its military prowess (an ageing army and a few torpedo boats). If Vietnamese pride were just cockiness, ahead would lie hubris not riches. But Vietnam's self-assurance comes also from a down-to-earth feel for reality, from being able to look blunders in the eye and start over. 'Face', it is said, matters in Asia. Not in Vietnam, where being seen to be weak or wrong matters less than really being weak or wrong.'[6]

Historically, Vietnam's torments are fairly routine for the region. Almost every country in the neighbourhood has had fratricidal wars since 1945 — Burma, China, Indonesia, Korea, Malaysia. Each reached statehood under a nationalist banner — anti-colonial, anti-Japanese, pro-Communist or combination of these factors. All were poor at mid-century and have got far richer. The difference with Vietnam is that it all took so much longer.

But while US air power failed to live up to its pledge to return Vietnam to the 'Stone Age', the country's economic managers inadvertently made a good run at the task on their own. Vietnam, despite recent advances, still ranks among the world's poorest countries, in the same league as Ethiopia, Bangladesh and Mozambique. It even shares a dubious honour with sub-Saharan Africa as one of the last places on earth in the 1980s where masses of people were at risk of starvation. How could a nation that threw off the French colonial yoke and wore out the world's mightiest military machine find itself in such a fix?

A 1993 report by a panel of conservative American economists and Vietnamese expatriates, recruited by the Pacific Basin Research Institute and the Donner Foundation, offered some suggestions, among them a conclusion that an indefatigable will to sacrifice in the name of nationalism does not necessarily translate into economic success. After unification in 1975, Vietnam collectivized agriculture in the south along with nationalizing all manufacturing and most services. By even the government's admission, though, 'socialism building' was a disaster that left the war-devastated economy barely able to feed the nation.

Many thousands — some say a million — of southern soldiers, officials and intellectuals were sent to 're-education' camps after unification, while another two million people went or were driven into exile in the ensuing years of harsh rule, including many with the administrative and business skills vitally needed to rebuild a shattered economy.

These *Viet Kieu* (Overseas Vietnamese) are organized, particularly in America, and by Vietnamese standards they are rich. It has been calculated that they earned $17 billion after tax in 1994 — rather more than all the Vietnamese in Vietnam produced. Happily, some of this money is flowing back into Vietnam, and some of the refugees are now returning home to invest in new businesses.

Another loss to the nation were many of Saigon's Chinese traders, swept out in 1977–78 by a wave of anti-capitalism and xenophobia. In the otherwise bustling Cholon Chinese quarter of old Saigon, their bolted shops can still be seen. To the victims of this chauvinistic folly it was of little consolation that Hanoi's rulers were re-enacting a scene from history: in the early nineteenth century the Nguyen emperors, groping for national unity after civil war, had shackled commerce and harassed Chinese traders in the same way.

PRE-1980 POLICY

The Harvard-educated economist Nguyen Xuan Oanh — whose credentials are such that he was able to overcome the black mark of being a leading member of the southern administration during the war to take a leading role in rebuilding the reunited country[7] — describes the basic characteristics of the Vietnamese economy, like those of other socialist states, at that time as 'severe misallocation of natural resources and a serious neglect of worker motivation. The development strategy was driven by a heavy industry-orientated policy with deference to all costs.

'The misdirected, or rather suppressed flow of national resources represents a severe misallocation which nurtured inefficiency and low productivity. Coupled with a total lack of incentive to the workers, economic activities were gradually and severely curtailed. Sooner or later, the economy would grind to a halt.'

North Vietnam's model from the 1950s, extended to South Vietnam from 1975, showed the following few characteristics:

- The state determined all important economic activities of the entire country through a system of production plans and goods distribution; there were also strict regulations on pricing and interest rates.
- The state and the collectives constituted the foundation of the economy, the collectives being heavily subsidized in activities such as investment and credit loans and they quickly developed to become a sizeable part of the national economy.

- Large-scale private enterprises were not encouraged to expand further, but were singled out to be finally incorporated into either state or collective units.
- The market mechanism operated only in small businesses and the household economy (i.e. only part of the agricultural, handicraft and consumer goods retailing sectors). Many capital goods used for production were not allowed to be bought or sold on the market but were allocated by the state's planned distribution system.
- The state monopolized foreign trade. Due to historical circumstances, this trade was mainly with the Soviet Union and Eastern Europe through bilateral treaties. Foreign trade companies under state control would implement these treaties, and the profit-and-loss account of foreign trade was entirely taken care of by the state.
- The finance of the state was not separated from that of state-owned enterprises. The state undertook to compensate for losses incurred by these enterprises through subsidies, and when they managed to chalk up a profit, this was returned to the state budget. All productive activities were subsidized by the state through its provision of raw materials and other imputs of production, machinery, and equipment imported with aid funds and credit loans, and sold at low prices to the state-owned enterprises. For this reason, the budget deficits and foreign debt would have increased along with any increase in output.[8]

Such policies 'had helped the state to rapidly realize its goal of industrialization, and at the same time provide for the basic necessities of the population and help it tide over the aftermath of war. [They] were not, however, conducive to motivating individuals and companies to boost enterprising economic activities. [There was] no room for private individuals' creativity or dynamism'. At the same time, the policies were heavily subsidized by foreign aid that made up a considerable proportion of the state budget.[9]

The post-war economy from 1976 to 1980 was stagnant. Industrial production grew an average of 0.6 per cent a year, agricultural production gained 1.9 per cent. At the same time, the population was growing by nearly one million a year.

FALSE STARTS IN REFORM

In 1979, the first stirrings of reform were apparent with the introduction of a contract system in the agriculture. Essentially, this consisted of the government contracting an output quota with individual rice farmers instead of the cooperatives as before, with imputs provided by the State at pre-determined rates. Since private initiative and personal efforts were encouraged, output increased in a range of four to 10 per cent in the early 1980s, depending on local conditions, allowing the government to drastically reduce the substantial amounts of yearly rice imports.

As soon as the success in agriculture became apparent, the experiment was extended to other areas of the economy. Price controls were eased and enterprises permitted to sell to private markets once they fulfilled state quotas. Somewhat hesitantly, but no less significant, the reforms also aimed at eliminating subsidies for both consumers and enterprises, along with structural reforms to the banking system to free more cash for investment in key development areas.

But while the reforms led to growth, they also widened income differences between the north and the commerce-minded south, leaving the warrior half of the country with little to show for decades of suffering. At the same time, it became clear the initial reforms were not going to be far-reaching enough because, essentially, they were little more than adjustments to the state administration of wages and prices, side-stepping the workings of the market mechanism. Much reliance was placed on the effective working of both the Planning Commission and the State Price Commission

The result was that the use of State bank advances to finance an ever growing budget deficit, and indiscriminate bank credit to state enterprises led to an inflationary explosion which saw prices rising by annual rates up to 500 per cent. Rationing and subsidies were quickly reintroduced, leaving worker incomes in real terms probably lower than in the earlier years. With inflation running far ahead of bank interest rates, it was not surprising that this provoked a substantial draining of cash from the banking system. Starved of investment cash, enterprises began looking for surreptitious ways to retain revenue to keep themselves in business, rather than handing it over to the government as was required — thus worsening the State's indebtedness.

The price increases also destroyed the effectiveness of the contract system. The arbitrarily determined prices encouraged a siphoning off of essential commodities and factors of production to the free market, and encouraged exploitation by speculators. Much less essential goods were delivered to farmers, who were, however, required to pay for the imputs anyway because they had previously been incorporated in their production quotas. With farming incomes eroded, the result can be imagined: paddy-production fell once again and Vietnam faced another food crisis.[10]

TRADE BARRIERS

Foreign trade was another problem area. Firstly, it was almost non-existent, and, secondly, the trade that did exist was closely controlled, and stifled, by the central government. Hoang Ngoc Cu,[11] Deputy General Director of the Foreign Investment Department, Ministry of Trade, has no hesitation in admitting the main problem. 'Under the old system, the government exercised a trade monopoly. There was no way to create a favourable climate for trade to grow, no encouragement for the producer or the entrepreneur to develop their capacity. That's why the state-owned enterprises suffered heavy losses, which were partly disguised by subsidies. But what was happening was that the firms were forced to eat their own seed capital – the money that should have gone into acquiring fixed assets being swallowed up in wages and other day-to-day expenses.'

Another handicap was that there were several government agencies involved in handling aspects of trade, and they were not necessarily cooperating with each other. Mr Cu recalls: 'The Ministry of Foreign Trade would import certain machines, but for a variety of reasons these were not bought by the potential end user [whose interests, anyway, were supposed to be looked after by the Ministry of Supply Materials]. Yet the ministry continued buying more and more equipment, which ended up being stockpiled at great cost.

'Because domestic producers had no control whatsoever over the foreign markets, there was no way they could understand what was required, so they continued to turn out very low quality products which they were unable to sell. Toothpaste is one good example. For years, companies turned out products that were so bad nobody wanted to buy them at any price.'

According to another authority:[12] '[The] government managed foreign trade transactions through trade agreements with foreign governments. Institutionally, it had a dual foreign relations system, with separate procedures for handling trade transactions with convertible and non-convertible areas. Central planning authorities intervened directly to control all exports and imports with [Soviet bloc] countries according to five-year plans and annual protocols. These plans were to ensure that the state enterprises had adequate supplies and consumers were not short of supply either.

'The usual practice was that under the barter agreement there was a balance in trade since the currencies involved were non-convertible. Thus, traded goods were valued at fixed prices. The Foreign Economic Relations Ministry was responsible for the execution of the plans because it needed to ensure the fulfilment of export obligations. Targets for exports/imports were set by the ministries and localities, and actual transactions were executed by foreign trade firms under the jurisdiction of the ministries or provinces.

'This policy brought about the production of goods of inferior quality since exports to the [Soviet bloc] did not call for good quality and domestic firms had no incentive to produce quality goods.'

REVIVAL THROUGH *DOI MOI*

By 1986, famine conditions prevailed in some areas. Something drastic needed to be done. And the answer was: *Doi Moi* (economic renovation), of which the key policy elements were:

- Decentralization of state economic management and decision-making autonomy to state-owned enterprises in relation to production, distribution and financing.
- Replacement of administrative measures and controls by economic ones and, in particular, the use of market-oriented monetary policies to control inflation.
- Adoption of an outward-oriented policy in external economic relations. Exchange rates were allowed to float in response to market forces and interest rates were made responsive to market conditions; free gold import was allowed.
- Adoption of agricultural policies which allowed for long-term land use rights and greater freedom in marketing of products.

In addition, farmers could buy production inputs at mutually-agreed prices rather than pre-set contractual ones.
* Reliance on or acceptance of the private sector as an engine of economic growth.
* In trade, handing over the right to selected state-owned and private enterprises deal directly with foreign markets for both imports and exports in most products.

Politburo member Dao Duy Tung[13] summed up the change in this way:

'In the past, the model of building socialism as far as the economy was concerned [involved] two kinds of ownership, state and collective with a centrally planned mechanism. Now, Vietnam has transformed this into a multi-sectoral market economy, although the public sector still plays a management key role. Vietnam has decided to combine economic growth with social progress, the expansion of social welfare, encouraging people to make their fortunes legally and at the same time eliminate famine and alleviate poverty, improving education and health, reducing excessive subsidies and the slavish reliance on the state.'

In compliance with the strategy of shifting to a market economy, improvements are being made in the business environment, including the creation of so-called 'level playing-field' for all economic sectors regardless of ownership (although see below for more detailed analysis of this aspect suggesting that there is still a long way to go).

A *Law on State Enterprise* was passed to separate 'state social and commercial responsibilities' by establishing two different categories of state enterprises: commercial and non-commercial. The former are fully subject to competition from other sectors. They are given full management autonomy, and must be self-financing and accountable for the use of state assets. Competition and anti-monopoly legislation, meanwhile, were due to appear in 1996 to support the development of a competitive market economy.

Improving the performance of the state-owned sector through restructuring, management contracts, improved financial monitoring, clarifying state enterprise ownership issues are important issues now being undertaken. A new General Department for the Management of State Assets and Capital in Enterprises was established in 1995 for this purpose. Generally, state enterprise reform is a priority issue in the process of economic reform.

The question of the right mix of public and private sector remains a complicated one for Vietnamese planners. But according to Ha Dang, Head of the Department of Ideology and Culture of the Party Central Committee,[14] what the government is trying to achieve is a 'a multi-ownership economy' in which it will still retain a high degree of control, but it will be driving from the back seat, using more indirect means to control industrial and commercial activities such as taxation policies.

There are different types of ownership 'State ownership with state-owned enterprises, cooperative ownership with different forms of cooperatives, and individual ownership often in the form of small businesses and handicraft enterprises. There is also private capitalist ownership and state capitalistic ownership in two forms: joint ventures between the state and foreign or domestic capitalists.

'The distinction of economic ownership plays an important role in making appropriate economic, political and social policies. This distinction cannot be replaced by the distinction by types of scope of enterprises. The different types of ownership are legally equal but do not have the same role and position in the establishment of a new socio-economic regime. Each type of ownership, if properly used can contribute to build the socialist regime. This does not mean that all of them have the same socialist elements, and of course we cannot simply base it on the productivity of the type of ownership to consider it to have more socialist elements.

'State ownership, together with cooperative ownership, represents a more advanced production mode and should be constantly amended and developed. The state ownership sector must play the leading role, and together with the cooperative ownership sector it gradually forms the cornerstone for the national economy. Only by developing state and cooperative ownership of the economy can we create a firm ground for the new regime to develop, to take full advantage of our strengths to curb our weaknesses, to regulate and orient the develop of the others towards socialism.

'[But] we intend to promote extensively different types of state capitalist economies, being the direct joint effort between the state and private capitalist economy in nature, in order to create stronger positions and power for Vietnamese entrepreneurs to expand their business overseas and at the same time orient them towards socialism.'

ASSESSING THE RESULTS

Many parts of the country have been transformed by the new policies. Capitalism is thriving on the streets of both Hanoi and Ho Chi
Minh City (Saigon). The economy has moved from negative growth
to a rapid expansion at rates more akin to those enjoyed for years
by the other Asian 'tigers'. Gross domestic product has grown an
average of 8.2 per cent since 1991. It reached a record 9.5 per cent
in 1995, compared to 8.8 per cent the year before, mainly on the
back of rapid growth of construction, increased exports and industrial growth. Ho Chi Minh City, the country's engine of growth, grew
by almost 15 per cent, although Hanoi and the north in general is
catching up.[15]

In late 1995, the Ninth Party Central Committee Conference met to
consider the second five years of *Doi Moi*. According to Ha Dang,
head of the Department of Ideology and Culture of the Party Central
Committee,[16] the general conclusion was that 'we have overcome
our past economic crisis. Jobs have been created for more people.
The standard of living has generally improved. Above all, we have
brought about these achievements with our own minds and hands,
without aid from the socialist community as before.'

But there were still threats, inter-related and dangerous, that
could undo progress:

- The danger of lagging behind economically;
- Deviation from socialist orientation;
- Red tape and corruption; and
- Peaceful evolution.[17]

'The first threat of trailing economically behind our competitors is
important and has serious implications. Red tape and corruption also
include personal moral decadence. All these evils among part of
the Party members and officials have weakened the Party and the
state mechanism, eroding people's trust, distorting the implementation of new policies, and making fertile ground for 'peaceful
evolution'. There is always a dialectical relationship between opportunities and threats. Our strategy is to actively take advantage of
opportunities to develop rapidly and steadily, creating new positions
and power, at the same time making the best efforts to overcome
these threats to ensure smooth development of the nation.

'We are entering an era of industrialization and modernization.

The objective is to make Vietnam an industrialized country with an up-to-date infrastructure, appropriate economic structure, progressive production relations to suit the country's production capacity, high standards of spiritual and material life, stable national security and a richer and stronger equitable nation.

'The direction of future growth [. . .] involves developing and restructuring the economy towards industrialization and modernization, allowing a multi-ownership economy, continuing to renew the economic management mechanism, developing science and technology, education and training and building up an advanced culture while maintaining national identity, solving some social problems, national defence and security, external relations, national solidarity, promoting the people's role of ownership, and continuing the reform of the state mechanism. In short, perfecting the Socialist Republic of Vietnam.'

Despite all the brave talk, there are many causes for concern. A resolution issued by the Party Central Committee in early 1995 called for faster 'industrialization and modernization', a catchphrase reflecting growing concern over the country's ability to reach the ambitious target of doubling per capita income by 2000. The resolution added that Vietnam was facing 'acute difficulties' because of low economic growth, loose control of inflation, limited funding sources and increased competition – reflecting increased candour in the way policy-makers are dealing with the country's progress to a market economy.

And amidst an impressive list of achievements, it has to be acknowledged that the results of economic reform so far have been felt mainly in Hanoi and Ho Chi Minh City. In both cities, a growing class of new rich is enjoying increasing spending power. But they account for only a small percentage of the population. Most are still locked into the low-paying agricultural sector, where unemployment is increasing.

Hanoi's income per head in 1994 was around $600 a year, Ho Chi Minh City's $800. Income per head in the two poorest regions is a quarter or at best a third of that in or near the two big cities. Nghe An, between Hue and Hanoi, is a typically poor province, with income per head half that of the national average. The capital Vinh, shows scant signs of America's heavy bombing, but scars of backwardness are everywhere. The province has long produced people who want to change things one way or another: scholars, soldiers and rebels.

Ho Chi Minh came from there, while General Giap, who bested the French and Americans on the battlefield, was a near neighbour.

Vietnam's present worry is not so much that the south will outstrip the north economically, as that jobless people from provinces such as Nghe An will flood into towns in both the north and south creating social unrest similar to that already experienced in some parts of China by vast migrations of rural poor.

'The main issue is to get people out of the agricultural sector and into industry,' a Washington-based official at the World Bank's agricultural division says, pointing to estimates in 1994 that industry accounted for only about 20 per cent of gross national product.

There are also some worrying signs. Inflation has begun to creep up again — 17 per cent in 1995. Some economists are urging the brakes to be applied to the rapid economic growth to keep the indicator from climbing back up to the alarming levels of the recent past. Domestic savings contribution to the growth figures, an indicator of public confidence in economic stability, have more than doubled from the disappointing low level of 7.4 per cent in 1990. But this still compares very unfavourably with other countries in the region — China, for instance, with 35 per cent. Progress has been slow in mobilizing domestic savings, estimated in 1995 at about $2 billion, and channel them into the banking system where they can be used for national development because of a traditional public distrust of banks.

STATE SECTOR DOMINATION

While there has been an often chaotic rush towards an open market and competition in some sectors, the bulk of the economy remains within state control. Only three out of an estimated 6,000 public concerns have so far been sold off. Much of the banking sector is insolvent and unable to harness funds for development. The formation of a proper capital market is still some way off. 'Vietnam has a serious case of indigestion,' says one foreign fund manager. 'There is about $400 million in foreign funds plus several hundred million in various private ventures, ready for investing in the country. But it can't be absorbed. The system is just not ready for it.'

The government is often remarkably candid about mistakes and shortcomings. Prime Minister Vo Van Kiet says the economy is trapped in a 'vicious circle' of low productivity, low savings and low investment.

'In the areas of budget management, financial and monetary controls and taxes there are many hot spots, many problems,' he told the National Assembly. Politically, the Communist Party remains at the apex of power and there is no sign of it wanting to loosen its grip. A comprehensive state security apparatus remains firmly in place, largely unchallenged by the economic reform process.

There seems little possibility of any significant reversal in the *Doi Moi* process, but there could be a change of emphasis. Some badly needed changes have been made. In October 1995, for example, several ministries and state bodies were amalgamated in an attempt to streamline government and cut down red tape. The Finance Ministry now manages the property and finances of all state-owned companies in an effort to make them more competitive.

Nguyen Minh Tu, a director at the Central Institute for Economic Management, explained that the consolidation of powers in a single ministry will enable the government to set up a common legal framework. It should also lessen the conflict of interest some ministries have in acting as managers and regulators of the same firms. The move however, was resented and resisted by the authorities forced to give up their control, as state-owned companies were an important source of income for them.

Even if Mr Kiet and others succeed in pushing through more reforms, there is no guarantee that they will be adopted throughout the country. Although much of the economy remains centrally controlled, local Peoples' Committees and other pressure groups often have considerable power and at times contradict central government decrees.

According to government figures, state-owned firms account for 85 per cent of fixed assets and employ an even higher percentage of skilled workers. They provide at least half the state's tax revenues. Both the Communist Party and administration are now hammering out plans to lead the country into the next century and the future of Vietnam's remaining state enterprises lies at the heart of it. Further reform is likely to be both a crucial political and economic factor as the leadership faces questions of control and ideology while treading its careful path to market-oriented socialism.

In mid-1994, the government formed 14 conglomerates in sectors such as electricity, cement, textiles and rubber. 'The idea is to increase competition and to form more commercial establishments,' says Professor Phan Van Tiem, chairman of the State Enterprise

Reform Committee, admitting that Vietnamese policy-makers are using the *chaebol,* the big business conglomerates that powered South Korea's economic development, as a role model. But there are suspicions that the conglomerates may be just another way of strengthening state control over the economy.

At the same time, the professor points to the government's rigorous campaign to eliminate loss-making enterprises — which, at the beginning of the decade, accounted for an estimated 40 per cent of the 12,500 then existing. By 1995, the number was down to just over 6,000, of which only about nine per cent — some 500 enterprises — were still admitted to be losing money. Of the firms closed, about 3,000 were actually merged with other firms who, thus, took on some of the outstanding debts and partially avoided the problem of redundancies. Only 2,000 were completely dissolved. But, foreign economists are quick to point out that most of the operations closed down were small, town-based units in the provinces, with little economic clout even collectively. Less than 300 were based in Hanoi or Ho Chi Minh City — about 200 to 300. Professor Tiem confirms this, but adds that this imbalance was due to peculiar factors that existed when the state-subsidized economy was still in place.

'Many provincial enterprises found it easy to set up even though they were really not up to what we would now consider an acceptable standard. At that time, we also had a two-tier pricing system consisting of state-subsidized and market-oriented prices. State subsidies, for example, made some materials cheap. So, provincial enterprises bought them and sold them on the open market at a profit, enabling a lot of businessmen to become very rich. When the subsidy period stopped, such enterprises were faced with the rules of the market, and could not survive.'

Apart from the 500 survivors still in debt, the professor also admits that there are many potential lame ducks on the borderline. 'Many are small, capitalized at under $100,000. They cannot afford to update their technology and with poor technology, they can't compete. It's a downward spiral.'

Vietnam has a bankruptcy law, it has proved difficult to administer. One problem is a stipulation that some enterprises, especially in sectors regarded as strategically important, can enjoy a 'pre-bankruptcy' period until it is clear they cannot settle their debts. Many firms now want this status creating a heavy administrative burden as their cases are investigated.

At the same time, enterprises are normally considered unable to settle their arrears when their outstanding debts exceed their legal capital. But in Vietnam, 'legal capital' has not yet specified under law so that the courts have nothing on which to base a decision. Companies might be able to settle their debts if they were allowed to sell parcels of the land they occupy. But the land is not part of their legal capital, hence they do not have the right to sell it. In short, liability has not yet been clearly defined.

Given all the problems, why the continued insistence on the state sector maintaining the leading role? Professor Tiem's argument is that the private sector is not strong enough to take the leading role in key areas. In addition, Vietnam does not want foreign investors to dominate. 'We want to be independent in our development.' But, it isn't mandatory that the state control 100 per cent of operations even in key areas, as long as it has a controlling stake. It only has to take overall control of the operation. For example, the state can control 51 per cent and the private sector can take the remaining 49 per cent. So the concern is run as a joint-stock operation.

'The law does not restrict the private sector,' he insists. 'In fact, we give the state and private sectors the same opportunities and encouragement.' But the World Bank, for one, is not convinced. While acknowledging that much has already been done, it warns that Vietnam must demonstrate more enthusiasm for developing the nascent private sector if economic growth is to be sustained. 'Despite the success of state enterprise-led industrialization since 1991, a strategy based on developing large capital-intensive state enterprises, protected from foreign and domestic private competition and concentrated in selected 'strategic' sectors, will not deliver the kind of industrialization Vietnam needs,' it said in its 1995 country report.

The private sector is restricted to small-scale enterprises such as food processing, and the manufacturing of garments and some consumer goods. Local private businessmen complain of an unequal playing field on which they are forced to compete with privileged state-owned enterprises. 'The state sector has a monopoly of many high profit businesses like telecoms, real estate, export and import but the private sector is not allowed to take charge of them,' says Bui Huy Hung, president of Vietnam Joint Stock Commercial Bank, one of a handful of share holding banks. 'This is the biggest obstacle to the transition to the market economy.'

Privatization is certainly not a word one hears readily in the corridors of power in Hanoi. When cadres or the state press refer to the need for change in the state-owned enterprises, they prefer to talk of 'reform', 're-organization' or even 'equitization'. Whatever the word used, the first steps of reform undoubtedly have been taken. In theory at least, almost 6,300 state firms now stand free of state subsidies and are accountable to one office rather than a ministry. They can form boards of management, prepare audited accounts and, if they fail, face bankruptcy.

Pockets of dynamism now exist. State firms like Hanoi Electronic, a fast-growing ambitious consumer goods manufacturer, go from strength to strength in a string of joint ventures with Daewoo of South Korea. But for the most part, the bulk of the remaining firms stand like creaking monoliths run by managers who are simply unmotivated. There are huge cement and textile enterprises whose real balance sheet strength and land holdings remain a complete mystery. Cash-flow analysis, marketing and distribution strategy remain largely non-existent, fuelling fears of corruption.

But some Vietnamese economists privately believe 'hidden subsidies' remain, while many worry about the poor use made of new-found profits, often squeezed into housing cars and poorly thought-out investments. 'I was shocked to find a basic lack of entrepreneurism and enterprise,' said a foreign analyst, one of the first accountants with a state firm as part of a United Nations Development Programme aid project. 'It was black-hole management going from day to day. There was no strategy, no reporting systems, even before you tried to create balance sheets and value assets.'[18]

For foreigners, reform is also a key prerequisite. The bulk of industrial resources lies with state enterprises after years of Communist central planning. Here lie potential joint venture partners, access to land and the work-force. Here are the indicators of the economic vitality of the country. Progress in turning key state firms into respectable open firms of an international standard will be crucial for the formation and later success of any future stock market.

'Ultimately, there is no reason why the bulk of these enterprises cannot be cleaned up and auctioned off,' says Bradley Babson, the World Bank's resident representative in Vietnam. 'They know they want the state enterprises efficient and transparent, but how far they want to free them from the state is perhaps another matter.' Much is expected of an equitization scheme, whereby companies are evaluated and shares sold to managers and workers. An initial scheme involved three state firms in Ho Chi Minh City — a shoe factory, a transport firm and a refrigeration engineering shop — and the government as been trumpeting all three as unqualified successes.

'Rank and file workers have been retained and the enterprises have all increased their salaries paid to workers,' says state economist Le Dang Doanh of the Central Institute for Economic Management. 'Thus the reality . . . is completely different from the initial worry by some workers that there would be mass redundancies after the implementation of equitization. The enterprises all reported substantial progress in increasing levels of economic performance, output and export value, profits and contributions to the State budget.' Such words are likely to please both reformers and those with an interest in protecting the working class.

PRIVATE SECTOR STRUGGLES

During a question–and–answer session at the World Economic Forum in Ho Chi Minh City in April 1995, the Swiss–based organizers invited local business people, both state and private, to meet a delegation of business leaders from some of the largest corporations in Europe and America. One of the foreign businessmen asked a State Planning Commission official in which areas of the economy the private sector would be encouraged to participate. Instead, the official started to list the areas of the economy in which the state, 'for various reasons' would retain control, such as aviation, telecommunications, heavy industry, oil and gas. The official concluded his inventory with a short pause, then said '. . . and any other major area of the economy'. The largely Vietnamese audience of about 100 businessmen burst into laughter.[19]

The private business sector is growing in strength and number, but the playing field remains far from level. 'Our government considers the private sector an instrument to do things the government cannot reach. They forgot the private sector is a major instrument of a market economy,' said Nguyen Tran Bat, President of Investconsult, a private business consulting company.

Private businesses pay a profit tax rate of between 30 and 40 per cent, compared to 10 to 25 per cent for foreign invested firms. While 'one door' service for foreign investment has a long way to go, local business people chafe about red tape just as foreigners do, especially about licensing. Procedures for private companies to import machinery and raw materials are also more difficult compared to state companies. Freedom to travel abroad for business is restricted. Other than high-ranking government officials and select directors of large state companies, few private Vietnamese citizens actually have passports. Of these, an even smaller percentage are allowed to travel abroad on business trips at a moment's notice.

The Foreign Investment Law that opened the economy to foreign companies was passed in 1987. A domestic investment law that irons out some of the problems for local businesses exists, but the vital guidelines on how to implement the law have not followed. Access to credit is the most difficult hurdle. Few local banks are pursuing project finance for foreign joint ventures or state companies, much less for private companies. According to Lo Ky Nguon, director of the private Viet Hoa Commercial Joint Stock Bank, state policy dictates that borrowers must own assets, in particular houses or land, worth nearly twice the value of the loan before it can be granted.

For most private companies this is impossible. 'We can't get good loan conditions from private joint stock banks and it's very difficult to get any kind of loan from state commercial banks,'[20] says one vice director of a private furniture manufacturing company in Ho Chi Minh City. Many private companies such as this resort to simple connections to secure the loans they need.

The furniture company was established in 1992 when eight investors put up their private homes as collateral in order to receive a loan of $250,000 from Vietcombank, which they then used to buy a majority stake in a joint stock company. They were able to get the loan due to a long-standing relationship with the bank's directors rather than anything else. A similar loan from a private joint stock bank would not have been feasible because the interest would have been too high, says the vice director. Access to foreign currency loans is also difficult because the state sector gets the lion's share.

The fallout from Decree 18 issued in February 1995 requiring all land use right holders to pay rent to the state for the land they hold, hit private companies harder than state ones. The intrinsic problem with land use rights has been assessing the value of land in order to establish a collateral base for loans. Due to the uncertainty surrounding land policy, land use rights held by private individuals and companies tend to carry a lower value than those held by state companies. Thus, it is more difficult to secure loans using land as security and in addition private companies now have the unexpected costs of paying rent on their land.

Another problem is that private companies cannot donate land to a joint venture unless it's in agriculture, whereas state companies can. In effect, this makes it less attractive for foreign investors to enter into joint ventures with private firms, as they cannot contribute what Vietnamese entities normally bring to the table: land.

In summary, therefore, a chronic shortage of capital, complex and extortionate taxation, poor transport and distribution networks, regular power blackouts, a lack of modern management know-how and marketing skills, can all be identified as major constraints on the bright prospects for Vietnamese enterprises, whether in the public and private sector. And many of the Vietnamese businessmen's complaints strike a sympathetic chord with foreign investors as well.

This much can be gleaned from a survey, 'Assessment of Firm Responses to the New Business Environment,' jointly undertaken in late 1994 by the State Planning Committee and Japan's Overseas Economic Cooperation Fund, and which probed 101 sample enterprises from Hanoi and 107 from Ho Chi Minh City. These companies represent Vietnam's key industries: textiles and garments, chemicals, food processing, metallurgy, mechanical engineering, electrical and electronics excluding power generation. Among them, 85 were managed by the central government, 63 by local authorities and 60 by private businessmen.

A majority saw limited access to finance as their most serious impediment. They complained about formalities and cumbersome paperwork, collateral requirements and scarcity of funds at banks. After the money question, outdated machinery and equipment, insufficient marketing and transport facilities, further constrain their operations.

Apart from these obstacles, the enterprises complained about 'unhealthy competition' resulting from rampant smuggling and a lack of proper regulatory mechanisms — too heavy-handed where they are not needed and inadequate where they are essential. The government has pledged to reform its clumsy, time-consuming bureaucracy that breeds abuse and corruption. The companies' attitude that their growth rests in the government's hands underscores the urgency of administrative reform.

Almost half the state enterprises surveyed identified the state budget as their main source of finance, with bank loans next. With state funds off limits and bank loans difficult and expensive, 71.7 per cent of private companies said their business activities are mainly self-financed. A total of 80.8 per cent surveyed in Ho Chi Minh City say they rely on themselves, while the percentage in Hanoi is only 64.7 per cent. Some enterprises also look at joint ventures as a financial source of their business.

But private businesses do manage to prosper despite many difficulties. Take the Huy Hoang Joint Stock Company, founded in 1979 in Ho Chi Minh City with capital of $1,000 as a family cooperative by a former army engineer officer Le Van Kiem and his wife to produce colour powder for construction and various simple plastic appliances. In 1990, it became a joint stock company in anticipation of the eventual establishment of a stock market where it could raise capital by selling equity.

Today, it has an annual turnover of $10 million; Mrs Kiem supervises the output of two of the country's most successful garment manufacturing factories, devoted solely to the export market, while Mr Kiem oversees a growing construction business that has gained a toehold in some of Ho Chi Minh City's key infrastructure projects, as well as participating in the development of the local property market. It has tourist development projects in some of the South's best beauty spots, along with joint ventures with Korean and Indonesian companies, producing large diameter steel pipes and ceramic sanitary equipment respectively. The garment side contributed 70 per cent of revenues up to 1994, but in 1995 this sank to 50 per cent, with the construction business providing 40 per cent. In future, according to Deputy Director General Nguyen Van Hoan, the construction side will become the biggest earner.

The fact that both the company's founders previously worked for the government may have helped it prosper, even if only through knowledge of how to use the system to advantage. Another plus is that it contributes significantly to the government's job creation programme in the rapidly expanding former southern capital, employing more than 3,000 people. Thirdly, it is a significant foreign revenue earner.

But although it is one of the few private companies allow to carry out direct exports, it cannot expect any precedence over state-owned enterprises when it comes to the allocation of quotas for tightly-controlled key foreign markets [see chapter 4]. Huy Hoang's quota covers only 40 per cent of its total capacity, but it overcomes the problem by channelling the remainder through state companies who sell it on to the end user for a small commission.

As far as Mr Hoan is concerned, despite the company's success, it is still cannot get equal treatment with its state-owned rivals. 'Whether state or private sector, we are all contributing to national economic development, we are all providing much needed jobs at a time when available labour force is expanding rapidly. So we should be treated the same.'

But does a foreign company in Vietnam fare any better? That question will be answered in the next chapter

NOTES

1. Figures released by the colonial administration, disputed by the Vietnamese as being far below reality, for the years 1929 to 1931 give some flavour of the way dissent was handled. 1929 – 1,490 people arrested, three sentenced to death and 399 given long jail sentences. 1930 – 689 people killed during strikes and demonstrations, 2,693 people detained, 83 sentenced to death, 543 sentenced to a total of 3,648 years of imprisonment and 780 deported to such places as Guyana. 1931 – 1,419 people arrested of which 1,023 condemned to life imprisonment. Cited in *Contemporary Vietnam* by Nguyen Khac Vien. Red River Foreign Languages Publishing House, Hanoi 1981
2. Op. cit, p27.
3. It is intriguing to think how history might have been changed if the United States had taken the offer of friendship proffered by Ho at this time. Among the many touches of irony, given the later bloodshed, is the fact that Ho adopted the American Declaration of Independence virtually word for word.
4. Vien (op. cit. pp265–6).
5. It took 12 years for relations to be normalized once again, and it was not until 14 February 1996, that they finally reopened rail routes between the two countries closed by the 1979 clash.
6. Fawcett, E. 'Make money not war'.*Economist* Vietnam supplement, 8 July 1995.
7. Dr Oanh was Governor of the Central Bank of Vietnam (1963–67), and acting Prime Minister of the former South Vietnam in 1966–7. From 1983 to 1994, he was an adviser to the Vietnamese Government on economic policy, contributing many of the ideas on economic restructuring which have now been adopted. He now operates mainly from the private sector as a business management and international finance consultant with a number of multinational clients.
8. Adapted from an analysis by Vu Tuan Anh, director of the Vietnam Institute of Economics 1989–93, in a monograph *Development in Vietnam. Policy Reforms and Economic Growth*, 1993, Institute of Southeast Asian Studies, Singapore.
9. Ibid, pp4–5.
10. I am indebted to Dr Oanh for his comments which were of immense help in producing an analysis of this period.
11. Interview, 29 April 1996.
12. Than, M. 'Vietnam's External Trade 1975–91', in *Vietnam's Dilemmas and Options*. Than, M and Tan, J. (eds.), 1993, Singapore, Institute of Southeast Asian Studies.
13. *Vietnam Economic Times*, January 1995.
14. Interview with the *Vietnam Economic Times*, August 1995.

15. *Financial Times* survey 13 November 1995.

16. Quoted in the December 1995 issue of *Vietnam Economic Times*.

17. This phrase is also much used in China. It refers to 'hostile forces operating under the guise of peace which undermine the nation' and specifically relates to ideas prevalent in the West that as the market economy develops and capitalism takes a firm hold in places like China and Vietnam, Communism or socialism will naturally wither away in time without the need for any military or political threats to be applied. This is why the leadership in both countries place so much emphasis on the development of a market economy under firm socialist control.

18. Torode, G. 'Hanoi's hard road to the private sector', *South China Morning Post Weekly Edition* 17 September 1995.

19. See the *Vietnam Economic Times*. August 1995, p14.

20. Recognizing this, the World Bank announced it would open project offices in Hanoi and Ho Chi Minh City to help provide capital and technical help to the private sector, following a request from Vietnamese business leaders. The bank also said it was setting aside $40 million out of new concessional loans being granted to Vietnam in the 1997–99 period specifically to provide technical assistance to small businesses. [AFP, 10 May 1996].

3 Overview of Foreign Investment

DOUBTS APPEAR

'THERE will be doubters. There will be cynics. There will be resistance in some quarters,' declared a foreign joint venture partner at a ground breaking ceremony for a construction material project.[1] Hardly the language of a confident foreign investor in Vietnam, but seemingly representative of a growing mood of dissatisfaction among foreign investors.

Judged purely on the figures, however, it would be hard to imagine that anything is wrong. Foreign investment *promised* – as opposed to actually being put to work – up to the end of 1995 was in excess of $17 billion, against $10 billion the year before.

A World Bank report published in October 1995, however, put this into better perspective. It estimated the actual inflows of foreign investment funds in the first 10 months of the year at $812 million. For 1996, the projection was $919 million. Most of it went into oil and gas, hotels and tourism, property and light industry.

Vietnamese officials have been disappointed by the level of foreign interest, especially as, according to Finance Minister Ho Te, the government is hoping to attract enough foreign investment and create enough domestic capital to more than double per capita gross domestic product to $480 by the end of the century.

By July 1995, of the total foreign investment 58.1 per cent was from Asian countries other than Japan, 14.4 per cent from Western Europe, and 10 per cent from Japan.[2] Since President Bill Clinton removed the US trade embargo in 1994 and normalized relations in August 1995, American interest has increase ninefold and now accounts for 5.9 per cent of the investment funds. Taiwan and Hong Kong topped the table, as they have done since their arrival in Vietnam in the early 1990s.

However, for both the foreign investors and the Vietnamese, there has been a sharp and sometimes painful learning curve. Joint ventures have gone awry, investors have pulled out of high profile projects and there have been shrill calls in the Vietnamese media for curbs on the amount of equity foreign investors are allowed to take in joint projects. In April 1995, the independent Swiss customs inspection agency Societé Générale de Surveillance (SGS) parted company with its Vietnamese partner because of alleged irreconcilable differences. Two Japanese companies abandoned plans for a supermarket and a steel venture respectively in Hanoi after the Vietnamese told them that they were investing too little. There is an increasing tendency for foreign investors to explore wholly-owned foreign ventures as a way of avoiding what they see as the more troublesome joint venture route.

Investors also appear to be doing a lot more complaining. Capricious decisions by provincial authorities are still too common in an environment where the government is supposed to make and implement policy. Despite regular assurances that red tape is being cut and overlapping investment laws disentangled, investors see few tangible results. One automobile company given a manufacturing licence, for example, then spent many months trying to settle the key elements of parts import quotas and foreign exchange guarantees. Each specific request required a special seal for which a special application has to be made. 'Everyone is far more concerned about the stamp than the substance of the request,' a company executive complained.

Another potential foreign investor in Hanoi, seeking a representative office licence as a forerunner to factories to manufacture and export rice products, was still waiting to get started after seven months and 40 signatures on various documents. Other businessmen moan about a restrictive and complicated tax regime, a closed land market, high rents on top of all the bureaucratic complications and delays.

Brewing companies, which account for a large slice of foreign investment are also disgruntled. Although they are allowed to convert revenues in the local currency into hard currency for profit repatriation, they need a guarantee in writing from the central bank in order to do so. Such guarantees last only about six months, which is hardly a recipe for long-term planning.

Worries have surfaced over Vietnam's eagerness to accommodate as wide as possible a range of competing investors into one sector, ostensibly in the interests of free market economics. In the car industry, to be discussed in more detail in the next chapter, Vietnam so far has licensed 12 foreign manufacturers. The fear is that, having allowed so many investors in, none will be able to carve out a profitable piece of the small Vietnamese market. Industry experts warn that fierce competition as well as neighbouring Thailand's ambitions of producing cars by the year 2000 could force some car makers out of Vietnam after having made heavy investments with no chance to recoup.

Some observers believe the strategy could be deliberate. 'It seems they prefer letting everyone come in and compete, watching who's going to survive and shaking hands with the winner,' says Shiro Sadoshima, counsellor at the Japanese embassy in Hanoi.

INVESTOR WITHDRAWALS

One of Australia's biggest companies, Wesfarmers Ltd, which pulled out of proposed major investment to distribute and market liquefied petroleum gas, saying the country needed more time to develop its legal and corporate infrastructure. Managing Director Michael Chaney said the decision was influenced by significant changes in

Vietnamese taxes and import duties and changes in the conditions of its joint venture agreement with the Vietnamese Petroleum Import-Export Corporation. 'It proved very difficult for us in the end,' he told a news conference in Perth, Western Australia. 'They changed the rules and a number of conditions after we'd signed the joint venture agreement, and we didn't feel we could make a viable venture of it in the short to medium term.'

The venture was to have seen Wesfarmers, through a wholly-owned subsidiary, distribute LPG in three Vietnamese cities with a view to expanding nationwide. Cheney said the venture would have required a capital investment by Wesfarmers of $10 million in the first 18 months, but it had pulled out without making any of the investment. 'One of the expectations we had, or the undertakings received, was that there wouldn't be any more licences issued in some of these areas, but subsequently a number of licences have been issued. Import duties have been imposed, tax rates were higher than we anticipated and a number of other things like that occurred. While we think the industry has there has some potential in the long run, I think for us it is too early.' According to reports in the Australian press, the central government had increased the project's tax rate from 15 to 25 per cent and raised the import tax on LPG from one to 30 per cent after the joint venture agreement had been signed.

Asked how Wesfarmers' withdrawal would be viewed by other potential Australian investors in Vietnam, Chaney said: 'The message is that the Vietnam economy is at an early stage of development. They don't operate in quite an orderly a manner as they do in countries further down the development path. We always understood that, which is why we took a fairly low risk approach to it, with zero capital imput to date. But I think everyone recognizes the potential is there in a few years' time when certain things are more defined like laws — property laws and corporate laws — and people have more experience in operating in a commercial environment. There are a lot of companies up there operating and they will all have different experiences, and eventually there will be a data base of experience that maybe will have an influence.[3]

Wesfarmers was the second West Australian firm to run into problems over the definition of contractual exclusivity. In mid-1995, beach sands miner Westralian Sands acknowledged that the Vietnamese and Australian Governments had been called in to try and settle a conflict with its joint-venture partner in Ha Tinh province.

However, Westralian Sands' troubles actually started in November 1994, when the company discovered that its Vietnamese chief executive, also a senior cadre in the Ha Tinh People's Committee, was selling ilmenite from the joint venture mine to a Japanese buyer. Ilmenite is a black sand used in paint, plastic and paper production.

In 1992, Westralian Sands became the first foreign resources company to secure a mining licence in Vietnam. Part of the licence condition was that the company form a joint venture with a local partner — the Ha Tinh Provincial Government — and that the Australian company retained sole marketing rights to ilmenite mined in the province. Westralian had a 60 per cent holding in the venture, the Ha Tinh Provincial Government 30 per cent and the Vietnamese government's Department of Heavy Industry 10 per cent.

According to Vietnamese press reports, in the months following the discovery of the ilmenite sale to the Japanese there were five separate 'investigations' conducted by the Ha Tinh authorities, the joint venture had its bank accounts frozen, its executives were threatened, and placed under house arrest by the local authorities. Eventually, the central government's Department of Internal Affairs became involved in the 'investigation' process. If that was not bad enough, the Ha Tinh Government accused the Australian company of withholding financial information and urged Prime Minister Vo Van Kiet to revoke the joint venture licence.

The Vietnamese partner claimed that the Australian side had taken no steps to fulfil part of the original bargain to construct downstream rutin and pigment plants. The main goal, it arguued, had been not to exploit the mineral sands for export, but to create value-added processing within Vietnam — in the fifth year of operation for the rutin mill and the ninth year for the pigment plant.

Westralian Sands' senior executives continually stressed that the company had not breached any contract agreements and was committed to the project. Until the depth of the dispute became known, the joint venture had been seen as a good example of a small to medium-sized mining companies and foreign investors succeeding in Vietnam.

By May 1996, it seemed that the venture would collapse. According to the *Vietnam Dau Tu Nuoc Ngaoi*,[4] a weekly newspaper published by the Ministry of Planning and Investment, Westralian Sands had 'unilaterally suspended' production, although the licence had not yet been revoked. The newspaper said that in a letter dated

2 May, the Australian company had cited a worsening financial situation that could lead to early bankruptcy, following the failure of the two partners to resolve their differences.

The key issue appeared to be control of the project, in which the Australians held a 60 per cent stake. A symptom of the difficulties was a decision by the board of directors — three Australians and two Vietnamese — to borrow $4.5 million from the Australia New Zealand Bank in Hanoi to import mining equipment using the ilmenite reserves as collateral, according to a report in the tri-weekly *Tien Phong* newspaper[5] of the Communist Youth League, the imports cost three times the world price. When the equipment arrived packed in 48 crates at Haiphong port last year, the shipment was stopped by the customs on the grounds that it lacked the correct documents. At the end of April 1996, the local government fined the Australian company and warned that if the equipment was not removed from Vietnamese territory within 30 days it would be confiscated.

The ilmenite project was the first project in Ha Tinh, one of Vietnam's poorest areas, to attract foreign funds, so that its failure is likely to deal a major blow to the Hanoi government's hopes to channel more foreign capital into the less well-developed areas.

After the plight of Westralian and Wesfarmers became public, another Australian company, Portman Mining, decided to opt out of its $8 million silica sand operations in the central coastal region of Da Nang, while Arcourt Resources, a subsidiary of Australian Gold Development, stopped work on a project in Song Lo province, near the Chinese border, pending a local investigation. The official line from Portman was that its Da Nang venture was not financially viable, but reports from Vietnam claim that the Vietnamese mining company also had serious problems with its joint venture partner.

Portman abandoned the project only six months after receiving its joint venture licence. Originally, the licence had been for 30 years, but when the paperwork returned from the SCCI, the contract period had been reduced to 20 years, the area to be mined had been greatly reduced and a guarantee to allow Portman to mine a second substantial adjacent site had been scrapped. The company later discovered its local partner was negotiating with a Taiwanese company to mine the second site.

The provincial investigation into Arcourt Resources' Song Lo project followed local farmers' claims that the company was going to mine their rice paddies. Australian Gold Development insisted the farmers' refusal to allow access to some of the most prospective terraces were contrary to the official licensing agreement. On top of that, and after the agreement was signed, Prime Minister Kiet issued a directive that rice paddies should not be part of foreign investment projects. Around the same time, Arcourt discovered that illegal dredgers were operating near its site and that they had found gold, and the joint venture was hit with a $60,000 tax bill for equipment Arcourt was assured was tax exempt.[6]

The main problem for all these companies was that although a draft mining law had been prepared — ironically with Australian assistance — parliament was slow in giving it approval. This omission, however, has now been rectified.

But problems for foreign investors are not confined to the resources sector in Vietnam. Plans by a leading global eye specialist and lens manufacturer, Fred Hollows Foundation, to build a world class lens factory near Hanoi also ran into trouble. The lens factory was the centrepiece of the Australian Foundation's expansion into Vietnam, aimed at eradicating cataract blindness through introducing state-of-the-start surgery and lens implants. The Foundation's director Mike Lynskey said the plant had been ready for construction since September 1994, but it had been delayed because permits were required from as many as 24 government agencies before any concrete could be poured. Mr Lynskey added that rather than pull out of Vietnam, the Foundation was seriously considering moving the plant to Ho Chi Minh City where red tape and corruption was not so much a problem.

Arguably, some investors pulling out may have harboured unrealistic views about the opportunities in Vietnam at this early stage, and there are parallels in this regard with China when it first flung open the doors for foreign investors in the 1980s. The main complaint would seem to be the time and effort it takes for the necessary approvals to work their way through a cumbersome bureaucracy that is more in tune with the workings of a Soviet-style centrally planned economy than with a market-oriented system. While investors were initially attracted to Vietnam by low wage costs, delays and the shortage of essential services such as water and power, have created a larger than anticipated bill.

'Hype is dead and goodwill counts for little at the moment,' is the blunt assessment of one senior Asian bank executive in Hanoi.

'These are tense times, times of new commercial reality. The vast long-term potential is still as alluring as before, but anyone who is coming here for quick money is a fool.' Says a Japanese businessman: 'Vietnamese have neither the experience nor the understanding of modern economic realities.' While another complains: 'We are facing Vietnamese partners perhaps with nothing but land and debts to offer,'. But for major Singaporean property investor Antara Koh Development, delays and complications must just be coped with. Withdrawal is simply not an option. 'Anybody who came here thinking everything would be easy is just ignorant,' says general manager Robert Lai.

Vietnam so far has not suffered too badly from the adverse publicity generated by the withdrawals already mentioned. One major reason for this is that for every investor who leaves, another is keen to take its place. For instance, South Korea's Daewoo swiftly offered to replace the French oil firm Total when it withdrew from a project to build an oil refinery in a dispute with the government over its siting — although other foreign companies eventually seemed to have won the contract.[7] Daewoo is already Vietnam's biggest single investor and plans to pump some $2 billion into the country by 2000. Its chairman, Kim Woo Chong, who has been indicted for bribery at home, has made friends in Vietnam by signing up firms run by politically useful people as joint venture partners and by investing mainly in the less-developed north.

Daewoo, however, has also suffered frustrations of its own. In May 1995, a very high profile project it was building in Hanoi virtually ground to a halt because it was suddenly realized that three things were lacking — water, power and adequate telecommunications. This was unfortunate because it was one of the few projects that had managed to escape the quicksand of bureaucracy and land clearance problems faced by many other property developments in Hanoi. But one wonders why it took so long to realize that the basics were missing.

PROBLEMS WITH EXPORT PROCESSING ZONES

In the rush to attract foreign investment, enthusiasm can sometimes run ahead of practicalities. On more than one occasion, investors have been briefed about an industrial estate or zone that sounds like an absolute paradise. The brochures and the colour slides look most impressive. But go to the site and you may find nothing more than a few mounds of earth and an abandoned bulldozer.

In 1991, the Vietnamese government decided to create six export processing zones around the country in the hope they would become magnets for foreign investment. Two were to be located in Ho Chi Minh City, and one each in Can Tho, Danang, Hanoi and Haiphong. A consortium of Malaysian companies was formed and combined with provincial authorities to develop the Da Nang zone which was licensed on 1 October. 1993. At last report there was only one tenant on the site, which lacks both water and electricity supply. That brave pioneer only soldiers on because it has installed its own generator and sunk its own well. Da Nang province has now decided the zone should be incorporated into a larger and supposedly more flexible 'industrial zone'. Can Tho, meanwhile, seems to suffering the same problems with only one factory under construction at last report — for a Thai manufacturer of fishing nets.

At the same time, plans to turn Haiphong into a new Hong Kong suffered a severe setback with the collapse of an investment company that had wanted to build an export processing zone there. Hong Kong garment and property firm Very Good International VGI) pulled out of plans to develop 300 hectares (720 acres) of land into an area for factories, offices and housing, after failing to raise the required $1 billion development costs. VGI had advertised the project with a computer-generated video showing gleaming high-rise towers and executive homes, but the company never got beyond levelling the site just outside the port due to lack of foreign interest.[8]

Every country, region or individual city sees foreign investment as the panacea for all their problems. The idea sometimes seems to be: 'Lets get some investment and then we can use the money raised to provide the infrastructure.' Or, ideally, the investor will build or at least contribute towards the construction of the necessary infrastructure.

The approach has worked in other countries in the region reasonably well, offering not only fully-fitted factories with guaranteed power, water, light and road access, but also a range of tax breaks and financial incentives, as well as fast-track licensing approval. For provincial authorities in various parts of Vietnam clamouring for a similar approach, there is the attraction of thousands of jobs being created, an influx of investment dollars to rural areas, and an opportunity to build up a local parts manufacturing industry.

But although some provinces have been willing to make the leap of faith, the mixed results achieved so far have been less than convincing for the central government that EPZs are worth the risk. Hence, the Ministry of Planning and Investment decided to withhold licensing for any more zones, beyond the handful already allowed, until it can fully measure the success or failure of the concept.

One problem is that the authorities do not appear have a clear idea of what export processing zones or industrial estates really are and what they need in order to function well; nor is there a clearly defined industrial policy. The United Nations Industrial Development Organization has studied the problem and concluded that inappropriate choice of locations and expensive infrastructure costs made export processing zones in Vietnam a rather impractical choice at this stage in the country's development.

What were really wanted, it suggested, were simple industrial zones close to the main population centres that could tap into the growing domestic market for basic products. EPZs were unlikely to prosper in Vietnam until it developed a more liberal trade and domestic investment environment. For the moment, therefore, many foreign firms were more interested in building housing and golf courses than in providing areas for industrial development, Unido warned.

It seems to be a case of trying to run before one can walk. In five years time, export processing zones in places like Da Nang and Can Tho may make sense. But not now. And the danger is that the bad publicity generated by the experiences of those who have had their fingers burnt by going in now may discourage others from coming in later when, in fact, conditions have improved.[9]

Given all the problems with the EPZ concept, industrial parks do seem to be emerging as a better option. In northern Vietnam, Japan's Sumitomo Corp. envisions a 300 hectare park with a company operating under the auspices of the Ministry of Defence. In the south, Japanese trading company Nissho Iwai is looking at a 200 hectare site in Ho Chi Minh City, while Thailand's Bang Pakong Industrial Park 2 Public Company is investing in a 700 hectare park called Amata City in Dong Nai province just north of the old southern capital, and reported that it had signed up 30 foreign companies by the end of 1995.

The key difference is that EPZs cannot sell any of their output on the domestic market unless import duties have been paid. But, in compensation, the zones offer a 'one stop' licensing service, all the adminstrative requirements being handled by one body with claims that many projects can be approved in less than a month. In industrial parks, however, investors need to go to various ministries like the MPI, as well as the local people's committee, for approval, which can be a very frustrating experience.

Local people's committees, however, are pledging to improve their performance, and further changes could be underway. One possibility stems from an application by the various EPZ authorities to allow their investing companies to sell at least some of their output on the local market while still retaining most of the tax privileges granted under the EPZ law. This could lead to the emergence of a new 'centralized industrial zone' combining the best features of the EPZs and industrial parks.

RED TAPE

One reason for many of the difficulties that I have outlined above seems to be the 1987 foreign investment legislation, giving the Vietnamese partner the most power in a joint venture, irrespective of the size of its shareholding. Another factor is the central government's 1994 decision to only deal with large investors and to hand over responsibility of small and medium-sized foreign investment projects to provincial authorities. The latter are regarded by investors as largely unworldly, corrupt and unable to handle even the basic business and legal issues and responsibilities.

Le Xuan Trinh, Minister of the Government Office coordinating administrative reform, concedes that there is a problem here, requiring the Hanoi authorities to produce a clearer definition of the roles and responsibilities of central and local government, the organizational structure to carry out the defined functions, and clarification of the relationship between the two. 'In the process of economic reform, the government sees clearly the shortcomings of its handling and operation of the administrative apparatus. Red tape is certainly hindering development. Cumbersome administrative formalities required to get projects underway make the country a less attractive investment destination.'[10]

Addressing the issue in 1995, Prime Minister Vo Van Kiet told a meeting of national leaders in Ho Chi Minh City: 'The current management is failing to keep ahead of reforms and impedes development by letting prime opportunities slip through unnoticed. This failure paralyzes the nation's potential. The whole country must first be aware of the red tape crisis in order to participate in the common goal of creating a cleaner, more efficient state.' He warned that corruption still dominated some regions, fuelled by cumbersome bureaucracy.

In a move to improve the environment for foreign investors, the State Committee for Cooperation and Investment (SCCI), which has licensed all foreign investment since Vietnam's reforms began, was merged with the State Planning Committee (SPC) in October 1995 to become the Ministry of Planning and Investment (MPI). However, some businessmen are not convinced of the wisdom of dovetailing a body driven by business interests with another preoccupied with formulating national strategies.

Le Xuan Trinh explains: 'This affects both foreign and domestic investors. The responsibility and authority of government agencies needed to be clearly defined for the government to better manage investment projects. Previously, the SPC was chiefly responsible for national development and planning of the economy. However, foreign investment was the responsibility of the SCCI. In the past, the SCCI had to consult the SPC on the scale, types, modes and sites for any foreign investment project. Today, consultation becomes unnecessary as there is only one body, [so] the time taken for a foreign investment project to be granted a licence is much shorter.'[11]

This merger, in fact, was part of a much wider reform that so eight different ministries and agencies merged into three new ones: the MPI, the Ministry of Industry and the Ministry of Agriculture and Rural Development.

Finance Minister Ho Te has promised that procedures for foreign investment are being continually simplified and the domestic investment law will be 'applied in practice,' an apparent reference to complaints that provincial governments often refuse to recognize permits and rulings issued by the central government, leaving businessmen who think they have met legal requirements facing a new set of red tape.

This sometimes requires some ingenuity to get round, like the Western restaurateur in Ho Chi Minh City, who, frustrated by import taxes, waterfront delays and problems with refrigeration, decided to undertake some 'sausage diplomacy' by bringing his salami and chicken roll into Vietnam via a friendly diplomatic bag.[12]

A Hong Kong property developer in Ho Chi Minh City said that a little Asian patience was needed by anyone contemplating a plunge. 'It was never going to be a walk in the park here in terms of early investors. And anyone who thought it would shouldn't be there. Vietnam is seeking to do in 10 years what it has taken other countries 20 or 30 years. We've all got to get in early, make the contacts, corner the opportunities and wait. The market is so large and has so much potential for both retail and manufacturing, that people may be grumbling, but the bottom line is that they are not going to leave.' While such an attitude typifies the gritty Hong Kong and Taiwan investor, others less exposed to Asia, struggle to cope with Vietnam's new business environment.

CORRUPTION

As Vietnam's economy grows, the web of graft and corruption that surrounds it has expanded drastically, snaring many foreign businesses despite government campaigns to reduce the scourge. Tentative reforms of the bureaucracy and attempts to streamline the approval channels for investment have yet to do much in clearing away the frustrations faced by foreign businesses, whose executives complain that backhanders are needed to get any project through.

'Nothing gets done without palms being greased, it has become unavoidable,' said a Western businessman. Gifts are needed, he says, whenever one wants to clinch a government contract, ensure that a project is licensed, arrange meetings with officials and to lower companies' import duties and taxes. 'You have an all powerful public service and all these poorly paid officials are on the take'[13] A member of a Western law firm concurs. 'There is no getting away from corruption in doing business in Vietnam,' he says. One Western company went to the extent of agreeing to set aside nearly a quarter of its investment funds as 'speed money' to secure approvals for its operations.

To licence a foreign project, the former State Committee for Cooperation and Investment charged 0.01 per cent of total investment capital up to a ceiling of $10,000. But $20,000 was widely quoted in the business community as the standard price to illicitly fast-track an investment-licence application through various channels, and a Korean businessman claimed that one developer he knew had paid $100,000 for approval of a Hanoi project. 'At the start of the 1990s, officials were clean, even innocent. Now they know how to make money for themselves.'

Graft adds to operating expenses in a country that already has high urban rents, steep taxes and electricity bills that are twice as much for foreigners as for locals. Vietnam's decade-old economic reform drive has made wealth attainable and corruption a tempting way to grasp it. Under socialism, waiters shunned tips as a capitalist evil. Now, not only are gratuities ideologically acceptable. but less-innocent handouts are actively pursued. The issue comes near the top of long lists of complaints about Vietnam's business environment with such organizations as Japan's Keidanren raising it with the country's leaders. American companies, facing strict extra-territorial laws on corruption, have been made more wary by Vietnam's reputation and some are reported to have put off investment decisions, although it is hard to pin this down.

But there are others who insist that much of Vietnam's business climate is basically honest and that many Vietnamese shun illegal activities. 'If you know the right person you can still get things done without payment,' claims one Japanese businessman who admits to paying 'lubricants' when necessary. He accuses newcomers of being too willing to stoop to graft. 'They pay as requested. It sort of ruins proper business practice'.

Corruption seems to be basically the work of middle-level officials rather than of the top brass which is apparently 'preoccupied with the country's development,' according to one foreign businessman with several years experience in the country. One of the problems is that in many sectors the foreigners are obliged to work through middlemen, the businessman said. 'For the middlemen, there is nothing worse than a business that is running smoothly. So they think up schemes and pretexts to extract handouts from time to time.'

Vietnam's collegial approach to decision-making and the need to win approvals from both central and local governments provide opportunities for a single official, even those of low rank, to hold up projects. 'So you've got to make sure everyone's been paid off,' said a Western banker in Ho Chi Minh City, adding that it was easier in China where two or three key decision-makers could be identified. On occasions, a businessman finds himself paying for approval from departments who, it eventually transpires, actually have no jurisdiction over his particular project. But given the present bureaucratic confusion in Vietnam it is hard to find this out in a painless way.

One unique aspect of graft in Vietnam is that frequently many levels in a ministry need bribing, although often only petty sums are involved. 'You have to cover so many different levels in one organization,' says an Asian executive, adding that a payment at any one level that reaches into the thousands of dollars is extraordinarily high.

And it does not always have to be straight cash deal. Most Vietnamese want to see the world, so foreign investors who sponsor jaunts abroad reap appreciation. Trips to other Asian capitals often involve handing a Vietnamese a department store credit card valid for a few thousand dollars. The sponsoring company will arrange for the goods to be delivered in Vietnam, so its guests can return hassle-free through customs.

In January 1995, the authorities launched an anti-graft publicity blitz to demonstrate its resolve to combat corruption. And the undertaking seems sincere — official newspapers give prominent display to graft busts. Eradicating corruption in the civil service is a key aim of Prime Minister Vo Van Kiet's drive to renovate the state sector. 'The biggest challenge facing the government is how to implement reforms effectively to reduce opportunities for corruption,' says Nguyen Trung Truc, managing director of Peregrine Capital Vietnam Ltd. The idea is to clarify and modernize shrouded auditing systems, prune the layers of bureaucracy and remove the control of state-owned enterprises from ministries. Because ministries often own companies, conflicts of interest can arise when a ministry awards contracts. Because of this grey area, the government has begun shifting administration of state-owned enterprises to the Ministry of Finance.

Despite such good intentions, corruption will prove difficult to eradicate. 'Dealing with these problems is an uphill and complicated task,' the prime minister told an official newspaper. Many foreign investors appear resigned to graft for at least some of their business deals, perhaps comforted by the knowledge that Vietnam's anti-corruption-police sweeps have so far left outsiders alone.

CONSULTANTS AND MIDDLEMEN

Faced with the problems of corruption and red tape, many foreign investors prefer to keep at a distance by leaving everything to an outside consultant or middleman. Finding the right middleman is relatively simple. Just ask officials supervising a deal if they know anyone familiar with the industry. They will likely say no. But expect a phone call later from someone claiming expertise and offering to help. There are scores of consultants on the ground in Vietnam, but are any of them offering good service at value-for-money prices?

'A consultant,' said the American sitting at the bar in Hanoi's elegant Metropole Hotel, 'is an expediter, a legman, a baby-sitter, a lobbyist, a cowboy'. Speaking as a former consultant himself, the American went on: 'The start-up costs here are incredibly high. 'It takes six months just to get your feet planted [as an investor] – not to mention thousands of dollars to get phone lines and to set up an office. In this sense, you're not bad off finding a consultant to help.'

But he spoke disdainfully of the 'cowboys' who typically try to get a cut from both sides. 'What disturbs me are these guys who run around and say they can get you in to meet anyone, that they know someone who knows the prime minister. There are hundreds of consultants here, and most of them think they have a connection. But they don't know the first thing about due diligence, about creating a marketing plan,' he said. 'If you want to set up a meeting, you might as well just call up the Vietnamese Chamber of Commerce.'

Not that he held any grudges. Consulting had treated him well. He had come to Asia after college for 'adventure', become fluent in Vietnamese and had bootstrapped himself into a position with a boutique consulting firm in North America. Billing out at rates ranging from $800 to $1,500 a day ('more when the client was on the ground – it's like baby-sitting') the firm he worked for researched markets, prepared strategic plans and ran searches of prospective joint venture partners and distributors for investors. 'Really to do a proper search you need to visit 50 factories and evaluate which ones would be best for your client,' he said. 'That's what we did.'

While there are specialists offering well-defined areas of expertise, most consultants are generalists who stress their connections, their knowledge as to how the system works in practice, and their information gathering abilities. Having an ear to the ground they are possibly attuned to business opportunities, and – perhaps more than lawyers and accountants – are willing to play a direct role in the business aspects of deals. They do field research, shepherd a project through the bureaucracy and prepare the kind of market analyses that are outside the scope of most legal and accounting firms.

The obvious weakness of this, of course, is that as generalists, they can be jack-of-all-trades and masters of none, and may give short shrift to critical legal and tax issues. Since their fee is often in part based on getting a transaction consummated, they may be more concerned with doing the deal, than in doing it properly and in the client's best interests.

Accountants and lawyers, meanwhile, are rapidly developing a presence in Vietnam as investors seek specialized counsel on increasingly sophisticated transactions. Unlike general business consultants, accountants are not likely to be willing to become deeply involved in the identification of possible Vietnamese partners or in the collection of market data. Law firms pride themselves on attention to detail particularly in the documentation of transactions and a concomitant ability to understand and 'run' complex deals.

But these days with more people on the ground actually doing business, investors simply do not need the sort of early bird start-up advice that consultants used to offer. The pioneer generalist consultants whose duties ran the gamut from tour guide to legal draftsman are being forced to redefine their roles and seek new business niches. There are also signs that life could get tough for some of them given that some of the very large investors that are starting to look at Vietnam seriously have in-house experience of tapping underdeveloped markets and are unlikely to have such a great need for consultants' services.

So how do the consultants match up? Under Vietnamese law, all foreign invested enterprises must be audited by qualified accounting firms at the end of each calendar year. This would appear to give accountants the edge in consultancy. All the 'Big Six' accounting firms have offices in Vietnam, but Ernst & Young was the first with a representative office in December 1990 and getting its full office licence in November 1992. 'We are in a position to help people if they want a representative office, to guide them through the maze of paperwork and to get their applications structured to be processed,' said John Harvey, a Hong Kong-based partner who directs the firm's Indochina practice. There is some overlap with the type of work that lawyers and other consultants perform. 'We're able to help people to review joint venture contracts, to point out the pitfalls of doing things in a particular way, or the advantages of doing them in another way', said Harvey. 'We can also carry out feasibility studies and reviews of potential "marriage partners".' Fees are calculated on an hourly basis, in some cases to create a flat fee or monthly retainer, depending on the services to be performed.

The firm does not use success fees, or take equity positions in client's investments.

'What do attorneys do here? People have asked me that question before,' says Michael Scown, a partner at Russin & Vecchi's Ho Chi Minh City office. 'We advise people about legal issues; we draft documents, and represent people in negotiations.' The types of issues lawyers work on are associated with companies coming into an industrialized country: basis issues of entry, structuring and operations. Russin and Vecchi has the distinction of being the only foreign law firm to have had an office in Vietnam before 1975. The firm, which was started by partner Sesto Vecchi, kept its offices in Saigon open from the firm's establishment in 1967 until the week helicopters started taking off from the US Embassy. Invited by the Foreign Ministry to return in 1988, Vecchi became among the first American lawyers to open a law office in a united Vietnam. The firm has had an office in Ho Chi Minh City since January 1993, and counts among its clients several multinational oil and construction companies. It opened an office in Hanoi in April 1994.

'There's a lot of law here, and the law that they have, they take very seriously,' says Scown. 'You can find big holes in the law, but you can't necessarily ignore what's on the books. We see a lot of clients who would like us to represent them after the fact. They come in and try to do something quickly and informally, and have had problems.' Vecchi hints at why consultants are in a weaker position than in previous years when he says that 'deals which were being done three years ago could not be done today because the laws have become more specific.'

What about Vietnamese consultants? 'We have some important advantages compared to foreign consultants,' says Nguyen Trong Hieu, the head of Investip's Project Department, a Vietnamese consultancy operating under the umbrella of the Ministry of Science, Technology and the Environment. 'Our close relationship with ministries and other Vietnamese organizations means it's easier for us to source information and know policies and plans.' It is this kind of relationship that seems to give local consultants an edge over their foreign counterparts and it helps that most local firms are tied to ministries.

Only a few are independent. One is Investconsult, which offers a wide range of services including legal advice. 'With our independent role, we are under no [government] pressure,' says Nguyen Tran Bat, the firm's president. 'Our service deals with development, change and knowledge of the political and economic systems to help foreign companies define their approach to Vietnam.' He points out that foreign consultants should look to their Vietnamese counterparts for specialized information. 'There's no way for a foreign consultant to have success if there's no cooperation with local consultants,' he says. Investip and Investconsult cooperate with large international law firms. 'I think cooperation with foreign consultants is very necessary,' says Bat. 'But we're not joined fully or exclusively with any foreign company.'[14]

RED LIGHT, GREEN LIGHT

Foreign business people doing business in Vietnam often ask: 'If there's no red light, does that mean I've got a green light?' The emerging consensus, says Fred Burke, an American lawyer based in Ho Chi Minh City, is 'no'. Every form of foreign business activity in Vietnam must have a specific legal basis.

When Vietnam launched its economic reforms several years ago, there was a widely held view that a *laissez faire* economy would emerge to replace the state-planned economy, recalls Baker. In that atmosphere of change, there was little consensus among legal authorities as to whether all foreign business activity in Vietnam required a specific approval or permit from an authorized government agency to make it legal. For example, some observers took the view that the Law on Foreign Investment was merely precatory — that it was simply one of several options for establishing a long-term business operation in Vietnam.

These observers took the position that so long as the foreign business activity was not contrary to any law, it would still be legal. In the words of one foreign trader: 'Unless there's a red light, that means it's a green light.' In the years since Vietnam's legal framework for foreign investment was introduced, it has become increasingly clear that while more and more legal options are becoming available to foreign investors, it is indeed necessary to have a specific legal basis for doing business in Vietnam.

The consensus that seems to have emerged is that that foreign business activity must fall within one of the following categories:

- Forms of foreign investment provided by the Law on Foreign Investment, namely Joint Venture Contracts, Business Cooperation

Contracts, Enterprises with 100 per cent Foreign-Owned Capital and Build-Operate-Transfer projects;
- Joint Venture Banks and Bank Branches;
- Representative Office;
- Technology transfer and intellectual property licensing contracts; and
- Traditional forms of foreign trade.

All foreign investment activities must be licensed by the MPI. The essential elements it will consider in evaluating a project are the legal and financial standing of the foreign and Vietnamese partners and the suitability of the project to the country's economic and social development goals. Any entity of reputable standing may endeavour to invest in Vietnam and there are no restrictions as to country of origin. Vietnam's Foreign Investment Law allows foreign-invested projects a maximum duration of 50 years with extension to 70 years for special cases. The desired project length should be stipulated in the licence application.

As a general matter, business forms such as branches, franchises, shareholdings in Vietnamese companies, agencies and distributorships are not yet available to foreigners in Vietnam unless they can be structured in one of the forms specifically provided for above. Moreover, for these forms of doing business that are available, each implies a specific governmental licensing, permit or approval requirement. The point to note here is that the positive categories of business activities provided for under current legislation are exhaustive. Forms of foreign business activity which do not fall squarely within any of these categories run the risk that any contractual relationships underlying the activities may not be recognized, and will therefore be unenforceable; and the activity may be considered as an 'illegal investment' thus attracting administrative and even criminal sanctions.

In the first case of its kind, a Hanoi-based British businessman was fined $50,000 in 1995 by the Ministry of Trade for 'operating a company representative office without a licence', while several other foreigners were 'disciplined' in Ho Chi Minh City for a similar offence. Clive Cartwright said he was running Clive Cartwright and Associates as an offshore firm while awaiting the result of an 18 month-old application for an office licence for the London-based auditing and accountancy firm RSM International, which his own company represented in Indochina. The RSM office licence was due to be issued on 4 May, 'but just as they were about to issue it they held back and came to investigate my office. I had been effectively operating on the basis of expecting the representative office licence to be issued,' Cartwright explained, adding that the government did not understand the link between the two companies and had penalized him for operating an illegal representative office.[15]

The simplest form of presence for a foreign company is the REPRESENTATIVE OFFICE.[16] This option is open only to companies operating in certain sectors such as banking and finance, import-export, transport, communication and post, scientific and technical cooperation, tourism services. Licensing of representative offices, except for credit and banking offices, is under the jurisdiction of the Ministry of Trade. Even after a representative office is licensed by the ministry and registered with the relevant local People's Committee, a number of important restrictions on its scope of activities apply and these restrictions have been troublesome for many foreign companies. Representative offices are permitted to engage in preparatory work for long-term investments, technology assistance projects and trade in goods and services. Their role is to provide market research, feasibility studies, customer support and liaison services.

A representative office is not allowed to execute commercial contracts except where a special power of attorney is granted to it by the head office of the company (and there may be tax consequences in so doing). It cannot receive payment for products or services provided in Vietnam or offshore. Trading activity of any kind, is barred. Minimal amounts of samples may be held and displayed, and product showrooms are allowed, but no stocks of products, whether imported, sourced locally or intended for export, may be held. Also banned is any subleasing of office or residential space even to affiliate companies; nor can it act as a correspondence address or representative of any company that is not the specified licence holder.

Representative offices may open an account in either foreign currency or Vietnamese Dong backed by a foreign currency at a bank established under Vietnamese law, but such an account may only be used for the purposes of paying the administrative expenses incurred by the representative office. It cannot be used for the purposes of receiving payments on behalf of the head office.

A representative office may import into Vietnam, subject to import duties, only those items which are necessary for its operation and the personal use of its staff.

Some foreign companies are trying to get round the restriction by working through Vietnamese nominees to conduct business on their behalf. This is a rather a grey area, but what has to be borne in mind is that a representative office is not a Vietnamese legal entity with limited liability, as other investment structures are. Therefore, representative office staff risk a greater degree of personal liability and possibly even accountability under the criminal code than they would at home.[17]

If you are going to go beyond that limited business activity, the Vietnamese would prefer you to establish a JOINT VENTURE with a partner ideally from the state sector chosen by the government. Later in this chapter, I will discuss the options for joining forces with a company in the private sector. The minimum legal capital requirement for the foreign party in a joint venture is 30 per cent. There is no maximum limit, though approval is rarely granted to projects with over 75 per cent. And, as mentioned earlier, even if the foreign partner does have a majority shareholding that fact will not be reflected in the administrative control of the enterprise where the law favours the local side even in minority.

It is possible to set up a WHOLLY FOREIGN-OWNED COMPANY, and given some of the problems foreign businessmen have faced in joint ventures, as already outlined, this might be an attractive option. But this form is less favoured by the Vietnamese authorities and an applicant would have to offer strong justification for the need for 100 per cent ownership – although only one sector, hotel management, is officially barred.

John Pike, Chief Investment Officer of fund management company Finansa Thai, argues that though most investors start with joint ventures, agreements for these often involve arduous negotiations in unknown legal territory so that valuable time is lost. 'There are partners who can give rise to misunderstandings and different interpretations of laws and operating details. Many licensed projects fail to get off the ground because debt finance for projects is largely unavailable in Vietnam. To address this problem the authorities have to build a legal framework that will allow lenders to take Vietnamese assets as security for debts. Parallel to this should be an ability to take title of such assets in the event of loan default to enable the lenders to recover their unpaid loans. The government has made consider-able efforts to draft new laws, [but] it's a Herculean task. Some 65 foreign banks have set up offices in Vietnam illustrating how serious they are about doing business here if only the legal means were available to begin mobilizing capital.'

According to Pike, an allied issue for foreign bank lending is the value of 'land use rights' and its acceptability as collateral for debts. Recent changes in law have imposed the need on the Vietnamese parties with 'land use rights' to pay the annual land use tax at 100 per cent. Many Vietnamese organizations lack the cash to pay the rent, so it often falls on the foreign partner to provide the money. The knock-on effect then is to question the validity of the Vietnamese asset contribution to a joint-venture arrangement based on the 'Land Use Rights Certificate'. It is a lease rent obligation that has to be paid. It cannot also be an asset of value for use as collateral by a lender.

'This issue furthers strengthens the case for a 100 per cent foreign-invested project which at least guarantees the state the payment of rent for the land and a faster track to getting the project licensed. For 100 per cent foreign-invested projects, operations can start up more quickly and there is less likelihood of failure. There are no part-ners to give rise to misunderstandings or different interpretations of laws and operating details. There is an earlier transfer of technology and know-how through job creation and on-the-job training of local staff. Also important, foreign investors are able to see that the investment process is less problematic at the outset when entering Vietnam. This is not to say that other forms of projects are to be avoided, but they can be entered into later when it becomes clear that there are mutual advantages to such relationships.'

DISTRIBUTORSHIP AGREEMENTS are not specifically provided for under the Law on Foreign Investment or any other law. While regula-tions on the subject are under consideration, in some cases these agreements may therefore not be recognized as valid and may thus be unenforceable in the event of a dispute between the parties. Also, because of the restrictions applicable to representative offices, for example, it is not possible to use this as a vehicle to participate in the active management of a distributor in Vietnam. The provision of training, technical and marketing support, which usually forms part of a distribution arrangement, may also fall outside the scope of what a representative office is permitted to do.

In the area of infrastructure development in particular, Vietnam is now experimenting with the BUILD-OPERATE-TRANSFER (BOT) concept. A BOT contract creates a cooperation between the foreign investor and an authorized state body for the development of infrastructure projects. This cooperation gives the foreign partner control for a period deemed sufficient to retrieve investment capital and profits, and then transfers the whole project to the Vietnamese government. This will be considered in more detail in Chapter 5 on infrastructure.

BUSINESS COOPERATION CONTRACT: This form allows foreigners to do business in Vietnam by effectively creating an unincorporated joint venture between the foreign investor and the Vietnamese business enterprise.

Two common forms of indirect foreign investment that have been particularly problematic are proxy trading companies and proxy real estate investments. Frustrated by the fact that Vietnam does not yet have a branch form for trading companies, and that foreign companies may not establish trading companies under the Law on Foreign Investment, some foreign traders have set up local proxy companies which, with the foreign party's financing and management, give it a local import and distribution capacity. Typically, the foreign party will provide enough capital for the local entity to obtain the necessary business and import licences. In return, the local entity acts under the control and direction of the foreign trader. Similarly, because Vietnamese law does not allow foreigners to buy real estate, foreigners sometimes finance the acquisition of land use rights or building by local parties.

The authorities have now made clear that such arrangements have no legal basis.[18] In most cases, the economic police only become involved if the relationship goes sour. However, in a variety of circumstances, competitors or other adverse parties may be counted on to cause trouble for such investors. When this happens, the economic police may use their extensive investigatory powers to obtain information about the relationship between the foreign and Vietnamese party. If they determine that an 'illegal investment' has taken place, the sanctions may be serious. Not only is the contractual documentation evidencing the relationship invalid and unenforceable, but administrative fines and even criminal sanctions may apply as well.

The advice to foreign businessmen, therefore, is to make sure their Vietnamese partners have or can and will obtain the necessary authorization and licences to enable them to fulfil their obligations under an agreed contract. Special licences are needed, for example, to import and retail foreign products. Indeed, the Ministry of Trade has indicated that a Vietnamese company without a licence to import products would be acting contrary to the law if it entered into an agreement with a foreign supplier after the goods have been properly imported by a licensed Vietnamese importer.

This can all be summed up in one sentence: If you do not have a green light, consider it a red light!

CIVIL CODE

The provisions of the laws affecting foreign business operations will be presented in detail in Appendix 3. Before leaving the issue of the regulatory framework in this chapter, however, I would like to refer briefly to one other aspect of the legal environment as it affects foreign individuals — namely, the creation of a Civil Code.

Continuity and change, and the delicate balance between them, may explain why it took 14 years of complex lawmaking, sometimes heated public discussions and 15 written drafts to engineer Vietnam's new Civil Code. Finally in November 1995, the National Assembly approved the weighty tome which spells out the individual citizen's civil rights and responsibilities, including issues of inheritance, contract and property ownership. The code also addresses such foreign investment concerns as technology transfer, compensation, land use and intellectual property.

'At the moment, when Vietnam is opening its doors to the world, you want the stability of a legal code that cannot be changed too often or too lightly. At the same time, it must be flexible enough to deal with the country's dynamic growth and rapidly changing socio-economic conditions,' says Dr Dinh Trung Tung, head of the Department of Civil and Economic Laws at the Ministry of Justice.

Chapter seven of the code, for instance, deals with foreign individuals and business entities, outlining broad principles while leaving ample room for more specific legislation in future. 'It provides the legal basis for the fundamentals of the market economy, which are property rights an contract rights,' says John Bentley, a legal adviser for the United Nations Development Programme (UNDP).

While the code's passage probably will not affect investor decisions in the short term, it is a healthy sign for Vietnam's long-term prospects. Like the 1992 constitution, the new code underscores the country's commitment to the rule of law, and serious attempts to normalize civil relations between two parties in Vietnam. 'It's the kind of thing foreign investors like to see,' agrees James Finch, a partner of the American law firm Russin and Vecchi.

Vietnam's last successful attempt to write such a code occurred in the fifteenth century during the reign of Emperor Le Thanh Tong. The scholarly ruler penned a manuscript that protected citizens against abuse by mandarins and permitted women to own property and share inheritances. A striking feature of the code this time around is the efforts of contemporary lawmakers to open up the process to the public.

For the past 18 years, UNDP's Bentley has proffered advice to developing nations on how to attract foreign investment and build a market economy. Vietnam's approach to drafting a civil code seems anything but typical, he says. 'I have never seen a developing country like this that would go to so much effort to get a consensus on the civil code. And they were very open to advice and comments from others.' In early 1995, the lawmakers went public with draft 12 by publishing its contents in newspapers and inviting public comment.

A civil code lives or dies on the ability of the state to enforce the law's provisions fairly and consistently. Still to come in Vietnam is a judicial civil code, for example. Although economic courts already exist, it is questionable how effective they can be given that they don not have much practice. In the past, precious few Vietnamese judges had any training whatsoever. To beef up judicial standards, the government is shifting from electing judges to appointing them along the lines of a national merit system.

VIET KIEU

Vietnam encourages persons of Vietnamese origin (*Viet Kieu*) to return to the country and invest. However, there remains a substantial degree of misunderstanding on the issue of whether such persons are entitled to invest in forms of business that would not be open to other foreign investors. Although overseas Vietnamese may enjoy tax and other investment incentives not available to other foreign investors, a consensus seems to have emerged that they are restricted to the same forms of doing business in Vietnam as other foreign entities are.

For example, the Law on Domestic Investment provides that *Viet Kieu* are permitted to contribute capital to a Vietnamese enterprise which may then act as the domestic party to one of the forms of investment under the Law of Foreign Investment. But there remains a substantial degree of disagreement among various government authorities about whether such investment is really permissible. Moreover, the rights and liabilities of *Viet Kieu* investors who choose this investment route remain relatively undefined.

Nevertheless, the central government has high hopes for the *Viet Kieu* playing a significant role in economic catch-up, given the capital they have amassed and the business skills they have acquired while living in exile. There is hope that they will act as an economic catalyst as Overseas Chinese have done since China opened the door the foreign investment at the end of the 1970s. But the Overseas Vietnamese community has neither the resources, the numbers or the length of residence abroad to match the powerful Chinese communities in places like Hong Kong, Indonesia, Singapore, Taiwan and Thailand, who are now pumping billions of dollars of their fortunes into the motherland.

Since 1990, an estimated 800,000 Vietnamese exiles have returned home, many bringing in money for their families to start small businesses.[19] Most of the money goes on helping the families in their daily living, however, and only a small fraction ever gets into the business sector.

'I'll tell you frankly, their investment isn't enormous. It's minimal, not even one per cent of foreign invested capital,' says Dr Nguyen Ngoc Ha, President of the Ho Chi Minh City Committee for Vietnamese Living Overseas. 'The economic potential may not prove to be enormous compared to other populations like the Overseas Chinese.'

The MPI at the end of 1995 had 34 active *Viet Kieu* licences on file with a total capital of $107 million, the largest being a $21 million, wholly foreign-owned pharmaceutical project in the southern province of Dong Nai. By comparison, there were almost 240 licensed Japanese representative offices in the country.

Other *Viet Kieu* return as 'pointmen' for multinational corporations, operating as the first in-country manager to get operations rolling. Born in Vietnam but exposed to international practices, they should, in theory, be able to act as an important conduit to straddle the cultural and linguistic barriers between East and West. The reality can be somewhat different. They are not immune to the complexities of doing business in Vietnam; they often experience as much culture shock as other foreign expatriates when they return, especially the younger ones who, having left the country as babies, have little or no memory of it.

Being at *Viet Kieu* can bring the worst rather than the best of both worlds — a point made forcibly by Nguyen Anh Nam, a young man working for the venture capital fund Peregrine Capital Vietnam. 'In Vietnam, you never have enough experience, your Vietnamese is never good enough.' he says. 'Vietnamese expect you to act in a certain way, and these are expectations that can be hard to live up to.'

'*Viet Kieu* are often placed in untenable positions, caught in a crossfire of suspicion and misunderstanding from both sides. Foreign companies often see them as super-human problem-solvers, while local Vietnamese in some cases show even less understanding and sympathy for their overseas cousins, failing to take account of their strengths and the reasons behind their cultural missteps.'[20]

There can also be jealousy within a company from local Vietnamese who feel they can do as good if not a better job than the highly-paid *Viet Kieu*. Know-it-alls, waving Western degrees, rarely last long or accomplish what they set out to do, instead earning enmity of the very people they need in order to succeed. 'Arrogant people are definitely not effective here because the Vietnamese won't listen to you if you act like that,' says Nam firmly.

All this should be borne in mind by Western foreign investors who might see the *Viet Kieu* route as an inside track to success in Vietnam.

PRIVATE SECTOR

For the more adventurous businessperson there is always the private sector. There are three types of private sector companies available to foreign investors, but only a very select number of these will likely find themselves listed on the stock market where your investment, originally in the form of a loan or a low-interest bond, can later be transferred into shares. Aside from setting up a full joint venture with a private company, the only direct investment possible by foreigners at this stage is in joint stock banks.

In reality, the Vietnam Bank for Private Enterprises (VP Bank) is the only option since it is the only bank that the State Bank has allowed to sell shares to foreigners. Direct investment in other private companies, joint stock banks, or joint stock companies is not allowed.

'The problem is one still cannot invest directly in a private sector company. They're off limits, as are state companies. We have to go through a convoluted exercise of convertible debt,' says John Pike of Finansa Thai.

There are many potential pitfalls in convertible debt financing. No one knows precisely when a stock exchange will be set up, if foreigners can take an active role or at what price if they are allowed to do so. If a convertible loan is made today, the financial position that loan is buying when the shares are actually issued has to be negotiated. This would include the actual number of shares in the company to be held, the percentage stake in profits and loss, management role, and other factors.

Investors also have to predict how fast or slow the company will grow due to the use of the newly invested capital. Pike spent eight months trying to negotiate a convertible debt arrangement with a provincial state company that Finansa Thai knew well and that had been listed for 'equitization' (privatization). The $1.5 million investment had a three-year term, after which the fund reserved the right to get its money back if shares could not be issued by the company. The fund managers asked for a state commercial bank guarantee but were rejected. Also, while determining equity share, assets were overvalued and arriving at a percentage share reflecting future growth proved very difficult. 'There was no apparent legal problem. What we don't know is if they'll guarantee a convertible debt,' says Pike, who writes the failed negotiations off as a solid learning experience.

The Vietnamese private sector is made up of three types of companies:

- **Private Proprietorship Company**: This is an unlimited company owned by just one person, who is 100 per cent liable for all business activities. These companies are most commonly found on the retail level and have probably gained the lion's share of overseas Vietnamese investment.
- **Limited Liability Company**: This is like a joint venture in which a minimum of two investors have a percentage interest in the company but do not have actual shares, as in a joint stock company. Technically, each individual investor is only liable for the amount of capital that he or she puts into the company. However, there is no clear legal policy on the investor's limited

liability in the case of bankruptcy. Legal sources say that in some cases the company, in particular the director, may be liable for debts beyond their original capital imput.

- **Joint stock company**: This is a company with a minimum of seven investors each holding an identical number of shares (and thus percentage interest) in the company. In some cases, the state will be an investor along with private investors. Individuals and private companies can be shareholders and different state companies can join forces to set up a joint stock company. Due to having an identifiable number of shares that can be bought, this type of company is attracting the most attention for convertible loan investment.

NOTES

1. Quoted in a Vietnam survey published by the *Financial Times*, 13 November 1995.
2. World Bank figures.
3. 'Aust company says Vietnam needs more time to develop'. *Bangkok Post* 17 August 1995.
4. 'Australia–Vietnam mining venture near collapse,' *Bangkok Post* 'Inside Indochina' supplement 14 May 1996.
5. Ibid.
6. Macrae, M. 'Joint ventures shot down by Communist bureaucrats', *Asian Business Review*, August 1995, p16.
7. South Korea's Lucky Goldstar, Conoco of the United States, Petronas of Malaysia and two Taiwanese firms, China Petroleum Corp. and China Investment & Development all made bids and were allocated shares, but immediately began arguing that the allocation was spread too thinly over too many companies. Although Total pulled out because it felt the new site at Dung Quat, Quang Ngai province, was uneconomical – having first been interested when the refinery was to be built in Vung Tau, centre of the oil extraction industry, the company was reported to have expressed interested in bidding for a second planned refinery. PetroVietnam said it would give this application the 'same consideration' as it would any other contenders.
8. Despite this setback, the prime minister gave the go-ahead in principle for another massive investment scheme in the city to build an industrial zone and port. American International Group (AIG), Thailand's Asian International Development and International Port Engineering Management of Belgium are to develop a 973 hectare site with an investment of $556 million. The zone is expected to include oil and chemical storage facilities, a deep water port and a large industrial zone. Japanese financial giant Nomura, meanwhile, is currently building a $120 million industrial zone in the city that will cover 153 hectares. AFP report in the *Bangkok Post* 26 Aug., 1995.
9. Extracted from a speech the author delivered to an Asia–Pacific conference on 'Technology Opportunities & Manufacturing Business in the 21st Century' in Singapore, 13 September 1995.
10. Interview with *Vietnam Economic Times*, February 1996.
11. Ibid.
12. Torode, G. 'Overseas firms trip in Hanoi's red-tape jungle'. *South China Morning Post Weekly Edition* 11 December 1995.
13. Salaries for many officials range from $20 to $50 a month, yet these are the people who hold sway over contracts worth tens or even hundreds of millions of dollars. The temptations are obvious, and many foreign businessmen seem to show some understanding of this. After

decades of war and socialist mismanagement, Vietnamese are finally tasting the good life. Honda motorbikes, colour TV sets and VCRs and French perfume are within reach of city dwellers. After being banned until 1990, advertising is again filling Vietnamese with materialistic aspirations. The influx of foreigners and access to foreign media give the locals a glimmer of a sophistication that many want to emulate. Economic growth will satisfy these desires over time and limit at least the poverty motive behind corruption. Trimming layers of bureaucracy and introducing better accountancy practices should diminish opportunities for bribe-taking. But agencies are expected to fight against losing power and revenue sources. 'All of this is not in the interest of provincial authorities and ministries,' says an adviser to the government. In a country where the Asian Development Bank says unemployment hovers around 20 per cent, petty officials have few opportunities to become rich aside from underhanded payments. While firing squads are one way to deter corruption, wage increases and more sophisticated accounting procedures might be Vietnam's best hope in the battle against graft.

14. *Vietnam Economic Times*, December 1994–January 1995.
15. Reuters news agency 7 July 1995.
16. Information in this section has been gathered from personal investigation and several published sources, including the *Vietnam Economic Journal*, *Vietnam Business Journal*, and *Vietnam. An Investment Guide* published by. Citibank, Hanoi, March 1995.
17. Information supplied by Hal P. Fiske of Russin & Vecchi.
18. *Vietnam Business Journal*, October 1995.
19. The government says $600–700 million a year is being remitted to Vietnam by exiles through official channels, and much more is probably flowing in through the back door.
20. *Vietnam Economic Times*, February 1996.

4 Industrial Profile

GROWTH CONSTRAINTS

ADDRESSING an international manufacturing conference in Singapore in September 1995, Bui Ngoc Hien, a senior economist with the State Planning Committee's Industry Department, described the many challenges and difficulties that were an important constraint on economic growth for Vietnam, and which could only be alleviated in the longer term. The physical infrastructure was very poor, especially the road and rail network and port facilities,[1] he said. Per capita income made Vietnam one of the world's poorest countries, and its low level of savings was a severe hindrance in accessing new technology. The capital market remained undeveloped, making it difficult to mobilize the finance needed to modernize and expand production.[2]

Many industrial products still faced difficulty competing in international markets, and even at home. Productivity and profitability were very low due to continued use of obsolete technology.

This implied a need for investment in both modernizing existing industry and in moving into new areas where Vietnam held a potential comparative advantage. But there was also an important need for strong employment growth in Vietnam. Based on estimates that an additional 1.2 million potential workers entered the labour force each year, Vietnam, at least in the short term, needed a strategy aimed at creating as many jobs as possible. Priority should be given to labour-intensive industries for the moment, therefore, even while looking for ways to balance this with vital technological upgrading.

At the same time, the concept of a market economy remained new to Vietnamese, Mr Hien said. The competition that could promote production and business, and encourage the application of high technology, had yet to be reach optimal development. The lack of competition, given the dominance of the state-run sector and the weakness of private business, continue to constrain development.

But the economist felt Vietnam still had some advantages. Being a country with a long agricultural tradition, it had benefited from the green revolution to become a major rice exporter. Rice and other agricultural exports have been critical in generating the hard currency needed to import new technology and other raw materials necessary to develop industry. A large and relatively well-educated population provided a strong and professional labour force for the industrial sector. And the country had considerable valuable mineral resources such as oil and gas, iron ore (currently proven and untapped reserves of 540 million tonnes), bauxite (seven billion tonnes), coal (three billion tonnes), apatite (crystallized phosphate of lime, three billion tonnes) and chromate (salt of chromatic acid, 19 million tonnes), which could be exploited with the right imported technology to generate vital export earnings.

He went on: 'In order to take advantage of the emerging technical opportunities for the twenty-first century and to rapidly develop the Vietnamese economy to reduce the economic gap with our neighbours, [my] government has launched a programme for achieving average growth in industrial output of 15 per cent per annum during the period 1996–2000. We understand, however, that this is a challenging task for an agricultural-based, less developed economy.'

He identified the priority industrial sectors as:

- **Oil and gas.** Crude oil production is now seven million tonnes per year, mostly for export. 'Proven gas reserves amount to three billion cubic metres of which half can be brought onshore with a newly-built pipeline. These resources provide many opportunities for the development of Vietnamese industry. Most of the gas brought onshore is now mainly used in power generation. There is an immediate need to build a refinery with a capacity of five million tonnes. Because oil and gas are basic raw materials for many other industries, this sector is accorded the highest priority.'

- **Cement.** Vietnam has very large resources of limestone and anthracite coal providing a good base for the development of this industry. Annual cement production is now about six million tonnes. Production is planned to increase to about 15–20 million tonnes by the year 2000. A number of new production units with capacity of around 1–2 million tonnes are being implemented, and other projects have been formulated with the sponsors actively seeking foreign joint-venture partners.

- **Iron and steel.** The steel industry has developed strongly in recent years with annual growth rates of up to 40 per cent. 'Although total design capacity is one million tonnes of rolling steel bar and coil, the industry cannot meet the growing domestic demand for steel needed to develop infrastructure and production facilities.' There are plans to build a large integrated steel mill with a capacity of 1.5–2 million tonnes using gas and anthracite coal for reduction. A project to develop a large deposit of around 10 million tonnes of iron ore at Thach Khe [in the north] is seeking foreign investment.

- **Food and foodstuff processing.** 'There is a great potential for strong expansion, but the industry has developed very slowly and its products often do not meet international quality standards. In this area, there are many opportunities for both domestic and foreign investors to do business.'

- **Textiles and garments.** 'Vietnamese have a good tradition in this field and the industry has been renewed in recent years with modern equipment from Japan and European countries. As a result, quality has improved and Vietnamese products have gained access to international markets. Exports in this sector have increased from $156 million in 1991 to $800 million in 1995. This sector also has high priority because it is relatively labour intensive and we have a comparative advantage in providing quality labour at a competitive cost.'

With this brief overview from the Vietnamese side, I now want to look at various key sectors in more detail. In some instances, this will be done through a case history approach dealing with one particular company in the sector. These 'snapshots' will also give some of the flavour of doing business in Vietnam today and provide anecdotal evidence of pitfalls that can face the unwary foreign investor. This theme also will be taken up in the next chapter on infrastructure development.

TEXTILES

Korean garment manufacturer Jung Kyung Seong is playing a multi-million dollar waiting game. Seong is general director of Hanjoo-Viet Thang, a joint venture garment company in the Thu Duc district of Ho Chi Minh City. Like many foreign and local investors, he was waiting for news on revised European Union quotas while at the same time crossing his fingers for Vietnam to obtain Most Favoured Nation (MFN) status from the United States, which would make the modest EU quotas relatively meaningless.

In 1994, the garment industry racked up over $500 million in earnings, but Vietnam-based manufacturers, blessed with an inexpensive labour force, believe this could be dramatically expanded if it was not for the quota system in key markets. 'Quotas are very difficult to control, and its hard to survive without them. For the hot items, it goes to the local companies only,' says Seong.

Quotas on most profitable items, such as jackets, are dealt out to state and private Vietnamese companies first, followed by the non-hot quota categories — simple styled shirts and work uniforms — issued to joint ventures. A limited number of more simply styled quota items (trousers, T-shirts) go to the 100 per cent foreign-invested companies, which account for most foreign investments in the industry. The garment industry so far has attracted 62 foreign companies investing over $130 million.

Seong estimates that about a half of most joint ventures' business involves quota-affected garments, compared to only about 20 per cent for 100 per cent foreign-invested companies. Most of the latter deal in non-quota garments for export to their home countries. However, even existing EU quotas affecting 161 categories of garments cause problems. 'Our company is unfortunately very much affected by the EU quotas. The quantity we received in 1995 is approximately only 15 per cent of our total production capacity this year,' said F.Nonnenmacher, General Manager of Triumph International (Vietnam) Ltd.

Another problem for investors relates to local sourcing of raw materials. Exporting companies need to have a Certificate of Origin (CO–Form A), which confirms that at least 60 per cent locally-procured raw materials have been used in their product, if they are to benefit from reduced import tariffs under the Generalized System of Preferences (GSP). Unfortunately, there is a definite lack of domestic raw materials to produce export-quality goods. Triumph International, for example, imports almost all of its raw materials for lingerie manufacture, and this applies to most export-oriented operations. 'It's not possible to source locally. The quality and delivery is not good,' says one foreign garment manufacturer.[3]

The Huy Hoang Company, the private enterprise mentioned in Chapter 2, also imports all its materials for precisely the same reason. Quality control is vital for this company as its entire stock is exported. The materials are provided by its customers to be made up into designated garments — primarily jackets, T-shirts and golf-wear — to designs either provided by the client or by Huy Hoang itself (these days there is a fairly even balance between the two). The company has big markets in France and Germany, and hopes to enlarge a small bridgehead in Britain, as well as in Japan. In the first year of operation, its two garment factories — a small one in the city and a much larger one in the suburbs on the road to Bien Hoa — only supplied the domstic market. But in the second year, the first foreign clients came knocking, and gradually the switch to processing for export expanded.

Because Huy Hoang has to import its materials at high cost, it needs to keep its prices down to take advantage of lower labour costs against other rivals in the Asian region. According to Nguyen Van Hoan, its deputy director-general, this is done by shaving profit margins to a maximum of 10 per cent, mostly for reinvestment, even though the end user will add huge mark-ups to the product price. Thus an average jacket priced at $40–60 in Vietnam will end up in Europe at anywhere from $280 to $350. 'Vietnam needs the jobs so we have to keep our prices down to keep receiving the orders,' explains Hoan.

Huy Hoang normally produces a sample garment for the client for approval before going into mass production. Should the quality not be up to scratch, and the customer returns the garments, they are usually offloaded in other markets, largely in Asia but also in Eastern Europe, Hoan admits.

The company is ambitious to move further upmarket and become a player in the high fashion field if it can find customers or a suitable joint venture partner. The suburban garment factory is also diversifying, with two workshops producing sports parachutes from imported material again. One workshop supplies the French market, the other Japan.[4]

STEEL

Vietnam's embryonic steel industry received a significant boost in January 1996 with the commencement of a $70 million steel plant in Ba Ria-Vung Tau between Vietnam Steel Corporation (VSC) and three Japanese partners: Kyoei Steel, Mitsui and Itochu. The Vina Kyoei plant, capable of producing 240,000 tonnes of steel bars and wire rods per year in its inital stage (with a second production line in the planning stage), is one of four that came on stream about the same time, pushing steel production up to 1.2 million tonnes from 360,000 tonnes in 1995. This contrasts with the demand for construction steel in 1995 of one million tonnes. Demand is growing about 20 per cent a year and the southern market alone was expected to take around half a million tonnes in 1996.

Another joint venture involves the Taiwanese company Ho-Asia Co. with several Vietnamese partners in the establishment of a steel mill at Can Tho in the Mekong Delta to produce 120,000 tonnes of bars and rods annually. The Vietnam Steel Corp., whose subsidiary Southern Steel Co. is one of the partners, said the joint venture was likely to be the last of its type allowed for some time. 'We are not encouraging more steel-rolling mills at present because the market is becoming rather crowded. Instead, we want steel mills that process iron ore in blast furnaces.'[5]

Survival of the domestic steel market hinges on imports. To protect domestic production the VSC has been lobbying the government to ban the import of all construction steel rods. Vietnam imports about 600,000 tonnes of steel each year. Despite a 40 per cent import tariff, the low price of imported steel makes the locally produced product expensive. Steel makers have also been urging the government to impose a tax levy on foreign joint ventures which currently import construction steel free of charge.[6] But the real issue is the domestic industry's high transport costs and low productivity which pushes up costs. 'Even with new steel plants, Vietnam will still need imports as the price of domestic products is always higher than imports,' predicts Thanh Van Hung, manager of the trading firm Polimex.

The industry's largest producer in the north and the biggest headache is the steel complex at Thai Nguyen, a provincial capital 80 kilometres from Hanoi, which produces about 100,000 tonnes a year. Built in the 1960s with Chinese aid, the sprawling site is a grim and blackened wasteland of outdated equipment that has poor transport links with its markets. While the more modern steel plants in the south of the country are profitable, Thai Nguyen's creaking equipment and work force of 13,500 have kept productivity low, according to the plant's general director Duong Khanh Lam.

Expanded in the 1970s with help from East Germany, Thai Nguyen is a relic of Vietnam's centrally planned past with ore mines, blast furnaces and rolling mills integrated into a vast but inefficient plant. According to official reports, the plant ran at just half of its capacity in 1994 an ended up stockpiling 13,000 tonnes of steel it was unable to sell because of competition from cheaper and higher quality products from overseas. But production is still cheaper at Thai Nguyen at around $310 a ton than at foreign joint ventures, which pay much more for labour, electricity, water and transport.

Reforms have broken down some of the elements of central planning by separating VSC from the Ministry of Heavy Industry, establishing it as a conglomerate controlling everything from production to marketing, plus the freedom to negotiate loans and other sources of additional capital for modernization and expansion.

It remains to be seen how independent state conglomerates will be under the reforms as they will have limited scope to take politically-charged decisions to cut excess labour, a key factor in raising productivity. One answer has been to transfer workers to new joint ventures, but VSC has been pushing for foreign companies to take more people than they need, raising labour costs. 'Contrary to what we expected labour costs are expensive because there are so few skilled workers,' said a foreign steel executive, who complained that the numbers required to run plants was much higher than in other countries.

Despite the difficulties, the industry has remained attractive for foreign investors. Among the giants of the steel world already in Vietnam, apart from the Japanese, are South Korea's Pohang Iron and Steel Co (POSCO) with five joint ventures, while German firm Mannesmann Krupp has for some time been studying the prospects of developing a combined iron ore mine and steel mill. However, in late 1996, the government said no more steel joint ventures would be allowed before 2000.

PAPER

Vietnam's paper industry is being reborn, Increasing domestic demand and rocketing world prices have set antiquated paper mills buzzing. In Vinh Phu province, Bai Bang Paper Co, initiated in 1974 with Swedish help, expected to put out 42,000 tonnes of relatively good grade paper in 1996, but Viet Tri Paper, born 22 years earlier, is struggling with 1950s Chinese technology and no money to upgrade its equipment.

If Bai Bang Paper Co. is a 'cat with nine lives' it has used up at least three of them in the last two decades. In its latest cycle, the pulp and paper mill can at long last see signs of prosperity. The Swedish and Vietnamese governments signed a pact to create a paper industry complex out of paddy fields in 1974, although it took eight years before the mill was completed. In 1975, when Vietnam had just emerged victorious in the war with the United States, it thought it could accomplish anything, including industrialization. Many mammoth projects were launched in the post-reunification period, but with insufficient resources available to the government, many were starved of cash and were delayed for years or their scope was drastically scaled down.

Bai Bang was one such example. Initially, it was planned to have a production capacity of 100,000 tonnes per year. But the Swedes persuaded Hanoi to be cautious and give serious thought to conservative choice of technology and the need to strike a balance between hopes and reality. The mill eventually was designed for an output of 50,000 tonnes with 1960s Swedish technology. Even in the mid-1990s, it was still not running at full capacity – 42,000 tonnes in 1995 against 34,000 tonnes the year before.

Through much of the 1980s, when Vietnam's economy hit rock bottom and the massive Swedish commitment to the Bai Bang project [$70 million and the involvement of some 5,000 Swedish experts from 1974 to 1990] drew criticism at home, the mill barely survived. The Soviet Union, until its demise, supplied most of the paper that Vietnam could not produce, while Hanoi's resources went to fund its occupation of Cambodia. No additional capital has been invested since the Swedes withdrew in 1990.

The company saw daylight again when aid from the Soviet Union dried up in 1990–91 and Vietnam absorbed anything Bai Bang could turn out. But an influx of cheap, smuggled products including writing and toilet paper from China between 1992 and mid-1994 quickly stalled the recovery. 'We suffered heavy losses as we could not sell products in stock until the first half of 1994,' recalls Tran Ngoc Que, the general director. In 1995, however, the company finally made its first profit as domestic demand for anything from packaging to white paper for photocopiers took the relatively high-end products from Bai Bang, which accounts for about a third of the country's paper production capacity.

Prospects look good for the industry, with Vietnam's demand for paper doubling to 400,000 tonnes by 2000, so Bai Bang wants to expand its annual production capacity to 70,000 tonnes by 1998. That goal seems realistic, provided Vietnam can resolve another problem — raw material supplies. Attracted by high prices of wood chips, the Forestry Ministry has in recent years been exporting chips to other paper producing countries such as Japan and Taiwan rather than ensuring supplies for domestic producers. 'We have to import pulp from Thailand and Indonesia while the Forestry Ministry is exporting wood chips. But we hope to be self-sufficient with the latest reorganization efforts,' said Que.

The situation is improving. The newly-formed National Paper Corporation, the core group of all state-owned paper producers, has set up its own subsidiary exclusively to handle raw materials to ensure steady supply. The government, meanwhile, has banned wood-chip exports.

Twenty-two years older, but only 20 kilometres from Bai Bang, is Viet Tri Paper Company, part of an industrial zone China helped North Vietnam to put into place in the 1950s. Viet Tri and Bai Bang date from different periods of industrialization and it shows. The former resembles a smaller version of the vast, decrepit Thai Nguyen Steel Complex, and has the same gloomy, grey appearance; the Bai Bang mills, meanwhile, shows lively touches of red, blue and green in its production facilities.

Maintained largely because its loyal workforce of 700 throughout wartime could not be laid off, and their children needed to be employed, Viet Tri has recently found the key to survival in a very successful line — toilet paper. Most urban Vietnamese have shifted from using second hand newspapers to toilet rolls. People in other major provinces are catching up. Completed in 1958 and opened in 1960 as a key plant designed, built and funded by the Chinese government, the Viet Tri factory produced paper for school text-books. Half of the plant was damaged by American bombing from 1967 to 1972. The Chinese designed a factory that could produce 18,000 tonnes of paper a year. But by the time bombing ended, production averaged 3,000 tonnes.

Vietnam's wave of reforms touched the factory in 1993 with the purchase of equipment from China to improve product quality. Despite domestic demand for paper, the factory knows it cannot expand production on machinery dating from the 1950s. 'This year, we can produce only 4,500 tonnes owing to the condition of these machines. It's very difficult to modernize,' says Doan Trung Can, the company director. The fiercely loyal workforce showed initiative by modifying equipment to enable toilet roll production without the use of new technology.The company also makes textbook paper, cardboard and hard paper for book covers.

'Our main market is in the north of Vietnam and we have plans to export to Russia, which is a big market for our good-enough products at competitive prices,' says the director. Output stands at only 500 tonnes a year, maximum capacity given the age of the equipment. There is room for growth as current demand in the north is about 1,500 tonnes a year, with the supply shortfall met by China. In the south, where demand is estimated at 2,500 tonnes, local production so far has only reached only 400 tonnes as year.

Viet Tri Paper's staff earn an average of 300,000 dong a month, less than half that of Bai Bang. Most of the former's 700 employees have followed in the footsteps of parents who worked at the factory before them. Nguyen Thi Thanh, 28, is a example. Her father and mother, who are now retired, worked for Viet Tri Paper for 25 years and have sent four of their children to the factory. 'I couldn't get into college, so I came to work here seven years ago,' said Thanh, 'A few years ago, it took me such a long time to save money to buy a set of clothes. But now life is much better. I intend to work here as long as this mill can survive.'

Her bosses have the same idea. The government promised to help increase Viet Tri Paper's annual production capacity to 20,000 tonnes, of which the company decided to use 1,500 tonnes to make toilet paper. According to Can, the paper mills in Bai Bang and in Tan Mai of Dong Nai province in the south are the only two factories in Vietnam that can get anywhere close to using advanced technology.

'The rest of the mills around the country are operating with anti-quated machines. We are gradually replacing them as we can't afford a whole new set all at once.' The Vietnamese say no foreign investment commitment has been made in their paper industry, probably because of the slump world-wide. 'It's necessary for a factory like Viet Tri Paper to enter joint ventures since expensive production modernization needs capital we don't have,' said Can. He wonders why Vietnam's promising paper industry fails to attract these investors. 'Are they worried about the investment environment, raw material supply or costs? They shouldn't, because this is going to be a growth industry.'[7]

AUTOMOBILES

Early in 1996, Japan's Mitsubishi Motors Corp. decided on a drastic cut in its projected vehicle output from Vina Star Motors Corp., its joint venture with the state-run Vietranscimex.[8] The figures are somewhat startling. Output was to be reduced from the earlier target of 2,000–3,000 vehicles to 600–800 units — the sort of production figures one might have expected for the hand-built vehicles from the earliest days of the automobile! Mitsubishi's Tokyo headquarters said the decision had been taken because the joint venture only sold 500 small buses and trucks in 1995, mostly to state-run enterprises.

Mitsubishi said an inadequate sales network of only 10 dealer-ships nationwide and an inflow of cheaper used foreign vehicles accounted for the poor performance. The joint venture had been due to start passenger car production in 1996, but decided to concentrate its efforts on improving the dealership network instead. Mitsubishi established Vina Star in 1991 with Vietranscimex and the Japanese company's Malaysian affiliate Proton, with an original output target of 1,000 small buses and trucks per year. The Japanese firm also began making the Pajero, an off-road vehicle, at its Vietna-mese factory to take up some of the production slack.

Edgar Chiongban, vice-president of Vietnam Motors Corp., assembler of various German, Japanese and Korean models,[91] has similar problems. Although VMC got the biggest share of the government's 1996 assembly quota, the allotted number of vehicles had all been built by the middle of April. What, he asks, 'are we going to do for the rest of the year?'

These experiences are fairly typical of the Vietnamese automotive market at present. Yet, in what may seem akin to putting the cart before the horse, most foreign car-and-truck makers still seem keen to assemble cars and trucks in Vietnam. This is optimism indeed, considering the fact that much of the country's road network remains in tatters, the result of war damage and poor maintenance. In the two main cities, Hanoi and Ho Chi Minh City, taxis fight a constant battle for road space with waves of bicycles and motor cycles, and travel between virtually any two places throughout the country is a time-consuming and often dangerous experience.

Never in the history of the automotive industry can such a poor country (where the average annual income at the time of writing wouldn't even buy a set of tyres) with such a small market[10] have attracted such intense interest from investors. The government has issued 12 vehicle-assembly licences in an effort to jump start the fledgling industry. But at the same time, a series of measures designed to build up a domestic components sector is actually stalling the industry just when it should be moving into second gear. The assembly quotas issued by the Ministry of Trade, necessitated by its ban on import of semi-knockdown units (SKDs) and strict controls on complete-knowndown (CKD) kits, are so restrictive that one assembler says the 'ministry is our biggest competitor'.

To illustrate the way the government is keeping its foot on the brake, one only has to look at the ministry's 1996 import quota for vehicles with under 12 seats. Completely built-up units (CBUs), whether new or used, were restricted to 1,500. CKD kits were pegged at 3,500. Of this total, VMC received an allocation of 750 units. To put that into some sort of perspective, one might consider that South Korea now produces two million cars a year, and its factories could cope with Vietnam's entire CKD quota in one eight-hour shift.

In desperation, mainly to keep the plant open and to avoid massive layoffs, VMC in 1995 decided to keep producing its Korean KIA trucks even though there were few buyers. These ended up packed into its warehouses for months on end.

And yet, foreign companies are still knocking on the door — although perhaps a little less loudly than before.

So why is Vietnam so irresistible? The Americans, it seems, want to avoid losing another Southeast Asian market to Japan. The Japanese are moving aggressively because they have had good experiences in other Southeast Asian markets and would like to block the competition out of the region completely which dominance in Vietnam would certainly accomplish.[11]

The Japanese are also keenly aware of their failure to recognize the early potential of the Chinese market where their late arrival has put them at something of a disadvantage against their European and American rivals.[12] Toyota, whose Crown model has virtually replaced the Soviet Volga as Vietnamese government officials' preferred means of transport, has eventual plans to assemble 20,000 cars, minibuses and vans a year, which, if successful, would make it the big fish in a small pond. In October 1996 it began modest production of its Corolla Sedan and HiAce commercial vehicle from semi-knockdown kits.

The Europeans and South Koreans, meanwhile, are also seeking gains from getting in on the ground floor. Hyundai Motor Co. surprised everyone in August 1995 when it announced it had signed a joint venture agreement with Corporation 990, a firm under the control of the Ministry of the Interior, for a $200 million car factory near Ho Chi Minh City. Until the announcement, nobody knew the Koreans were planning any such move. Hyundai said it would hold a 65 per cent stake and the Singaporean firm Sae Yong International 15 per cent in the venture to create a plant capable of turning out 20,000 passenger cars, vans and light trucks per year.

Alas, the Korean announcement proved premature, as the authorities in Ho Chi Minh City rejected the application on the grounds the project did not offer sufficient technology transfer nor an adequate commitment on the use of local spare parts. But Hyundai remained hopeful the problems could be resolved in time — although another stumbling block appeared to be a demand by the local authorities that the Koreans pay land rent up-front for the entire 40—year span of the joint venture as well as the cost of site clearance.

Given the size of the market — conservative sales projections of 40,000 vehicles a year by the turn of the century from the government, and 60,000—80,000 units among more optimistic market analysts — even if Hyundai fails to get in, there will still be too many manufacturers, so that an eventual shakedown will be necessary in which a number will either have to merge or retire from the fray.

The attractiveness of Vietnam is twofold. With economic growth expected to average between eight and 10 per cent until the end of the century, vehicle makers and the government believe incomes will be high enough to justify making and selling cars and trucks domestically. But for the next few years, the product mix will swing in favour of commercial vehicles, a direct result of the government's tax regime which penalizes private car use. The likelihood is that Isuzu, Toyota and Mitsubishi primarily will assemble light commercial vans – pickups and passenger vans; Ford and Chrysler will likely counter with mini-vans, sports utilities, compact cars and maybe larger pick-up trucks; Mercedes, meanwhile, will concentrate on the heavy commercial vehicle segment, as it has done in Thailand and Indonesia.

Undaunted by the plethora of competition, Japan's number two manufacturer Nissan Motors threw its hat into the ring in spring 1996 when it obtained permission for a joint venture to build cars and pickup trucks in Da Nang. The venture is owned 25 per cent by Da Nang Automobile Mechanical Factory and 75 per cent by Nissan TCM, an investment company formed with Tan Chong & Sons Motor of Malaysia and the Japanese trading company Marubeni. It was hoped to start production in 1998 at 1,000 vehicles a year rising to 3,000 by the turn of the century.[13]

Nissan's move towards Da Nang is in line with the trend for most manufacturers to concentrate in the south, especially Ho Chi Minh City, where demand accounts for 70 per cent of the national total, with Hanoi taking another 20 per cent. 'That's where the largest market is at the moment and for the next few years to come,' says Dr Sieghard Ehner, regional manager of Mercedes Benz based in Hanoi. His parent company, Daimler-Benz, plans one plant in the north and one in the south, representing a total investment of $70 million and focusing on the assembly of trucks and vans.[14] It sees demand for commercial vehicles reaching 11,000 by 2005, but also aims to be selling between 500 and 600 of its luxury saloon cars in Vietnam by then. The company has a car dealership in Ho Chi Minh City, where it sold its first car to a Vietnamese businessmen in July 1994.

Germany is already represented in the north, where BMW assembles luxury sedans at a plant in Hanoi. But Volkswagen postponed its plans for a passenger car plant citing the 'very low market for cars in the foreseeable future'. This is in sharp contrast to China, where VW was the first foreign company to launch car production in the mid-1980s, reaping the rewards of enduring a traumatic opening few years with a current large market-share and the gratitude of the Chinese government.

Certainly, there is no argument that on current figures VW's caution may be justified. But ultimately, the various foreign vehicle makers hope to use Vietnam as a springboard to export some of what they produce to other countries, particularly other Asean members. 'I think there is a good opportunity for exports here,' predicts Vance Peacock, director of local operations for Chrysler, which is investing around $200 million in making Jeep four-wheel drive vehicles, light trucks and a version of its Neon saloon. 'We realize that you can't wait to enter a market until it's fully developed. It's too expensive.'

Chryler's initial strategy was to have its manufacturing facility fully operational by 1997, although, as I will shortly discuss, this is now in doubt; at full capacity, the factory was supposed to be capable of producing 17,000 vehicles a year, starting with Dodge Dakotas in 1997, the Cherokee Jeep in 1998 and the Plymouth Neon in 1999. Domestically, the company identified four potential customer areas – a growing Vietnamese middle class, fleet sales to government, joint venture companies, and the 140,000 owners of ageing Russian vehicles still on the road.

When it came to selecting a local company for collaboration, the now defunct Ministry of Heavy Industry first directed Chrysler to Vietnam Engine and Agricultural Machinery (VEAM) who then guided the company to its eventual partner, Vinapro. Chrysler officials say they accepted Vinapro because it was based in Dong Nai province where the Americans wanted to locate their plant, possessed 'technical savvy' from experience building small diesel engines for export to Taiwan and from obtaining Japanese process technology, and had a knowledgeable, experienced management committed to make the proposed venture succeed.

Dong Nai Province was chosen because of the proximity of a deep water port at Vung Tau and commercial centre of Ho Chi Minh City; there was a relatively good road network (Highway 51) for transporting heavy containers from Vung Tau to the plant site. The site located in the Thanh Tuy Ha industrial zone avoided having to displace and relocate local residents or 'squatters', a costly and time-consuming aspect of construction projects in Vietnam, as will become clear in a subsequent chapter.

Highway 51 is slated to become an 'industrial corridor' connecting Vung Tau, Bien Hoa (site of a giant American air base during the war) and Ho Chi Minh City, with good access to new deep water ports along the Saigon River, a new international airport between the former southern capital and Vung Tau and an expanded road and rail network to the rest of the country.

Dong Nai, incidentally is also the site of a light truck manufacturing factory being built by Suzuki Motors. It is the main partner in a $21 million venture with the Japanese trading company Nissho Iwai and Vietnam's state-owned Vikyoo, to initially produce 500 trucks a year, eventually rising to 3,500, with 10 per cent allocated for export.

If all the proposed projects are built, by the year 2007, foreign joint ventures will be assembling more than 120,000 cars, trucks and buses each year. This worries some investors. 'The government is issuing too many licences for this small market,' said Naoko Tatebe, general director of Mekong Corp., which has been assembling four-wheel drive vehicles since 1992. 'One or two is enough,' agreed Wann Lee, former general director of Vidamco, owned partly by Daewoo Corp. Some of the cars assembled in Vietnam hopefully will be sold to neighbouring countries. In fact, Vidamco's operating licence requires it to export one-fifth of its output to earn hard currency. But most companies are counting on Vietnam's 72 million people for the bulk of demand.

The government, which sees kit assembly as the first step towards fully-fledged domestic manufacturing, initially encouraged operations by setting tariffs on unassembled kits as low as 20 per cent. At the same time, it levied tariffs of 200 per cent on new passenger cars and 150 per cent on new minivans. The Trade Ministry shocked the industry in May 1995 when it recommended limiting the year's imports of car and minivan knockdown-kits to 2,000, barely five per cent of domestic capacity. The ministry quickly appeared to back off from that policy, but left it unclear how many kits would be allowed. Alarm over the quota erupted as car companies already were fuming about the government's removal of a ban on importing second-hand vehicles, Used cars, mostly Japanese and Korean, are a popular alternative to pricier new ones.

Executives doubted the government would stick to its plan to phase out second-hand imports over the next few years. 'It's just like a drug addict,' said Thomas Cook, Ford's director of new business in Asia. 'Once you start with used cars you can't stop.' Hanoi lifted the ban as a way to supply buyers with more affordable cars and generate tariff revenues, explained Nguyen Xuan Chuan, Vice Minister of Heavy Industry. Chuan acknowledged the imports would reduce sales of domestic assemblers, but urged foreign investors not to lose heart. 'I think the risk of not being in Vietnam for ever is a bigger risk than facing second-hand cars,' he said.

But Chrysler for one is unconvinced. It has set its key target as lobbying the government to make sure regulations in place to protect those who decide to invest.'We have decided to make an investment here and don't want to be overwhelmed by cheap imports coming into the country and hurting our markets,' said one official.

There is considerable frustration among investors at what they see as Hanoi's erratic policies. State planners originally said they would allow only four firms to set up in the sector, but then threw the door open to all-comers when Japanese manufacturers complained about the restrictions. Chrysler, for one, said its decision to enter the Vietnamese market was based on what it considered a government guarantee that no more than six assembly licenses would be issued. A company source, while denying rumours that it planned to scrap its project, did admit that the country's 'extremely low' vehicle sales made Chrysler's initial assembly target of January 1998 somewhat unrealistic. At the time of writing, the company was reassessing its investment plan on the assumption that profitability of any sort was likely to be a very long-term proposition.

Import duties and assembly licensing requirements have been altered several times since 1992. In a policy designed to shift demand in favour of domestically assembled vehicles, a July 1994 directive raised the import duty on passenger cars by 200 per cent and banned imports of used cars. Six months later the government reversed part of the directive and authorized the import of used cars. As the used car imports were counted as part of total imports, this had the effect of drastically lowering the quota on completely knocked-down (CKD) kits for vehicles with 12 seats of less to 2000 in 1995 (as already noted this was raised to 3,500 in 1996).

The two major domestic manufacturers, Vietnam Motor Corp.and Mekong Corp.[15] quickly petitioned the Ministry of Trade to reconsider as they had already fulfilled their allocation for the year. VMC, the biggest player in the market with 850 passenger cars sold domestically last year, compared with 400 for Mekong, pointed out that it had received a quota of only 600 kits when it had an *annual production capacity of 20,000 vehicles*. As a result, the company said it would have to lay off at least 500 workers at its Hanoi plant.

Nguyen Huy Phong, deputy general director of Mekong Corp said his company's plans to start assembling up to 3000 Fiat cars a year at their plant in Ho Chi Minh City would be jeopardized. 'Annual output of below 1,500 units means a certain loss to any manufacturer in this market, since turnover from low sales would hardly cover the high production costs,' he said. Meanwhile, Vu Kuoc Binh, VMC's Material Supply Manager, said the company wanted to set up a spare parts plant in the South to produce water cooling system and seats, but 'whether this operation will get off the ground will depend largely on how much we can get off imported kits supply. Because, if we can only produce 600 cars there is no economy of scale to make any investment worthwhile'.

The decision to limit imports of kits apparently was aimed at building up a components industry in Vietnam. What officials did not seem to realize was that parts production of the quality insisted upon by foreign manufacturers would require massive investment that could not be offset by returns from the limited vehicle market.

Nevertheless, existing and would-be investors have had to agree to a government demand that five per cent of vehicle parts they use be locally made within five years, rising to 40 per cent after — a move clearly designed to weed out companies that are not deemed serious about technology transfer. Privately, however, some foreign executives say finding the right sort of local parts is likely to be tough in a country where even the indigenous bicycle industry has difficulty surviving with outmoded technology.

VMC, for example, was struggling to get a seat manufacturing joint venture in place, while admitting that even if they can persuade the Ministry of Trade to include the value of assembly labour in the localization percentage, it still would not approach five per cent of the vehicle value. 'Localization doesn't happen that quickly,' says Hanoi-based consultant James Rockwell, who advises on industry matters for American manufacturers. 'You won't be able to force the auto industry to use local parts just by enforcing the law if they aren't up to scratch on quality.'

The answer — as it has been in China — will probably be for the manufacturers to invite their key parts suppliers to join them in Vietnam. But these have so far been sparse on the ground. Manufacturers are working on a potential solution involving the sharing of components. If they could come up with a few dozen low-tech parts that were interchangeable among vehicles, so the argument goes, they would stand a better chance of luring components suppliers into the market with some sort of economies of scale.

A few pioneers have begun to appear. Apart from its car assembly project, Mitsubishi is looking to set up a $60 million tyre plant in Ho Chi Chi Minh City, while another Japanese firm, Storage Battery Ltd, was reported to be looking at a $15 million joint venture for battery production in the same area. MK Plastics of Japan already has a modest $9.6 million investment in the production of plastic parts.[16]

When Honda Motor Co. received a licence for its $104 million motorcycle assembly joint venture, its exclusive supplier of bulbs and electrical equipment in Japan, Stanley Electric Co., quickly announced plans for its own local production base. The company quickly formed a $4.3 million joint venture with the Import-Export Construction and Investment Co. of Hanoi for a factory in the Gia Lam district of the capital.

In Vietnam, the generic word for motorbikes is 'Honda', and the streets of Hanoi and Ho Chi Minh are a constantly moving advertisement for the Japanese firm. For years, Honda exported its machines from its factories in Japan and Thailand. But production was scheduled to begin in Vietnam by the end of 1997. Its joint venture, in which Honda has a 70 per cent stake and its local partner Vietnam Engine and Agricultural Machinery the remainder, will use frame parts shipped in from Thailand and engine components from Japan in the initial stage.

Stanley's commitment, however, will make it easier for Honda and its rival Suzuki — which is spending some $33 million on its own production venture — will have a slightly easier time meeting the government's insistence that 60 per cent of the total value of assembled parts be locally produced by the end of the fifth year of production. Honda planned initial production of 200,000 machines, while Suzuki's target was 100,000. Kotaro Uchiyama, Stanley Electronic's chief representative in Vietnam, said the company's proposed project would be able to supply not only these two, but also Yamaha, which is also anxious to begin assembling as soon as possible.

Another Japanese company eager to move in is Sumitomo, which proposed a $20 million joint venture with Vietnam Gold Star Rubber Co., to produce an estimated 600,000 tyres and inner tubes per year. There are also 14 Taiwan-invested manufacturing facilities already operating in various parts of Vietnam producing motorcycle parts ranging from piston rings and batteries to plastics.

ELECTRICAL GOODS

In April 1996, South Korea's Samsung Electronics opened a $36.5 million factory in Ho Chi Minh City to manufacture television sets and refrigerators for the growing domestic market.[17] This is a sector which is just beginning to take off and Korean companies, such as Daewoo, Hyundai and the LG Group, have been among the prominent early birds, along with Japanese giants like Sony.

Of particular interest in the Samsung deal is that its local partner is a private company rather than a state-owned enterprise – Trade Import-Export Co. (TIE). The Koreans have a dominant 70 per cent stake in the joint venture, which will initially produce 70,000 television sets and 30,000 refrigerators a year. Samsung hopes, however, that it will not be too long before production can rise to 350,000 televisions and 100,000 refrigerators. 'We'll increase slowly as the market evolves', says Shin Seung-Taek, president of the joint venture known as Savina.

Samsung Electronics, a subsidiary of Samsung Corporation, began selling black and white televisions in Vietnam in the early 1980s and claims to have built this into a 20 per cent market share. Total annual sales were running at around 700,000 sets by the mid-1990s.

'We expect total demand to grow to 1.5 million sets by the turn of the century, so if we can retain our current mrket share we'll easily reach our target production capacity,' says the Savina president. Samsung will import components for the first three years, but expects to have a local component level of around 50 per cent by the end of that period, with a long-term goal of being totally self-sufficient once the necessary technology transfers can be arranged and absorbed.

Even as the television/refrigerator plant was being completed, Samsung Corp. was launching a feasibility study for another plant to produce household electronic products such as stereos, video cassette recorders and air conditioners.[18]

The Dutch electronics group Philips is also in the process of establishing a strong presence. Philips has been supplying kit parts for 14-inch televisions to Vietronics Bien Hoa, near Ho Chi Minh City,

with an annual production of 6,000 sets, along with the trial production of electric irons with a local company Cholifax. Now it is
moving on to the next stage of producing its own television sets in
the country. The company said it would be establishing a 'significant
industrial presence' although manufacture of large-scale electronic
products would only take place 'after a significant market presence
has been obtained in order to support the investment'.[19]

Sony, meanwhile, in early 1996 began building a new consumer
electronics plant in the Binh Thanh district of Ho Chi Minh City which
it reckoned would triple its existing in-country production capacity.
The Japanese were spending some $3 million on the project, in which
they hold a 70 per cent equity stake, with its local partner Vietronics
Tan Binh Co.(controlled by the Ministry of Industry). The new factory
was supposed to be operational by the end of 1996 with an annual
productive capacity of 300,000 television sets, a similar number of
audio products such as hi-fis and radio cassettes, and 150,000
video cassette recorders.

Sony began producing television sets and radio cassettes in
November 1994. At that time, said general director Masaaki Terada,
'our feasibility study suggested we would need to move to a bigger
plant after three years or so, so we have actually moved on much
earlier than expected.

One problem for the Japanese is a government demand that its
products, mainly intended for the local market, have at least 20 per
cent local content rather than importing everything from Japan. Part
of the new investment would be used for new equipment to produce
some of the key components, but efforts to persuade Sony's big
suppliers in Japan to follow the company into Vietnam so far had
not been successful, Terada said. 'The problem is that even with a
factory three times bigger than before, we're still not close to the
break-even point to make it worthwhile for our suppliers in Japan
to invest at present.'

OIL, GAS AND COAL

Since Vietnam's law on foreign investment was passed in 1987, Petro-
Vietnam, the state oil agency, has signed 29 production-sharing
contracts, but the results to date have generally been modest. Up
until mid-1995, about 100 wells had been drilled with 11 potential
commercial oil and gas discoveries. While that has raised some

pessimism about Vietnam's oil/gas reserves, it might be well to remember that substantial investment in exploration took place in the North Sea with little encouragement prior to the discovery of the Forties Field in 1970. To date, comparatively few wells have been drilled offshore Vietnam.

Big names such as Shell, BP, Lasmo, Total and Australia's BHP started prospecting in the early 1990s in an area 350 km south of Vung Tau known as the Nam Con Son Basin hoping for big finds. At the time, the talk about Vietnam's oil and gas potential had Vietnam down as one of the largest prospects in Asia and by 1995, the total investment by some 30 oil companies had reached $1.5 billion. However, most major oil companies have been disappointed. None of the eight operators who had drilled wells so far in the Nam Con Son have made significant discoveries and in many cases they have concluded that the geology is too complex to justify further exploration investment.[20]

Shell alone invested $150 million in exploration in Vietnam since 1988, with mixed results and in 1996 it decided to pull out, leaving only its downstream ventures in lubricants, bitumen and liquefied petroleum gas. America's Mobil Oil, which prospected for oil before the end of the Vietnam war forced it out in 1975, failed in its first two atempts on return in the mid-1990s, but tried again with a third well, the deepest ever drilled in Vietnam at 5,000 metres, in the Thanh Long (Blue Dragon) field. Britain's Enterprise Oil, an early arrival, continues in hope despite having drilled four wells without commercial success just off Vung Tau.

But promising oil strikes in adjacent blocks by Japan Vietnam Petroleum Company, a subsidiary of Mitsubishi Corp.and Petronas Carigali of Malaysia, in June 1995 did encourage some companies to bid for exploration rights in other unassigned blocks in the Cuu Long (Mekong) basin north of Nam Con Son in the hope of finding the elusive pot of gold. The Cuu Long Basin is unique in that the bulk of the oil found so far has been in the 'basement' (at depths greater than 3,000 metres). This could lead to complications, since basement-level drilling is difficult to predict. Oil discoveries in the Nam Con Son are above basement level and therefore more coventional.

Total proved, probable and potential reserves offshore are estimated at anywhere from a conservative 1.7 billion barrels to a more optimistic 3.5 billion barrels, but industry analysts feel it is still too early for accurate predictions. Nevertheless, there are some in the government and industry who feel that the oil industry may not fulfil its early hopes and that, in fact, natural gas may prove to be the saviour of the country's hydrocarbon exploitation process.

Crude oil already is the country's top foreign exchange earner,[21] most of it exported to Japan.The bulk of this comes from the Bach Ho (White Tiger) field, a venture between Vietnam and the former Soviet Union known as VietSovPetro. However, these amounts are not enough to ensure Vietnam achieves targeted double digit growth by the year 2000 unless other viable amounts are discovered. Industry analysts already predict that Bach Ho production will decline by the turn of the century.

Even a promising strike by BHP at Dai Hung (Big Bear) field in the same area, initially thought to contain 750 million barrels of oil, was subsequently downgraded to an estimate of recoverable oil totalling 100–500 million barrels. Daily output by late 1995 had slumped to just over 15,000 barrels per day (bpd) from the 35,000 bpd achieved when production started in October 1994, forcing the Australian firm to say it would either have to renegotiate its production sharing contract (PSC) with PetroVietnam or withdraw as further development of this field would be uneconomic.

One problem that quickly surfaced was that the Melbourne-based company became involved largely on the basis of two dimensional seismic data recorded by VietSovPetro, the Russo-Vietnamese joint venture. Only later was it able to do a full appraisal using 3D seismic data which revealed a highly compartmentalized and faulted structure that added considerably to the extraction costs. BHP has been along this route before. It first arrived in Vietnam in the late 1960s, working in a joint venture with a former subsidiary of Shell, pulling out in 1972 abortive exploration of the Nam Con Son Basin. In 1989 it returned to bid successfully for two blocks southeast of Da Nang. But after drilling two unsuccessful wells, it relinquished the PSC in April 1994.

Vietnam's image. and its ambitions in the energy sector, were not helped when Total of France abruptly withdrew from involvement in a planned $1.2 billion oil refinery which would have been the country's first. Total had conducted a feasibility study for a site close to the oil fields, but the government asked the company to look instead at Dung Quat, a remote site on the country's central coastal belt. the area had been chosen for political rather than commercial reasons – the aim being to boost the economy of the poor central region.

However, the move backfired when Total concluded that Dung Quat was too far from crude oil sources to make it economically viable and that the area lacked basic infrastructure. Industry experts were left wondering whether Vietnam's policy-makers understood the commercial realities behind such a project, despite strong interest from other companies to take Total's place. Indeed, with an anticipated refining over-capacity in Southeast and North Asia as a result of ambitious plans by South Korean energy companies, some analysts question the wisdom of Vietnam building any refinery at all.

To encourage more offshore investment and establish a legal and fiscal regulatory framework for the management and conduct of offshore operations, the National Assembly passed the Petroleum Law in July 1993, followed shortly after by various regulations covering the the conduct of petroleum operations, the health and safety of the offshore work force, the protection of the offshore environment, the fiscal and royalty rates, and the management and inspection of petroleum operations.

Investment in Vietnam's industries other than oil and gas have been prone to failure, due in part to inadequacies in the domestic legal framework. This cannot be said to hinder upstream investment in the oil and gas industry, where the legal regime is similar to that which regulates the industry in most parts of the world. Many oil companies now have specialized downstream lubricant, lpg or bitumen joint ventures, but there does not appear to be any clear policy on the future development of other sectors of Vietnam's downstream industries, including the distribution and marketing of gasoline and diesel.

This may be due to there being no oil ministry in Vietnam which would be responsible for, among other things, the drafting of a downstream petroleum policy. While a number of foreign companies have agreed on sponsorship arrangements with the owners of retail sites in Vietnam — whereby they upgrade the facility and provide advice on basic environmental, health and safety issues, in return for which they are entitled to display the corporate logo of that company — only five state companies are licensed by the Ministry of Trade to import, distribute and market petroleum products. These are: Petrolimex(Ministry of Trade), Petrochem (PetroVietnam), Saigon Petro (Ho Chi Minh City People's Committee), Kerogasimex (Ministry of Defence) and Vietnam Air Petro Company (Civil Aviation Authority of Vietnam).

On the domestic side, the key role is played by PetroVietnam, which is being turned into a semi-autonomous state agency with wide-ranging powers and ambitions. After years as a state-owned enterprise, the first move towards restructuring came in January 1995 when the government defined it as a corporation. It has a new four-member governing board headed by Finance Minister Ho Te.

The next stage of the transformation was to win control over its budget and start to have a consolidated profit-and-loss account. Previously, revenue from oil exports went directly to the state budget controlled by the treasury department of the Finance Ministry. Any spending by PetroVietnam theoretically had to be approved by the same ministry. With the restructuring, PetroVietnam is able to collect and keep oil revenues, while paying tax on them in line with international practice. The funds it accumulates are then supposed to go towards further business expansion. To ensure it will become the 'spearhead body' for the national industry, PetroVietnam received a capital injection of some $800 million at the end of 1995.[22]

Looking ahead, General Director Ho Si Thoang says the firm has ambitions to produce and supply fertilizers, petrochemicals — based on estimates of average 30 per cent growth a year up to 2010 — and PVC, and wants to supply power to power plants. It is also doing a feasibility study on a planned second oil refinery.[23]

If there is some scepticism about Vietnam's oil future among foreign operators, the picture is slightly better as regards gas. On the Vietnamese side at least there is confidence the country can support a major gas industry, but billions of dollars of investment will be needed to build links between producers and consumers. After years of focusing on oil production from Vietnam's three offshore fields, interest has turned to gas, with BP and its Norwegian partner Statoil announcing three important finds in the Nam Con Son Basin. But a number of crucial issues remain to be resolved. Development of gas production and markets needs to be simultaneous, requiring huge sums of capital and coordination of pricing and policy.

Unlike oil, the gas market works on long-term contracts often up to 25 years, that tie producers and consumers into close relationships. A master plan was due out in 1996 which foreign companies hoped would address three key issues: Vietnam's position on exports, the allocation of the energy source to particular industries and pricing policy. 'If gas is undepriced, wastage will be encouraged and the country will fail to make the most efficient use of a valuable resource,' says BP General Manager Ian Forbes. 'If it is overpriced, gas will fail to compete effectively with other fuels.'

Because of the heavy subsidizing of the power industry, there are worries that the prices set for natural gas will be unrealistically low. To generate power using the gas, which is the most obvious use, requires a reasonabkle price to be paid by the state electric company. But the price currently charged for power is far below the rate necessary for generators to make a decent profit. In fact, electricity for years has been sold below production cost.

BP and Statoil estimate reserves in two fields already explored at 57 billion cubic metres. But BP said a third significant gas find in the Nam Con Son Basin increased confidence that Vietnam can develop a 'substantial offshore gas industry'. Estimates of Vietnam's total recoverable reserves, including associated gas from oil fields, are up to five times the BP figure. That could provide Vietnam with energy for power stations, materials for petrochemical plants to produce fertilizer and heat for steel furnaces as well as the possibility of exporting LPG. Vietnam's potential is modest compared to other areas in Asia, such as Indonesia's Natuna field, where Exxon Corp is to develop reserves estimated at 6.3 trillion cubic metres at a cost of $34 billion.

The evolution of the industry in Vietnam began in November 1993 when, after numerous delays, Hyundai Corp. of South Korea won a contract for a $80 million 125–kilometre pipeline to bring associated gas ashore from the Bach Ho oil field. Prime Minister Vo Van Kiet opened the pipeline in May 1995 to feed a 270–megawatt power station in Ba Ria providing electicity to Ho Chi Minh City.

In July 1995, Bouygues Offshore of France and Samsung Heavy Industries of South Korea, were awarded a $122.8 million contract to supply a gas compressor platform for the Bach Ho field, beating off 19 other groups who had bid for the contract. Samsung will build the platform, while Bouygues Offshore will install it in the oilfield, where the bad weather at times is comparable to Britain's North Sea oil fields. The platform due to be operation by mid-1997, will have a capacity of four million cubic metres, which its operators plan to double over an unspecified period.

The project was to be operated by the Vietnam Oil and Gas Corp., a planned joint venture between British Gas plc, Japan's Mitsui & Co., and VietSovPetro, the Russian-Vietnamese venture now operating at Bach Ho. But it suffered a setback in November 1995, when Mitsui announced it was pulling out, while British Gas said it was scaling back its involvement because of apparent problems in setting terms with the government.

The key issue seemed to be that establishing the necessary infrastructure for bringing the gas onshore would push up its price to two to three times the level prevailing in similar projects in Indonesia and the Middle East. Despite this, British Gas said it was still interested in the lpg plant alone, and the government said it would proceed with the offshore side of the project by itself.[24]

Shell Vietnam has an agreement with state-owned Shipbreaking and Industrial Gas Production Co. to a lpg plant in Haiphong.[25] This includes a LPG import terminal and bottling plant. Local press reports quoted Shell officials as saying the company chose the northern site because rivals were more advanced with similar plans in the south. At the same time, the north would eventually account for 40 per cent of national demand. Taiwan's Ching Fong Group is also involved in a $11 million LPG plant in Haiphong. But a proposed joint venture between the Vietnamese Petroleum Import-Export Corp. and Wesfarmers Ltd. was terminated before it got off the ground after a re-evaluation by the Australian firm concluded that with new import duties and tax regime, allied to doubts over market conditions, the project was no longer as attractive as originally envisaged.[26]

In October 1995, meanwhile, a consortium including BP, Statoil, Tractabel of Belgium and Tomen Corp. of Japan, signed a memorandum of understanding with Vietnamese partners for a feasibility study for a huge power station and urea plant near Ho Chi Minh City using the gas found by BP in Nam Con Son. The partners could end up spending as much as $1 billion building production facilities offshore and an undersea pipeline to make use of the gas it found. A further $1 billion could be needed to develop a market for the gas onshore.

The gas will be supplied via a 400 km pipeline to the $800 million Phu My combined power/fertilizer plant — comprising four generators producing 600–Mw, and a 750,000 tonnes-a-year urea fertilizer plant — which is supposed to come on line by early 1999 at the latest. This is expected to consume 1.3 billion cubic metres of gas a year by the turn of the century.

Apart from power generation, the benefits to agriculture from the gas developments are also significant. Most of the foreign exchange earned through rice exports is swallowed up by the import costs of urea fertilizer, so local production of this commodity will considerable improve the balance of payments. And although Vietnam needs the gas domestically, it is also keen to export as much as possible, possibly to Thailand, which is known to be looking at further import sources.

The coal sector, meanwhile, was on the verge of bankruptcy in 1994 with output of only three million tons. But, after the government undertook a streamlining of management and marketing practices, the 1995 figure was more than doubled to 7.6 million tons. One key step was the decision to centralize all production activities under the Vietnam Coal Corporation, creating a monopoly in seeming contradiction to the country's general moves towards a market-oriented economy. The corporation has now been given the task of expanding the exploration and exploitation of coal deposits, especially in the Red River Delta, where deposits are thought to be larger than those currently being tapped in Quang Ninh Province, the current main producing area.

Prime Minister Vo Van Kiet has urged the coal industry, one of Vietnam's major exporters, to produce 10 per cent more per year to achieve annual output of 10 million tonnes by the end of the century. The prime minister also called for drastic measures to stop coal 'pirates' who appear to be holding back efforts to boost national coal production. The pirates mine illegally on the fringes of open-cast mines or loot coal trains. The government reckons 20 to 25 per cent of national output in recent years is currently siphoned off illegally.

PHARMACEUTICALS

Vietnam's health-care system is being resuscitated from the verge of collapse by regular infusions of foreign aid and foreign investment. Over 20 joint ventures and wholly foreign-invested projects are providing a huge shot in the arm with commitments of $122 million. These include France's Rhone-Poulenc, CIBA of Switzerland and Bayer of Germany. The biggest single investment, however, is the $33 million by the Australian trader/distributor Gateway Pharmaceuticals.

The Vietnamese market in 1996 was estimated at $300 million, and while optimistic analysts estimate annual growth at between 25 and 100 per cent for at least a decade, not all the signs point to success for foreign pharmaceutical companies. Rigid laws and inex-plicable delays on drug import and distribution make life hard for manufacturers and doctors alike. Counterfeit drugs, some allegedly sanctioned by health officials, are rampant and growing in number. Some sources say corruption 'threatens to undermine the industry as a whole'.[27]

But some of those involved in the industry are not pessimistic. Rom Koziol, general manager for Gateway Australia, decided to move into local manufacturing after considerable success in the sale of drugs such as the pain-reliever Panadol. In 1995, Gateway signed an agreement with VIDEMEDIX of Hanoi to build a major pharma-ceuticals plant in northern Hay Ting Province producing at least 16 brand name drugs beginning in 1997.

The Hanoi government is now keen to encourage more such investments, admitting that the quality of locally-produced pharma-ceuticals is poor. But there is also concern at alleged 'dumping' – passing discontinued, expired or low-grade drugs which could not sell in the originating market into a developing one like Vietnam. One Western doctor in Hanoi claimed many of the foreign drugs entering the country would never meet quality standards in the West. 'We're taking unnecessary risks with this rubbish.'

Drugs are switched or diluted and low-grade fakes are sold in the original packaging. 'Medicine is like any other commodity,' said Arun Nayyar, chief representative in Vietnam for Ranbaxy, India's largest pharmaeutical company. 'Distributors and importers want it at the cheapest price. They're making profits and at times overlooking quality.'

This damages Gateway's premier product Panadol, which has been sold in Vietnam since the beginning of the 1990s. The drug's success has encouraged the emergence of about a dozen copies, some of which are watered down versions of the original, while others have different ingredients and slightly different names like Paradol, according to Rom Koziol.

Smuggling also accounts for a growing percentage of drugs appearing on the shelvs, while *Viet Kieu* have for some years been sending drugs through various channels back home for relatives to re-sell.

The ready availability of drugs over-the-counter, rather than via a doctor's prescription, and a seeming blind faith among urban Viet-namese at least in the efficacy of Western medicine, also tends to undermine efforts to create higher quality pharmaceuticals. Le Thi Hau, a licensed distributor of a Ministry of Health-affiliated pharmacy in Hanoi, said: 'Many Western drugs do not pass quality tests because of the shortage of modern equipment for checking drugs. But people still buy them largely out of ignorance.'

Gradual improvements are anticipated by the end of the century. Gateway, for example, has promised the Vietnamese Government that it will export at least 35 per cent of its output within five years of operations – a virtual mandate for meeting international medicine standards. As more foreign invested-projects come on stream, Health Minister Nguyen Phuong has promised to streamline approval procedures and also crack down on copy-cat drugs. Training quality control and provincial-level health care coordination and inspections are also high priorities. Ministry officials also agree that the entire import and distribution system needs overhauling to close loopholes.[28]

AGRICULTURE

Speaking at an anniversary celebration for the National Farmers Association in 1995, Party Secretary General Do Muoi praised those in rural areas for their long years of hard work and suffering. 'Without agriculture, there can be no stability,' he declared, describing farmers as a vital part of the economy and all important political force. Vietnamese society is still overwhelmingly rural. The agricultural sector employs more than 70 per cent of the labour force and accounts for more than 50 per cent of total export volume. Agricultural exports were worth about $1.5 bllion in 1994. Since *Doi Moi* was launched, agriculture's share of overall economic output has been steadily decreasing while that of the industrial and service sectors has been growing. It accounted for 34 per cent of gdp in 1994, compared to 40 per cent in 1990.

The fortunes of the agricultural sector have fluctuated because of various government policies and the impact of the weather. Government attempts to collectivize agricultural production in the north in the 1950s and the south in the 1980s resulted in serious shortages and famine with farmers rejecting the communist style centralized marketing system. The weather continues to wreak havoc with production. In the mid-1990s, more than a million tonnes of rice was still being lost each year due to flooding.

Yet there have been improvements. In 1989, the country was a net rice importer, unable to grow enough grain to feed its 72 million people. Today, Vietnam is the world's fourth biggest rice exporter after the US, Thailand and India. More and more farms are growing cash crops, such as coffee, rubber, sugarcane and cashew nuts. Land is being rehabilitated. New irrigation schemes are being put into place.

But agriculture limps behind the fast track development of other sectors. While the overall economy has been growing at a rate of between six and 10 per cent in recent years, agricultural output went up by 3.9 per cent in 1994. The World Bank estimates that 51 per cent of the population is living at or below the poverty line. Much of the rural economy is not monetized, but involves barter transactions.

Production remains backward, infrastructure is almost non-existent and product quality is poor. Food production has constantly to be increased, both to feed a fast expanding domestic market and to build up vitally needed export revenues. 'We cannot get rich through food production,' says Phan Van Khai, the deputy prime minister. 'But without guaranteeing safe food supply for 80 million people by the end of the century there will be no stability for development.'

Expanding agricultural production is limited by Vietnam's population density – one of thw world's highest. Sixty per cent of rice is produced in the Mekong delta region in the south while the rest is mainly produced in the northern Red River delta. Both areas are over- populated: The Red River delta contains nearly 900 people per square kilometre. Land plots average only 0.5 hectares. In early 1995, the government announced a ban on using rice land for other purposes. The decision was a controversial one. Some Vietnamese argue that more land should be given to industrial projects that are capable of generating jobs and higher revenues.

For every poor household in the gradually improving cities, there are 10 impoverished households in the countryside. Although the General Statistical Office indicates poverty throughout Vietnam has been reduced by six per cent between 1992 and 1994, the gap between rich and poor appears to be growing. If economic growth continues at its current rate, only 29 per cent of the population is expected to be living in absolute poverty by the turn of the century. But the risk is that the pattern could vary sharply from region to region. The economic growth rate varies from 2.5 per cent in the

North Central coastal region to 15 per cent in the South-east. If that pattern continues, poverty will have all but been eliminated in the South-east by the year 2000 but will still affect 68 per cent of the population living along the North Central coast.[29]

'Until about 10 years ago, with some exceptions, in Vietnam there were two groups: the poor and the less poor', explains Dr Pham Bich San, a deputy director at the Institute of Sociology at the National Centre for Social Sciences. 'Living standards in the rural areas were lower than in urban areas. but not by much. Now that is all changing.'

In a 1995 report, *Social Implications of the Economic Renovation in Vietnam*, Dr San pointed out that out that traditional Vietnamese society divided itself in four strata: Confucian literates at the top; farmers, considered the backbone of society, second; handicraft makers third; and, at the bottom, the merchants, those who contributed marginally to the prosperity of society because 'they too followed their own benefits and often neglected common interests'. If there has been a shuffle in the arrangements, it is at the expense of the farmers, who find themselves on the lower rungs of Vietnam's economic ladder. 'Cities are getting most of the benefit,' he says. 'What is the main benefit for rural areas? They are no longer so hungry, yes, but they cannot become rich.'

This urban/rural division was highlighted in a 1995 United Nations report, *Poverty Elimination in Vietnam*, highlighting the causes and constraints: geographic and cultural isolation; inadequate productive resources; lack of sustainability; and inadequate participation in planning and implementing government programmes.

Poverty alleviation will not be cheap. The State Planning Committee estimated that between 1994 to 2000 the programmes would require $12–13 billion. Subtracting the estimated amount that Vietnamese taxpayers will provide,the programme would require about one billion dollars per year from the international community for the next decade.

Dr Nguyen Le Minh, vice director of the National Programme for Employment Promotion, under the Ministry of Labour, Invalids and Social Affairs, ackowledges the rural dilemma. 'The farmer is getting relatively poorer. In 1990, one labourer occupied 0.27 hectares of land. In 1995, one labourer occupied 0.23 hectares.' And though work levels in the rural areas are high, production levels are dropping, meaning people are working longer hours for less real income. Combine that with the influence of television – which has recently allowed farmers to watch their cousins in the city getting rich – and internal migration becmes a national concern.

Few hard statistics are available, but Dr Minh says that, according to a pilot survey, 20,000 migrate from the countryside each year to seek a better life in Hanoi. Ho Chi Minh City's figures are 10 times that, putting 'tremendous pressure' on employment.

The government has seen the danger of wholesale migration of workers to the cities from the countryside and plans to encourage local job creation by moving certain industries into the agricultural heartland. Industry officials say the types of industries they have in mind are fruit canning, processing and handicrafts, although agro-nomists say this by itself may not be enough to make a significant difference as these industries are modest in scale.

But the most significant measure to boost the rural economy has been empowering farming households to be responsible for their own means of production. A move to disband collectives began in 1981 and has been very successful. State farms now have all but disappeared, contributing only three per cent of national output, and largely banished to border mountain areas requiring a great deal of expensive clearance work and development to create viable plantations. In 1987, 70 per cent of all farmers were grouped into some 45,000 cooperatives, accounting for a similar amount of production. Now, the number is down to 16,000 and their output contribution has shrunk to 30 per cent.

Most of these are located in the northern and central areas, where they still have a great deal of relevance. Ministry policy-maker Cao Duc Phat explains: 'Land is very limited and there is great popu-lation pressure in these areas. At the same time, these regions are prone to regular natural disasters. It makes sense for farmers to continue to work together in a cooperative way.' But, the official stresses, there is a big difference from the past. 'Before, the farmers listened to the cooperative director and simply followed orders. But the old style is no longer appropriate Now, the director is there in a support role only, and the farmers join the cooperative because they want to, and for their own benefit not that of the cooperative.'

Most farmers now own land-use rights and sell what they produce on their own account, often with the help of loans from the Vietnam Bank for Agriculture. Farmers are now able to make investments by themselves for development of production., and can mortgage and inherit land. The government is now working on schemes to improve the land ownership system, providing farmers with stronger guarantees on security and length of tenure.

A rural credit scheme was introduced in 1994 by the Vietnam Bank for Agriculture through its 2,300 branches. Apart from direct loans to farmers' households, the VBA also offers deposit accounts to boost farmers' savings. However, although the rural credit scheme has got off to a good start, only about half of the farmers have received loans due to a critical lack of capital. A $96 million World Bank loan will go some way to alleviating the problem, but the extent of the shortfall will require more drastic treatment. The aim in the five-year period 1996–2000 is to raise the percentage of farming households receiving credit to at least 80 per cent, as well as increasing the amount involved in individual loans (now about $80–100). At the same time, the emphasis will shift from short-term towards mid- and even long-term loans to provide farmers with a greater degree of security and allow them to plan ahead with confidence.[30]

According to a World Bank evaluation, as much as 51 per cent of the Vietnamese population lives below the world poverty standard, with rural populations being hardest hit. Basic subsistence has been solved at a national level but it is still a pressing problem for many families. As the Minister of Agriculture and Food Industry Nguyen Cong Tan has put it: 'The most basic solution should be to raise people's intellectual standard and enable them to create funds, create jobs and raise incomes in order to overcome poverty by themselves.'

FOOD PRODUCTION

Though Vietnam has benefited from an increase in world rice prices in 1995, problems have been caused at home. Inflation rose from five per cent n 1993 to around 15 per cent in 1995, largely due to a steep increase in foodstuff prices, particularly rice. The problem has been exacerbated by widespread smuggling of rice, especially to China. Many shipments of rice from the starved to the rice-starved north have gone astray. Estimates are that as much as a million tonnes has gone across the border into China where prices are up to 30 per cent higher than on the domestic market.

The government has taken measures to halt the smuggling, which it says is threatening the nation's economic progress. At one stage in 1995, rice exports were banned. The government has also announced plans to create two state enterprises which will have a virtual monopoly on rice distribution and trading. Foreign traders complain that centralizing the rice business will create more problems than it will solve. In the past, such enterprises have been inefficient and corrupt.

The outlook is brighter for other crops. Coffee, backed by a sharp increase in world prices, has enjoyed a spectacular comeback. Luu Viet Huong, a manager of the state run Vinacafe firm in Ho Chi Minh City says coffee has now replaced rice as Vietnam's second biggest export revenue earner after oil. Coffee exports in 1994 were worth more than $400 million — 10 per cent of the total, pushing Vietnam up to fifth in the ranks of world producers. Ambitious government plans call for the doubling of land used for coffee plantations over the next five years.

The London coffee broker E D & F.Man has established the country's first bean processing joint venture in Buon Ma Thuot in the coffee-rich central highlands. The $10.6 million enterprise has a projected annual capacity to sort and grade around 25,000 tonnes of beans a year to sell on to roasters around the world. The general manager of the company's representative office in Hanoi, Michael O'Donnell, says: 'Coffee people are becoming aware of Vietnam, but outside that people don't yet know. We're very excited. It's such a good product, with a neutral taste that makes it fine for blending. They have beautiful soils and good water and the husbandry and care the Vietnamese take with their plants is tremendous. We're finding yields here higher than anywhere else in the world.'

Cashew nuts have been another success story, with Vietnam now the world's third leading producer. Extensive work is going on to rehabilitate rubber plantations, many of which were destroyed during the war. However, capital shortages and a serious lack of processing capacity is hindering onward development. One interesting development occurred in 1995 when the government handed over the deeds of a major rubber plantation to a Russian firm as part of a debt-equity swap arrangement designed to reduce Vietnam's massive debt incurred at a time when the two countries were close communist allies.[31] About 972 hectares of land in southern Song Be province was leased to the Russians for 25 years.[32]

Vietnam has made a pitch to foreign investors for more than $1 billion by the year 2000 to build up its agriculture, fisheries and forestry sectors. Improving still-backward agriculture is a vital part of the country's plans to increase overall economic growth at an average 10–12 per cent per year over the next five years. The government already offers tax and land rental reductions and other incentives to investors moving into, and has hinted that more are being considered. Agriculture Minister Nguyen Cong Tan has laid out plans plans for government investment totalling $1.78 billion for development, including $800 million for livestock breeding, $600 million for rubber, $200 million for food production, $40 million each for silk and tea, $20 million each for coffee and for cashew nuts, and $5 million for cotton. Plans include:

- **Rice and food production**: raising annual output to 32 million tonnes in 2000 from 26 million tonnes, maintaining reserves for security in staple food while increasing the quantity and quality of exported rice to two million tonnes a year. Classifying and sorting plants are planned in the Mekong and Red River deltas.
- **Coffee**: Investment is needed in deep cultivation to increase productivity and quantity, expanding to 40,000 to 50,000 hectares of arabica. Vietnam produces about 150,000 tonnes, mainly robusta. New processing units are needed.
- **Sugar**: investment is needed to expand the production area, plant new seeds and to expand and build many new sugar mills to increase processing capacity to 55,000–60,000 tones of sugar-cane a day from the present 14,000 tonnes.

Vietnam's food industry has grown rapidly in the 1990s. By the end of 1995, nearly 100 food processing projects had been licensed, including pineapple, coffee and cashew processing plants. These projects, when fully invested, will have capital from abroad which will exceed $500 million. In 1994, gross sales of exported fish exceeded $450 million, almost $100 million more than in 1993. Despite these successes, there are quite a number of regulatory and practical hurdles to be overcome by the foreign investor who wishes to process and export foodstuffs in Vietnam.

If a foreign investor in food processing is applying for an investment licence in Vietnam, the investor's feasibility study must include the standards by which the product will be processed, packaged, labelled and stored, which will be assessed by the Standards and

Quality Directorate.of the Ministry of Science Technology and the Environment. For large-scale plants (over 10,000 tonnes a year), an environmental impact statement is also required. Before starting operations, a project also needs a 'certificate of hygienic conditions' from the Ministry of Health at provincial level.

Each year, the Ministry of Science, Technology and the Environment issues a list of goods which must be registered for quality. If the product being produced is on that list, prior approval to operate the plant must also be obtained from the Directorate. Once the plant is operating, it must receive approval of quality on a yearly basis from one of the Directorate's three centres in Hanoi, Ho Chi Minh City and Da Nang, unless it approves a provincial office for the purpose.

For every product the initial and yearly procedures to get this approval are slightly different but always involve the filling out of a form, submitting copies of relevant trade marks and submitting a certificate of quality from an accredited laboratory. Generally, a plant may use an international company which provides these services, or a lab locally accredited by the Directorate.

For a number of products designated periodically by regulation such as tea, coffee and rice, there are regular on-site inspections by the Directorate, whose inspectors may also visit as a result of complaints from customers or others. Adherence to the standards already mentioned place the investor in a position to export the product. There are, however, a few additional factors to consider. The application for the licence from the government to invest in Vietnam may include an application for the overall right to export the product. But even in if this is approved, a license from the Ministry of Trade for each specific shipment is still required.

Cao Duc Phat, the Ministry of Agriculture and Rural Development's policy director, admits that the inflow of foreign investment has been disappointing so far — some $1.2 billion, most of it directed into the food processing sector which is considered the least risky. 'We have got to encourage foreigners to take a serious look at all sectors of agriculture — planting crops, livestock, fisheries, processing — as well as development of the infrastructure, especially irrigation schemes.'

His department was at the time of writing rushing to finish a set of proposals for 'making the sector less risky and more profitable.' These proposals would include changes in land policy to give foreigners greater access to land use rights easier, more certain, cheaper, and for a longer period. Investors willing to put their money into rural development or 'township enterprises' (the concept of industrialization decentralization that has been adopted very successfully by the Chinese) should also pay lower taxes, Mr Cao said.

NOTES

1. See Chapter 5 for a full discussion on infrastructure development.
2. See Chapter 8 for a full analysis of Vietnam's financial sector.
3. *Vietnam Economic Times,* July 1995.
4. Based on a visit to the company, 22 April 1996.
5. Quoted by Agence France Presse, 20 June 1995.
6. Ibid., February 1996.
7. *Bangkok Post* 27 June 1995.
8. This section on the automobile industry has been prepared from personal investigation, as well as from material published over a period of several months in 1995 and 1996 by a variety of publications – the Associated Press, *Bangkok Post, Financial Times, Vietnam Business Journal, Vietnam Economic Times* and *Vietnam Investment Review.*
9. Two from BMW, four versions of Japan's Mazda, and two models of the Korean KIA.
10. Just under 10,000 vehicles were sold in 1994, for example.
11. Of the cars and light commercial vehicles sold in 1994, imports from Toyota, Nissan and Honda accounted for 70 per cent; in fact, Japanese makes together accounted for 90 per cent of all new vehicle sales.
12. For a full analysis of the Chinese automotive market see Murray,G. China: The Last Great Market, Chinas Library (1994,1996).
13. *Financial Times,* 15 March 1996.
14. The Daimler Benz project is interesting because it is a truly multinational venture, involving the Singapore Government's Economic Development Board and the State-owned Sembawang Group, along with Saigon Motor Co. and the Ministry of Transport, Indonesia's Salim Group and Autostar, a subsidiary of Hong Kong's Peregrine Group.
15. VMC is a joint venture between the Philippines' Columbian Motors Corp., Japanese trading firm Nichimen and Vietnamese state-owned partner Hoa Binh Auto, while Mekong is owned by South Korea's Saeyong International and Japan's Saello Machinery, together with a local partner.
16. *Vietnam Investment Review,* 8–14 April 1996.
17. The growing consumer market, and the potential it offers for foreign products, will be discussed in detail in Chapter 9 on marketing and distribution.
18. Agence France Presse, 13 August 1995.
19. *Vietnam Investment Review,* 9 July 1995.
20. Another issue of concern is Vietnam's territorial rights to explore for oil in certain areas in which it is in dispute with neighbouring China. A 1995 legal opinion by a Washington DC law firm instructed by the Vietnamese Government supported its territorial claims in the South China or East Sea, and in the block awarded by the Chinese to the American drilling company Crestone. It seems that as long as the area remains an issue for both China and Vietnam, international oil exploration companies will have to be prepared for the contingencies associated with exploring in disputed areas.
21. $900 million in 1995, against $866 million in 1994, on exports of 6.4 million tonnes and 6.9 million tonnes respectively.
22. *Vietnam Investment Review,* 22–28 January 1996.
23. *Vietnam Economic Times* June 1995.
24. *Financial Times,* 13 November 1995.
25. Shell is also involved in a $10 million lubricants plant, with a total capacity of 25,000

tonnes a year, in collaboration with PetroVietnam and the Meking Company of Dong Nai province, and a bitumen joint venture in Vinh. Shell officials say further downstream developments may follow in future years, ibncluding the opening of fuel terminals and petrol filling stations, but this will depend on how Vietnam's oil industry policy evolves.

26. This, of course, is not Wesfarmer's first difficulty in Vietnam, as was discussed in the opening chapter.
27. *Vietnam Economic Times*, March 1996.
28. Ibid.
29. World Bank estimate.
30. Briefing by Cao Duc Phat, Director of the Department of Agricultural and Rural Development Policy, Ministry of Agriculture and Rural Development, in Hanoi, 26 April 1996.
31. Hanoi still owes the former Soviet Union an estimated $1 billion.
32. *South China Morning Post International Weekly Edition*, 26 August 1995.

5 Case Study: Infrastructure

KEY POINTS

- $20 billion need
- Aviation
- Construction
- Ports
- Roads
- Railways
- Telecommunications

BIG NEED, BIG MONEY

PITY the manufacturing investor arriving in Vietnam with a good idea and the capital to back it up. The options are either starting from scratch in a greenfield site or moving into an ageing state-owned factory. Either way, the enthusiastic entrepreneur can swiftly be brought to earth by power blackouts, water shortages, poor roads, lack of telephones and expensive land rents. In simple terms, the infrastructure to support Vietnam's big ambitions is not there in many cases.

This is a country of 72 million people which has an installed electric capacity of only 3,500 megawatts, no more than 500,000 telephone lines and a crumbling road network of which only 40 per cent is paved.

In an investment seminar held in Hanoi in 1995 between the government and the World Bank, a detailed invoice was presented for $20 billion – the estimated cost of installing or overhauling the basic infrastructure. In detail, government officials said $3–4 billion would go to the energy sector, $2.5–3 billion into the development of new towns and industrial zones, while $2.5 billion would go on the country's dilapidated road network. In addition, $3.5 billion would be spent on telecommunications, a further $2 billion would go towards the supply and drainage of water, and at least $ 1billion each to railways, civil aviation and sea transport projects. The remainder of the money would be retained for contingencies.

Given the level of economic development in Vietnam, this is a great deal of money, and a substantial portion will have to come from foreign sources. In this chapter I will analyze some of the reasons why the spending is necessary, discuss some of the key projects, and identify areas where foreign businesses might profitably become involved.

AVIATION

There were no shortage of proposals from foreign investors, primarily British and Japanese, to upgrade Hanoi's Noi Bai Airport. But in the end the government decided to go ahead with building an entirely new airport without the involvement of any foreign contractors. The government did not explain why, but the most likely reason is that the decision was taken in the interests of security, given that the civilian part of Noi Bai borders an area used by the military. The airport was built in 1960 and was used as a practice ground for pilots during the Vietnam War.

With passenger traffic estimated to reach 2.5 million passengers a year by 1997 and four million by 2000, the need for an airport of international scale is urgent. Noi Bai currently handles 1.2 million passengers annually. 'The present airport is only a set of temporarily constructed buildings, If we don't build a new one now, we won't be able to meet ever-increasing demand in terms of passengers[1] and freight,' said Dinh Xuan Huong, a senior official of the Department of Civil Aviation. The blueprint for the airport envisages a five-storey, 53,193 sq.m terminal building on a 10 hectare site just north of the existing facility.

If any good came out of the Vietnam War, one aspect would be number of superb facilities bequeathed to the south by the United States Air Force. Ho Chi Minh City not only has Tan Son Nhat Airport, which at the height of the war was the world's busiest,[2] but the superb runways of the Bien Hoa Airbase a few miles north of the city along Highway 1. Tan Son Nhat is being upgraded at a cost of $4 billion, having become too small to handle the heavy traffic provided by the three domestic and 22 international airlines who now operate from there.

A total of $560 million will be invested in the first phase up to 2000 to help the airport accommodate up to eight million passengers annually (against 2.6 million in 1995). The main runway and terminal will be upgraded. In phase two (2000–2010), a new air terminal complex to be built to the northwest of the current buildings. A rail subway will link the two. This second phase will help Tan Son Nhat to handle 40 million passengers and one million tonnes of freight annually.

The airport at Da Nang on the central coast, another important American air base during the war, is also being modernized to cope with one million passengers a year.[3] Another wartime airport in the same area, Chu Lai, is getting a similar treatment.

CONSTRUCTION

Articles about construction in Vietnam usually start off with an anecdote about a building getting approved and built, only to be revisited by a fickle committee which requests the top five floors – or 15 – be lopped off.[4] Or taking three years to get basic approval only to learn it will cost another $500,000 to relocate residents who moved into the structure slated for demolition once they learned a foreign company was involved. Everyone has got a story and they are all true. Worse yet, often the would-be construction industry executives have brought their families with them, thus making a major commitment to Vietnam. Having to hang around for three years without a project to run can encourage the appearance of that famous glazed 'thousand yard stare' seen during the Vietnam War on people who had been 'in-country' too long and suffered too much stress.

Making things worse are several new 'Land Use Rights and Leases'. Regulations [Decree No 11–CP] introduced in January 1995 were designed to curb speculation and erratic escalation of land prices. In affect, foreign investors or their local partners had to lease land directly from the government, via a handful of state-owned companies, including Toserco, Haneco and the Housing Development Company of the Ministry of Construction. Previously, land use rights were synonymous with land ownership.

Even a newspaper published by the now defunct State Corporation for Cooperation and Investment (SCCI) ran an article about local construction entitled 'Lawlessness and the seeds of chaos.' A few pages later: '"Are there any rules at all?" asks top planner'. Another hard-hitting comment came from the *Vietnam Investment Review*, a must read for anyone wanting to do business in the country, which declared: 'Vietnam's hidden real estate market has made illegal millionaires out of many.

But the prime culprit in the construction mess is incompetent management of the State's authority. Obsolete regulations, red tape and law enforcement have turned the booming sector into a lawless output on the Doi Moi frontier, More than a few 'Towers of Pisa' exist, as Vietnamese jokingly refer to the teetering structures that give Vietnam's cityscapes the appearance of a craggy-toothed grin.'[5]

Even after the land use issues have been settled, the construction phase itself is full of pitfalls. Building materials from metal roofs to ceramic tiles can be difficult to impossible to source, or if available cannot be priced. Some state-owned companies supplying these materials are learning about quality control and marketing on the job; others are not learning. Considering all this, it might be said to be something of a miracle that any construction takes place in Vietnam at all. But, somehow, it is, as witnessed by the building boom in Hanoi and Ho Chi Minh City which will be described in detail in the next chapter.

PORTS

Not surprisingly for a country where the bulk of the population lives along its 3,260 km coastline, or by the Mekong and Red rivers, water transport has been a priority. The government wants the existing antiquated ports to handle a combined capacity of 70–75 million tonnes of cargo by the turn of the century, more than double existing levels. As everywhere, financing is going to be a major problem. The expansion plan has divided the ports into three regions: north, central and southern regions. It does not include ports that handle specialized cargo such as coal, oil and cement, however.

In the north, Haiphong, the country's oldest port having started operations in 1876, was a prime target for American bombing raid, as well as intensive mining of the approaches, to try and interdict the military supplies flowing in from friendly powers like the Soviet

Union to help keep the conflict going. The damage has long since been made good, while renovations some years ago raised port capacity to 3.6 million tonnes a year.

Concern has been expressed about thick sand deposits in its waters, but Haiphong's prime location makes it vital to keep the traffic flowing no matter what — not just for Vietnam's sake, but also for landlocked parts of southern China which are keen to use their neighbour as a vital channel for getting their goods to the outside world.[6]

Cai Lan is the second major port in the north. Officials there say geological conditions already allow the docking of vessels up to 160,000dwt, so the main work will be on expanding berths and adjacent roads and bridges to upgrade the handling capacity. Official projections show that Cai Lan port will handle 2.7 million tonnes of cargo by the end of the century and up to 18 million tonnes by 2010, to become the largest port in the north.

Ports in the central region of the country serve as a transit area for large volumes of commodities that are shipped into Laos, Thailand and Cambodia. Vietnamese authorities envisage that by the year 2000, the volume of cargo running through the ports in this region will be as much as 8.5 million tonnes a year. There are nine ports in the central region, including those that exclusively cater to the needs of the ore and oil industries. The largest is Da Nang. A major development project here aims to raise handling capacity to 3.75 million tonnes by 2000, and up to 10.5 million tonnes by 2010. The cost of upgrading this port is estimated at $17 million. Some $11.5 million will be sourced from the state budget and foreign partners will provide $5.65 million in soft loans.

The southern region includes the Ho Chi Minh and Thi Vai-Vung Tau ports, and a group of seven river ports in the Mekong River delta. Saigon Port, the country's biggest, is planning to upgrade its facilities with the installation of new piers, container parking bays, forklifts and cranes.

One of the largest single infrastructure projects is the $637 million Vung Tau container terminal, near the mouth of the Saigon River at Vung Tau, involving a consortium of investors from Japan, Malaysia, Singapore and Vietnam. The consortium, Tredia Vung Tau Port Development, intends to transform the oil and gas development hub into a major container port serving the needs of the Indochina region. A total of eight container wharves will be built and when completed

Vung Tau will have a total handling capacity for containerized and non-containerized cargo of about 60 million tonnes per year.

The government decided to approve the project in the belief that Saigon Port will be heavily over-used by the turn of the century. Tredia says the main attraction of Vung Tau is accessibility to ocean-going vessels. The port is also linked to a network of inland waterways in the Mekong Delta, which is served by barges.

But Saigon Port is not being neglected either. A major project there is the Keppel Bason Shipyard, a 60–40 joint venture project between Singapore's Keppel Corporation and Bason Shipyard Vietnam. It will provide ship repair, ship building and steel fabrication services, and its two floating and two dry docks will be able to cater for tankers, bulk carriers, trawlers, barges and supply vessels. But after a year of fruitless negotiations, P & O Australia pulled out of a joint venture to develop new container terminal facilities at Ben Nghe port in Ho Chi Minh City in late 1995.

Transport specialists at the Asian Development Bank have also recommended that river ports in the Mekong River delta – Can Tho, My Thoi, Dai Ngai, Tra Cu, Cao Lanh and My Tho – have huge development potential. Total volume of shipments in the southern region, which is three million tonnes a year at the moment, is projected to rise to five or six million tonnes by the year 2000. Officials estimate that shippers can realize savings of $10 to $15 million by using these ports for farm produce and commodities rather than going via congested Ho Chi Minh City.

Though privatization does not appear to be a major priority of the government, the International Finance Corp. (IFC), private sector investment arm of the World Bank, signed a deal to provide funds for what will be the first private port development project in Vietnam. IFC will provide around a third of the total $10 million required for the Ba Ria Secure Joint Venture Company to build a port on the Thi Vai River about 70 kilometres south of Ho Chi Minh City to handle ships of up to 40,000dwt. The joint venture will be 60 per cent-owned by two foreign firms – SCPA of France and Norsk Hydro of Norway – both of which are mostly involved in the fertilizer business.

POWER

If the Ministry of Energy has its way, more than $16 billion will be spent up to 2000 on developing and expanding the national power network. The Vietnam Power Corporation says that in order to achieve its goals, $5 billion is needed to build new power plants, $3.2 billion to upgrade the existing network, and $8 billion would be spent on rural electrification linking an estimated 8000 hamlets up to the national grid for the first time. Domestic financial sources, it is reckoned, can only cover 30 to 40 per cent at best, leaving the gap to be bridged by Official Development Aid from abroad and/ or commercial loans.

An estimated 300,000 new families enter the network each year, competing for the limited amount of power with commerce and industry, whose needs far outstrip demand. As discussed elsewhere, lack of a reliable power source is one of the biggest handicaps to the rapid industrialization of the country. But attracting potential foreign investment into power generation has been hard.

The government is dangling BOT (Build, Operate, Transfer) arrangements before foreign companies, but foreign power firms who have shown some interest tend to call for an increase in electricity prices. This may be acceptable to industry, but not to domestic consumers for whom higher rates would severely restrict their usage. Since 1994, the People's Committee of Ho Chi Minh City has been experimenting with charging different rates for certain categories of enterprises. For example, state administration agencies were required to pay 50 dong more per kilowatt while tobacco and liquor producers paid an additional 150 dong; foreign-invested companies and private local firms has to pay another 250 dong. But this has not proved sufficient to upgrade services to a significant degree so far.

At a seminar in 1995, foreign investors contemplating BOT arrangements in various types of infrastructure projects agreed that the current low pricing of all services was a major disincentive. Water costs in Vietnam are between eight and 20 cents were cubic metre while electricity is normally charged at a rate of around four to five cents per kilowatt. Responding to the complaints, Deputy Minister of Energy Nguyen Duc Phan, said the government was looking at ways to bring its pricing policy into line with other countries in the region.

For some time, the government has had to juggle power supply and demand. Northern provinces, for example, have tended to produce a surplus from thermal power stations taking advantage of cheap, locally-available coal, and this has been transmitted to the southern and central regions where rapid industrial development is creating a heavy demand. But it still is not enough. The Southern Power Company says current annual demand is about 7.2 billion KWH, rising to 12.5 billion by the turn of the century.

In the South, much reliance is being placed on development of the Phu My Thermal Power Plant No 2 (there are to be three plants altogether), with a projected output of 2.1 billion KWH a year, where the main generating equipment is being supplied by Japan's Marubeni Corporation and Sweden's Asean Brown Boveri. ABB is also supplying the new Song Hinh hydroelectric plant in Phu Yen Province. Another 3.6 billion KWH will come on stream in 1999 with the completion of the Ya Ly plant in central Gia Lai Province. The development of the oil and gas industries off the southern coast is also enabling the government to develop several gas turbine power plants in the Vung Tau–Baria Province.

In the North, there are ambitious plans for tapping hydroelectric power at Son La, Northwest of Hanoi, although the cost of this project could rise as high as $3.5 billion, according to government sources. If it goes ahead, the plant could be completed by 2007 with a 3.5 MW capacity. More conventional, and in the nearer term, the rich coal reserves in coastal Quang Ninh Province are to be tapped for a new power station at a site yet to be selected.[7]

RAILWAYS

Vietnam's railways are in a sorry state. Most of the rolling stock is either steam-driven Chinese locomotives or Russian diesel-driven engines dating from the 1960s sold to Vietnam some years ago by the Belgians. General Electric of the US and Germany's Siemens are interested in upgrading the rolling stock but the Vietnamese have little money with which to buy them. The train system that links Hanoi to Ho Chi Minh City, and provides affordable transport to a large number of people, has slowly got better. What was a 72–hour journey in 1989 now *only* takes 36 hours! The continued relative slowness is caused by the poor condition of the track, lack of modern signalling equipment and the delicate state of locomotives and carriages that would not be able to survive anything above pedestrian speed.

Old lines, disused since they were bombed during the Vietnam War, could also be reopened to improve movement around the country of goods and people — especially given the lack of a decent road network in many places (see next section on roads). But at the time of writing, Hanoi has not yet made the development of the dilapidated rail network a national priority.

Many foreign firms are interested in getting involved if the official commitment, and funding, is there. Balfour Beatty Railway Engineering produced a feasibility study on upgrading the single-track link between Hanoi and Haiphong in a project that could be worth about $70 million. The company originally envisaged upgrading a metre-guage railway all the way from the wharves at Haiphong port to Hanoi's French colonial railway station. However, after Vietnamese policy-makers said they wanted to reduce the flow of rail and road traffic into the capital, Balfour Beatty truncated its planned line upgrade, ending at Gia Lam, on the outskirts of the city, where a British subsidiary of Asea Brown Boveri was promoting a $30 million plan to upgrade a locomotive refurbishment plant. Davy British Rail, meanwhile, has been looking at doing similar track upgrading on a stretch from Hanoi to Lao Cai, on the border with China.

All three companies hoped to see much of the work financed by Britain's Overseas Development Assistance (ODA), but this was considered unlikely, at least until the Vietnamese Government gave clearer signals that rail development was a priority item. There was also some lobbying of the World Bank, but the latter so far has seen roads as a higher priority than rail.

If Vietnam manages to put its railway system in order, here are intriguing longer-term possibilities for a link-up with other parts of the region. Travellers with time to spare can now travel from Singapore to China via Malaysia and Thailand. There are now proposals for a branch line to run into the existing Ho Chi Minh City-Hanoi line possibly through the central highlands and across Laos via Vientiane before running into Thailand and down to Bangkok. The link in Vietnam might be made either at Da Nang, offering opportunities for that port to be used for goods to and from landlocked Laos, or further north at Nghe Tinh, also a growing port.

Vietnamese officials say there have been some preliminary suggestions from Thailand for such a link, especially as the Thais or also improving road and rail links with Laos from their side. But there are some doubts that a line through the central highlands would be feasible. American war veterans won't need reminding how tough the terrain is in this area, and even today there are few roads from the central plains for this very reason. Vietnam would prefer to see a rail link starting at Ho Chi Minh City, taking advantage of its growing port facilities, running down into the Mekong Delta and then through either Song Be or Tay Ninh Province into Cambodia and on to Phnom Penh. This proposed 240–kilometre line would present few technical difficulties, officials argue.

But all these projects are still mere paper ideas, it should be stressed.

However, the reopening of the rail link between Vietnam and China does open up possibilities immediately of travel all the way from Ho Chi Minh City to Western Europe, although there is some changing en route – notably in Hanoi and Beijing. Travellers can already get a 'soft sleeper' (four-bed private compartment) berth on a train twice weekly that makes the journey from Hanoi to Beijing in three-and-a-half days for about $100. In the Chinese capital, they can then join the existing rail network into Europe via Russia.

Meanwhile, given the population growth of Ho Chi Minh City and the emergence of sprawling suburbs and plans for the creation of new satellite cities on the outskirts, to be discussed in the next chapter, there are growing arguments in favour of a mass rapid transit system. But Nguyen Dinh Mai, Vice Chairman of the city's Cooperation and Investment Committee,[8] believes that although some sort of subway or light railway network will have to be established eventually, such a development is probably still 15 years away. Such projects cost a great deal of money and the city wants to concentrate first on upgrading its road and water links.

A Ministry of Transport plan already exists for an elevated railway extending some 200 kilometres to be installed in Hanoi and Ho Chi Minh City. This mass rapid transit network would be capable of carrying around 100,000 people a day. The idea was discussed in detail at an international urban rail conference in Hanoi in March 1996, when it was estimated that the minimum cost for each city system would be around $1.1 billion, funded mainly through foreign ODA.

A number of companies from Japan, Germany, Sweden and Romania were said to have indicated their interest in building the system, although they favoured a combination of an elevated monorail to be built in conjunction with underground and surface lines. Among the several branches of the Hanoi system would be one out to the Noi Bai international airport, In Ho Chi Minh City, there would be an elevated section out to Bien Hoa of some 53 kilometres, combined with 40 kilometres of underground track linking up four sectors of the city with the centre.[9]

ROADS

Vietnam has about 10,000 kilometres of roads, most of which have suffered from war damage and neglect Forty per cent of them are rated 'poor' or 'very poor'. There are 8,280 bridges half of which are dilapidated.[10]

The primary north-south Highway 1 linking Hanoi and Ho Chi Minh City, built by the French and bombed by the Americans, is a pot-holed, 2,300 km two-lane road in desperate need of upgrading. And primary stretches are among the first to attract foreign construction firms. About 430 kilometres are being upgraded initially. In the north, an American joint venture, De Leuw Cather International, is overseeing rehabilitation of 280 kilometres of highway from Hanoi south to the industrial city of Vinh, which during the Vietnam War served as a supply hub for the North Vietnamese Army and was decimated by US bombing. Vinh is now envisaged as one point in an economic triangle that also includes Hanoi and Haiphong.

In the southern part of the country, South Korean companies have been selected for four out of six contracts worth $317 million funded by the World Bank and Asian Development Bank. Three Korean companies, with Vietnamese partners, will break up the work into three sections — Ho Chi Minh City to Xuan Loc, Xuan Loc to Tuy Phong, and Tuy Phong to Nha Trang. Another contract won by the Koreans is upgrade a 150 kilometre stretch of highway between Ho Chi Minh City and Can Tho, a vital distribution hub for rice and agricultural products coming from the Mekong Delta. Transport Ministry officials make no secret of their admiration for South Korean road builders due to what they see as keen pricing and their heavy involvement in building roads in the former South Vietnam in the 1960s.[11] Other upgrades are planned on Highway Five linking Hanoi and Haiphong and Highway 18 also in the north.

Initially, the Ministry of Transport saw foreign investment as the key to rehabilitation of road and rail network, but this has yet to materialize in significant amounts — the foreign companies already involved doing so mainly because the money is being put up by international financial institutions, as already outlined. Many foreign contractors appear to be wary of the complicated, time-consuming bidding procedures, as well as doubts over the viability of projects under a BOT formula. The Hanoi authorities announced regulations covering BOT infrastructure developments in 1993, but the first foreign-invested project was not licensed until May 1995 – a modest $30 million water treatment project by Malaysian companies Emas Utilities and Sadec Malaysia to provide clean water to Ho Chi Minh City.[12]

A second project, approved in early 1996, was for the Indian Gadgil Western Group to build a $65 million power and fertilizer plan in the Binh Chinh district of Ho Chi Minh City. The plant intends to process 1,800 tonnes of city waste per day (compared to 3,500 tonnes currently produced) through a patented biological bacteria process to generate an estimated 12 megawatts of power and produce 4,00–5,000 tonnes of organic fertilizer a month. The Ho Chi Minh City People's Committee handed over 25 hectares of land free of charge for the duration of the 25–year BOT contract, and also guaranteed the Indian company minimum revenues for power and fertilizer.

But both road and rail BOTs are thought by many foreign experts to be unlikely to succeed considering the thin traffic volumes which are unlikely to generate sufficient revenue for a decent profit after covering construction costs. Few Vietnamese companies can afford commercial vehicles and still fewer individuals use cars. Few trucks ply Highway 1, and most other traffic is bicycles or ox-carts. 'There aren't that many projects on which you could recoup your money through BOT because the market isn't there,' says Cameron McCullough, a Hanoi-based lawyer.

The other worry is the non-convertibility of the local currency. Although Vietnamese law says that certain infrastructure projects – notably BOT – can apply for conversion of Dong revenues into hard currency, investors are jittery over the fact that, with its sovereign debt risk still relatively high, Vietnam is unable to guarantee the availability of foreign exchange with which to make such conversions.

Those with experience of bidding procedures for BOT say that because the concept is so new to the Vietnamese, it is taking a long time for the Ministry of Transport and other officials to get to grips with the complex documentation involved. Officials are also reluctant to offer investors commitments such as government guarantees which would ensure that investors receive compensation in cases where relocation of residents from, or near, a proposed site is delayed. 'They won't allow penalty clauses in land reclamation cases,' says a European roads contractors based in Hanoi.

Much of the reason for this is the legacy of a lumbering, socialist-style bureaucracy where officials are reluctant to make commitments unless clear policy guidelines from above say they should. This is rarely forthcoming. 'If you want to tender for construction on a particular project, it will be awarded to somebody they know and feel comfortable with, probably regardless of price,' adds the contractor.

TELECOMMUNICATIONS

Vietnam is gathering speed towards its ambitious aim of an all-digital national telecommunications network. Following the example of China, the government in 1995 took the first step towards creating a potential second network to challenge the existing state monopoly of the Vietnam Posts and Telecommunications (VNPT). In China, the challenge is provided by a consortium of the Railways, Electronic Industries and Electrical Power ministries using their existing private communications systems as a base for expansion into a variety of voice and data communications services. In Vietnam, it is the military who have been given the role through the licensing of the Military Electronics Telecommunications Corporation (METC). The Vietnamese Army, like its counterpart in China, has a well-evolved voice and data communications network. To date, it has outlined plans for a $100 million investment to establish nation-wide mobile 'roaming' services (allowing a mobile telephone to be used in any part of the country) and to extend its existing fixed-line network.

There was considerable confusion when the METC licence was first announced, particularly over the scale of its challenge to the VPT operating monopoly. The Directorate General of Posts and Telecommunications (DGPT) quickly stepped in to say that military would merely be allowed to use a part of the VNPT network for commercial purposes. It would not be allowed to operate its own competing network, and it certainly would not be allowed to involve foreign investors in this type of activity. But joint ventures would be allowed for the manufacture of telecommunications equipment.

The whole issue was further confused, however, when a Thai tele-communications company, Jasmine International, told the Stock Exchange of Thailand in July 1995 that it had signed a contract with Sigelco (as METC was previously known) to jointly develop and operate a Vietnamese telecommunications network nation-wide, including cellular mobile services.

The initial confusion over the content of the military's licence came amid intense jockeying by foreign telecommunications companies for a share of the country's largely virgin market. The phone system is so decrepit that, as recently as 1986, there were only nine lines out of the country, mostly to Moscow. Vietnam has bold plans to install three telephones per 100 people by the year 2000, up from a meagre 0.33 phones in 1995, and involving investment of about $2 billion. In particularly, it wants rural telephone penetration, presently at 26 per cent of villages, to reach 60–70 per cent.

The bulk of the money will have to come from foreign investment and domestic savings, as concessional finance sources – such as the World Bank and the Asian Development Bank – generally avoid funding the highly commercial telecommunications sector.

First into the market was Australia's Telstra, which recognized the business potential of a large Vietnamese expatriate population longing to phone home. Signing a Business Cooperation Contract with Vietnam Telecommunications International which handles over-seas calls to and from Vietnam for VNPT, Telstra installed a small earth station in Ho Chi Minh City to carry nine telephone circuits, which created a tenfold increase in traffic between the two coun-tries. That led to a six-year contract, signed in 1988 to upgrade and manage international communications services. The contract called for installations of Intelsat-A earth stations in Hanoi and Ho Chi Minh City, installation of equipment to improve international links from the domestic network and the training of Vietnamese personnel.

The Hanoi station became operational in 1989. Although Vietnam had long been an Intelsat signatory, its only satellite access was to the Soviet Intersputnik system. Other international traffic had relied on high frequency radio links, normally used only in marine and remote terrestrial environments. But Telstra's early act of faith paid off handsomely. In 1992, it won a $260 million contract to upgrade Vietnam's telecommunications capability, and more recently a $200 million expansion contract running to the year 2000, including installation of more international satellite gateways, a digital microwave backbone and Vietnam's first optical fibre submarine cable with direct links to Hong Kong.

The company suffered a setback in 1990,[13] when it bid to install a $15–20 million fibre optic cable 'backbone' down the length of Vietnam. Executives thought they had the deal in the bag, having arranged financing through Australia's Export Finance and Insurance for the DGPT – a $17 million loan at 8.3 per cent interest over 10 years. At that point, Telstra and others learnt an important lesson about the Vietnamese industry: think attractive financing. Italy's Marconi-Pirelli S.p.A. also wanted the deal, and working with its own government offered a mixed package of direct grants and soft loans, including about 20 per cent in 'direct grant aid', with the rest payable at 1.5 per cent yearly interest over an extended period. As a result, Marconi got its first Vietnam project.[14]

Attractive financing packages are also very much the concern of Motorola's Hanoi-based country manager Frank Marciano, who looks forward to the day when American government funds are available. 'For consumer items like telephones and beepers there is a quick cash flow and not a real need for any government help,' he says. 'But the infrastructure sector, which we are seriously looking at – such as satellite communications – would require financing packages (which are not available to American companies). Until that time, we have top use various forms of alternative financing. Many banks with Vietnam offices and access to government credit are not that interested, though, in getting involved, although they track it carefully.

'It's not the size of the projects, so much, but the risk,' explains one banker. 'In Vietnam, things take years and we don't want to carry Vietnam risk for 10 to 15 years.' Pierre A.Muyhl, general manager of Credit Lyonnais' Hanoi office, said that in many cases VNPT and DGPT are not interested in taking out loans for telecommunication projects. 'We are interested to lend in that sector because they are good earners, but local authorities prefer to borrow for projects like steel plants.' But another banker took the opposite view. 'We don't want to get involved. Frankly, we're looking for easier money. Trade commodity finance is the bread and butter market for all of us.'

For foreign companies wishing to sell equipment or otherwise become involved in the Vietnamese market, VNPT is allowed to handle procurements up to $100,000, while the DGPT can make decisions on purchases up to $5 million. Beyond that, deals must be decided on by the prime minister's office. VNPT also plays an important role in suggesting types of equipment needed, as well as instructing their procurement arms, Cokyvina and Potmasco, to make the purchases.

Firms interested in selling equipment should make sure their technology is the 'latest' and is well known to both DGPT and VNPT. Unlike other sectors, Business Cooperation Contracts are the only options for joining with a local partner. They are easier to dissolve than joint ventures, but give foreign partners less control. While some potential partners, particularly American firms, will not accept this arrangement, for most, the BCC is their first goal.

DGPT's Director for Information and Publishing, Nguyen Ngo Hong puts it simply: 'They (Vietnamese P & Ts) don't want foreign companies telling them how to run the telecom infrastructure of Vietnam. BCC allows them sole managerial control, while the business/profit side is shared.' Joint ventures can be formed for manufacturing telecom equipment, however, and to date there are more than 25 of these making everything from copper cable to digital microwave systems.

Equipment vendors can look to the growing need for digital switching equipment, digital microwave radio transmission systems, wireless local loop systems and access line equipment, and rural radio systems. With expected demand for three million line units by 2000, and investment to reach $116 million by 1998, the digital switching equipment market is considered one of the more attractive telecom opportunities for foreign players.

The downside is that three companies, Siemens (Germany), Alcatel (France) and Goldstar (South Korea) already control much of the market, with Siemens estimated to hold a commanding 60–70 per cent share, up from 35 per cent in 1994. Siemens has also entered into a $4.9 million joint venture to manufacture switching systems in Vietnam.

A similar situation exists in the digital microwave radio market, where demand is expected to increase substantially but operator-supplier relationships and competition with entrenched companies will make it tough going. Twelve companies currently supply Vietnam, with Alcatel holding a market edge in providing high-capacity and rural microwave transmission systems. Wireless local loop systems and access lines represent the best opportunities for equipment vendors to tap the network access market. DGPT has stated a desire to implement WLLs in both rural and urban areas because of the systems' suitability for Vietnam's geography, and the market remains relatively open. Copper cable, access line equipment, and rural radio could serve as important components in Vietnam's drive to connect rural areas, while a limited market will exist for fibre optic access loops, primarily for implementation in some urban areas.

But foreign companies are concerned about Vietnam's overall policy-making. To date, it has accepted no less than 12 different switching systems, most of them featuring different technology and many of them incompatible with each other. Provincial posts and telecommunications authorities are mostly to blame. In the early days, when foreign telecommunications companies first started investigating possibilities in Vietnam, it was often the P&Ts that were unable or unwilling to refuse technology that was being offered them, often regardless of quality. The result has been confusion.

Another question that is affected by the eventual choice of the number of operators is rural telecommunications. In countries where a high proportion of the population lives in the countryside, foreign companies are often faced with having to commit to setting a rural system as a component of clinching the more lucrative urban deals. Vietnam has made the introduction of telephones to rural areas a social priority. But if the government allows too many foreign companies into the country, either in Hanoi or Ho Chi Minh City or both, then the competitive attractiveness of investing in either place is reduced, especially where a loss-making rural element is concerned. 'Every operator here is prepared to do it (invest in rural telecommunications systems) as long as they get a good piece of the urban pie,' says one European executive.

NOTES

1. Anticipated as 1,325 passengers per hour in 1997 and 1,850 in the year 2000.
2. I can recall on many occasions sitting in an open-backed Caravelle or Hercules cargo plane thundering down the runway for take-off and looking back to see another plane already landing a few hundred yards behind us. Military and civilian aircraft were shuffled in and out of the facility around the clock at a rate — and with little margin for error — that would have terrified the administrators of civilian airports elsewhere in the world.
3. *Vietnam Economic Times,* July 1995.
4. See Chapter 6 for an example of this in Ho Chi Minh City.
5. *Vietnam Business Journal,* August 1995.
6. Haiphong's problems will be discussed in greater detail in Chapter 7.
7. *Vietnam Today,* March 1996, pp28–30.
8. Interview, 23 April 1996.
9. *Vietnam Investment Review,* 15–21 April 1996.

10. *Vietnam Business Journal,* August 1995.
11. The South Korean army was also heavily involved in the Vietnam War alongside the Americans and its troops were regarded by the Viet Cong and NVA as the toughest opponents they had to face.
12. See Chapter 6 for more details.
13. Telstra also suffered at least a temporary setback in mid-1996, along with three other foreign firms, when a $1.4 billion contract to install and operate land lines in Hanoi and Ho Chi Minh City failed to materialize as expected. The Australian firm, along with Cable and Wireless of Britain, NTT International of Japan and France Telecom had spent a year negotiating with VNPT, only to be told in early May that no contract was likely to be offered in the immediate future. C & W and NTT International were to share the installation of 400,000 lines in the capital, with Telstra and France Telecom splitting in the job of installing 800,00 lines in the south. The four would then have operated the networks and shared the income with VNPT. The negotiations seemed to have bogged down over the reluctance among some Vietnamese policy-makers to allow foreigners into a sector seen as important to national security.
14. *Vietnam Business Journal,* October 1995.

6 Tale of Two Cities

KEY POINTS

- Saigon restored
- Old southern entrepreneurial spirit survives
- Leading the way in *Doi Moi*
- Office/hotel construction boom
- Tourism potential
- New urban transit links
- Satellite city plans
- Infrastructure difficulties
- Hanoi transformed
- Anarchy on the Red River
- Overcoming water worries

SAIGON RISES AGAIN

IN THE days when American GIs roamed its streets and the Vietnam War gnawed at its edges, the Communists in Hanoi and their southern allies the Viet Cong denounced Saigon as a depraved city of greedy consumers, corrupt officials, drug addicts and 200,000 prostitutes. One tract at the time contrasted the 'insolent United States-style' high rises on central Nguyen Hue Avenue with the squalid tin-and-cardboard shanties of workers living along muddy canals, and there was plenty of truth in that.

Although there were still a few pretty tree-lined streets of elegant villas to hint at the reasons why the city had once been called the 'Paris of the East' (and these remain remarkably unchanged in the mid-1990s), Saigon was a pretty seedy place as a result of the war. In the suburbs, mountains of uncollected garbage rotted and stank in the tropical heat.

The stylish boulevards of the city centre wore a jaded look as hundreds of garishly named bars jostled for virtually every inch of real estate space in what were once graceful French colonial buildings. Meanwhile, tens of thousands of Honda and Suzuki motorbikes, belching out clouds of pungent exhaust smoke, fought for the right of passage with Mercedes and Datsun sedans of every colour and hue, numerous ancient battered Citroen taxis, as well as jeeps and other military vehicles.

When the Communists seized the former capital of US-backed South Vietnam, they vowed to transform the 'reactionary and rotten' city into a sober bastion of socialism. To underscore their intent, they renamed it in memory of their deceased revolutionary leader Ho Chi Minh.

But any foreigner with personal experience of the Vietnam returning today to Ho Chi Minh City will have little trouble adapting — because, on the surface at least, little has changed. As before, there is a wide gap between the rich and the very poor in this kinetic city of almost five million. The fetid, canal-side slums remain, although city officials are hopeful they can be eradicated by the end of the century.

Walking through the old central bar district, one finds these seedy establishments of high prices and broken promises long gone but prostitutes remain — now catering for rich Singaporeans and Taiwanese, rather than American soldiers. Marijuana and opium are still on offer by gnarled trishaw peddlers. Also back in force are the pickpockets and 'Saigon cowboys', motorcycle-riding thieves who can strip a watch off your wrist and be gone into the teeming traffic in the twinkling of an eye.

In fact, the raucous, chaotic streets show little surface evidence that this is the former capital of the losing side in the Vietnam War, nor, the ubiquitous pictures of the late Ho Chi Minh apart, that it is part of the *Socialist* Republic of Vietnam. Commerce courses through the city's veins. Smuggled television sets from Japan, pirated compact discs from China, fake Levi jeans from Thailand — everything is on offer in a city parts of which look more like Bangkok by the day. It is said America shipped an average 2,000 tonnes of equipment to Vietnam every day of the war. Much of it was left behind when the last helicopters fled on 30 April 1975, and can be found in backstreet shops and underground markets.

Down by the Saigon River in a line of shacks known simply as

American Market you can equip an army with dog-tags, night-scopes, boots, flak jackets and even parachutes. On Dong Khoi Street in the tourist district, dozens of shops get by selling GIs pens, cigarette lighters and dead men's sunglasses. Mini-helicopters made out of Coca-Cola cans and 'Good Morning Vietnam' T-shirts are brisk sellers on market stalls alongside supposed GI dog-tags which baby-faced vendors insist date from two decades ago. Most will want payment in 'greenbacks' — the dollar being the currency of preference.

Thus, perceptive returnees quickly realize that that the same brazen, stubborn, proud Saigon spirit, and the uncanny knack for making a quick buck in the most difficult of circumstances, typical of the war years remains undiluted despite years of attempted indoctrination. Given all this, it is little wonder that some residents believe Ho Chi Minh City should be renamed Saigon.[1]

Out of the upheavals of the last 20 years, in fact, has emerged a city which is economically more dynamic than in pre-Communist days. 'Then we were a country at war. Saigon was an oasis where we lived an unreal life supplied by the Americans. You could enjoy life if you chose to forget reality,' says Huynh Buu Son, a director of the South's central bank before 1975, now rehabilitated as deputy head of Saigon's biggest commercial bank.

In 'TV alley', where boxes of electric goods spill onto the pavements and block the roads, Pham Duong Long is selling the latest zoom-lens cameras. A former repairman in the South Vietnamese Air Force who used to service American fighter jets, he fled in late April 1975 as the North's forces closed in. 'We feared for our lives. But I was lucky. I was a junior rank and only had to go through a three-day re-education programme. Some of my officers were in the camps for years,' he recalls. 'Life now is not so different from the old days — shops and goods and bars and gambling. But not as many prostitutes or drugs, thankfully. It's a bit more ordered now and that's a good thing.'

Only 40 miles Northwest is small town of Cu Chi, whose surrounding woods and rice fields were among the most bombed areas in the Vietnam War. Now, the reconstructed tunnels of the Viet Cong guerrillas beneath the landscape have become a Vietnam War theme park, a kind of 'Cong World'.[2]

Tourists from Taiwan, South Korea, France and the occasional American war veteran come here in air-conditioned buses from

Ho Chi Minh City to hear how the guerrillas humbled the United States. They leave with armfuls of T-shirts depicting young women fighters clutching AK47 rifles and with toy guns and bullets fashioned from shrapnel. They can even fire off a few live rounds ($1 each), at a shooting range. One can crawl through miles of dusty tunnels widening for portly tourists to sip tea in an underground tea room. B52 craters still dot the landscape where only eucalyptus trees can grow now because of the agent orange defoliants dropped here during the war. There is even talk now of turning parts of the Ho Chi Minh Trail — the legendary jungle logistics route along the Laos and Cambodian border by which the North fed its war machine in the South — into some sort of tourist paradise.

LEADING THE WAY IN *DOI MOI*

Given Ho Chi Minh City's 'foreign contamination' — first by the French and then by the Americans — which the northerners were pledged to eradicate, it is somewhat odd while also being perfectly understandable, that it was here that the first experiments in *Doi Moi* were tried out.

Nguyen Son,[3] a high-ranking member of the local People's Committee as well as its spokesman, recalls years of hardship in the war weary city after the 1975 liberation. Things were so bad by 1978–9, that rice was no longer available and other grains had to serve as a poor substitute; many industries closed down due to lack of raw materials and power shortages often lasting three days a week. It was during this period that witnessed the major outflow of 'boat people' fleeing the country for economic rather than political reasons (the cause of the previous mass departure in 1975).

From 1983 to 1985, the Hanoi leadership, therefore, began experimenting gingerly with closely-monitored economic liberalization. The results were promising enough to lead to the official pronouncement of the *Doi Moi* policy in 1986. Again, when foreign investment began to trickle in, it was Ho Chi Minh that led the way — perhaps because foreigners felt reassured by the old entrepreneurial reputation of Saigon ready to burst forth again at the right moment. The old southern reprobate has more than repaid the government's faith, turning in repeated spectacular economic gains year after year — a decade of annual gdp gains between 12 and 15 per cent culminating in the 1995 figure of 15.3 per cent (against a national average of 9.5 per cent). The city and its environs account for a third of the country's industrial output and also leads the way in services and international trade.

According to Mr Son, manufacturing accounts for 34.7 per cent of the city's output, while trade, tourism and other services contribute 24.7 per cent. In future, manufacturing will remain dominant, but the extensive harbour along the Saigon River will be extended and upgraded to enhance the international trade role, while there will also be a strong emphasis on creating a major financial centre, especially after an experimental stock market is allowed to open.

Anyone travelling around the city's teeming streets will quickly appreciate its biggest problem: too many people. Natural growth is swelled by an influx of peasants lured away from back-breaking work in the rice paddies in the hope of richer pickings. Last year, the growth rate from births only was 1.5 per cent. But to this has to be added a further 1.6 per cent from inward migration.

The city authorities are now intent on easing the strain by building six satellite new towns to the east and south, each with its own industrial estate to keep residents from flocking back to the main city in search of jobs. This is important because an estimated 250,000 new jobs are expected to have to be created to meet the demands of a young post-war population now beginning to leave school and the migrants. In 1995, some 175,000 new jobs were created, but an estimated 230,000 people were jobless, raising worries about the inevitably social instability from high unemployment.

By 2010, when the towns are due to be completed, the population of the southern conurbation is forecast to be over seven million. But in the actual city area, the number will have been reduced to 3–3.5 million, which the existing and planned basic infrastructure should be capable of handling. Many of the migrants have ended up crowded into the canal-side slums, and the first task will be to move the estimated 26,000 households out to newly-built housing in the outer areas. Fortunately, there is still plenty of space available on the edges for expansion. The reduced population will also help avoid some of the environmental problems experienced by other Asian cities such as Bangkok and Beijing.

According to Mr Son, infrastructure development is the city's key priority. His shopping list, in order of need, is (1) improved water supply [see below in the section on Hanoi], (2) better drainage and the clean-up and dredging of the canals, (3) improved power supply, (4) road construction and upgrading, and bridge building, (5) enlargement of the port and airport. All of these areas will need heavy foreign funding.

CONSTRUCTION BOOM

Property speculation linked to economic reforms in Vietnam and an influx of foreign businesses have made Ho Chi Minh City and Hanoi among the most expensive cities in Asia. The average price per square metre reached $2,000 in the centres of both cities in 1995, while prices in the suburbs were $400 per sq.m in Hanoi and $250 in Ho Chi Minh City — unjustified when comparing the developed infrastructure and larger foreign communities of other cities in the region.[4] Prices have been pushed up not only by population growth but also by investments made by an increasing number of Vietnamese emigrants, especially from the United States, Australia and France. Many send money to family members in Vietnam, especially in the south to buy land against the day they return to Vietnam — or simply sell at a generous profit.

In the foyer of the office of Ho Chi Minh City's chief architect, the future shape of the business metropolis is laid out in white plastic scale models, accompanied by drawings of skyscrapers and huge layouts of new city centres. Images of the future city also clutter the hallway and are pasted on the walls. In the office of Luu Trong Hai, Architectural General Manager, large city maps and drawings are piled on shelves and spread over the conference table in the middle of the room. Yet perhaps the most important image is right above Hai's desk. It is a series of four small grainy pictures taped together to show a panoramic view of Bangkok and its many different downtown's rising above the smog and densely packed buildings.

'It's been a good model of development to study,' jokes Hai about one of the world's most notoriously congested cities. But will his city follow the same route? 'Of course, we have to worry about that. But I don't think we are like Bangkok. When Bangkok developed, they didn't have a plan. But we have a plan,' he says.

Vietnam is only 20 per cent urban, but the cities are growing and Ho Chi Minh City and Hanoi are the vital centres for the country's economic development. The two cities alone have attracted more than half of Vietnam's total foreign investment. So, as the cost of living and office and residential rents increase, city residents and property developers will need to look elsewhere to avoid the pitfalls of an urban nightmare like Bangkok.

For the moment, the city centre construction boom is in full swing. According to property consultants Colliers Jardine, over 90 per cent of approved office buildings under construction or in the planning stage are in District One, the city centre. These construction projects alone will probably keep Saigon's first district occupied for the next 10 years. It is this kind of construction frenzy that is developing an identifiable downtown Saigon, but it is also the reason the Bangkok syndrome is looming so heavily in people's minds. A significant part of the construction involves new hotels. Vietnam's first post-war international standard project was the Saigon Floating Hotel, towed in complete on a barge from Australia's Great Barrier Reef; the initial, very successful five-year lease was renewed at the end of 1994 after some tough negotiating. The first significant building projects were the Omni Hotel (250 rooms) and the New World (544 rooms) opened at the end of the year. In August 1995, another 500 international standard hotel rooms arrived on the market with the opening of the Saigon Prince and Equatorial hotels.

At the time, construction was underway on 11 more major hotel projects offering a total of over 3,200 rooms. These included the Hong Kong New World group's Ramada — a 388-room, 20-storey complex — the Malaysia's Pengkalen Holdings $48.5 million Grand Imperial Saigon Hotel and a five-star, 500-room hotel being developed by the Conrad Hotel Chain, part of the Hilton Group.

In the medium term, the city is convinced it will generate sufficient economic activity to mop up this torrent of new rooms and even support future double-digit annual percentage growth in supply. A study prepared by the city's tourist department and National Institute of Tourism in 1995 showed that while the number of international standard hotel rooms available or under construction amounted to 5,424, the current market required 7,000. The projected requirement is for 21,000 rooms by turn of the century when the number of visitors to the city is expected to double from the present one million to two million a year.

The optimism assumes that a strong tourist industry will spring up in Vietnam very quickly. But some hotel operators and airlines are somewhat disillusioned by the country's failure to develop the infrastructure and a marketing strategy that will support tourism growth.

After an initial flurry of visitors as the country opened its doors, hotel operators began complaining of declining occupancy rates and some airlines said passenger numbers had fallen.

Vietnam's 3,260 km coastline is mostly untouched by tourism and the few resorts that do exist like Vung Tau in the south and Do Son in the north have only drab and low quality hotels. Mammoth resort projects are planned in Vung Tau, Da Nang, Do Son and Ha Long Bay, but all the areas have very poor transport links to the main airports in Hanoi and Ho Chi Minh City. 'Wealthy travellers want to visit a developing country without being uncomfortable,' said an industry specialist. 'People who have visited Bali or Thailand are disappointed by Vietnamese standards of service.'

'Vietnam misses a lot of "last minute tourists" who decide to come while visiting other places in the region, but give up because of the administrative process,' said Chia Wing Chong, Vietnam area manager for Malaysian Airlines. 'People want to be welcomed, which is not the case when they apply for visas.' Efforts to improve airport formalities have had only limited impact and the border bureaucracy that often ties passengers for hours has become a common source of complaint.

The government also wants to keep as much of the business as possible in its own hands. In a 1995 newspaper article, the influential former Communist Party chief Nguyen Van Linh urged the government to keep foreigners from running hotels or restaurants. But tourism officials have begun to recognize that beaches and historic sites are not enough to keep the tourists coming back and that they need to move towards international standards in a highly competitive market. 'A scarcity of high-class hotel rooms and poor service are the main reasons few tourists return to Vietnam for a second visit,' Do Quang Trung, the country's top tourism official admitted.

Officially, the number of tourists visiting Vietnam rose by 40 per cent in 1994 to one million, but industry sources said the figure includes overseas Vietnamese on family visits who made up a fifth of the total. Vietnam wants the numbers to grow to nine million a year by 2010, when, according to a plan announced in May 1995, tourism will account for 27 per cent of gnp, up from the current 3.5 per cent.

Ho Chi Minh City draws most tourists, hence the rash of new hotel developments. But occupancy rates in many cases are around 50 per cent, less than breakeven. There are plenty of signs that the boom and bust cycle that has afflicted other Asian destinations will occur. 'Hotels have started a price war already,' said one manager in Ho Chi Minh City. 'Five-star hotels have targeted traditional three-star clients and three-star hotels have gone for the two-star clientele. Room rates have been slashed by up to 60 per cent.'[5]

Other big city centre developments in the southern metropolis involve a combination of serviced apartments and offices aimed particularly at the foreign businessman. In March 1995, for example, the government licensed the largest property project in the country, a $524 million scheme by Taiwanese Jin Wen Group to build a hotel, office tower and shopping mall in the centre of Ho Chi Minh City. Shortly after, another Taiwanese firm won a licence to build a $468 million residential and office complex. FYDAVICO, a joint venture between Dai Viet Import Export Company under the Ministry of the Interior, and Taiwan's Fei-Yuch Investment and Development Corp., will involve building nine high-rise blocks. The project, to be known as Saigon Happy Square, will include two office towers, two hotels and several residential and commercial buildings.

But while construction of hotels, offices and service apartments seems to be flourishing, the real estate industry, like all businesses in Vietnam, is not without its problems. The PDD Building, an 11-storey office block virtually completed in Ho Chi Minh City reportedly received legal approval and was built according to specifications. But then, Prime Minister Vo Van Kiet stepped in and ordered the top five floors be demolished. The reason cited was that it overshadowed a significant landmark – the beautiful French architecture of the old City Hall that is now the People's Committee headquarters.

Problems like this seems to show a lack of foresight by the authorities. While this appears to be a one-off circumstance, the thought of retrospective changes or revocation of already signed agreements does nothing to engender confidence in already timid investors. Businessmen complain that it is too difficult and time-consuming to know where to start or to get agreement on the appropriate use for certain land sites and compensation issues for displaced persons settled. The government has decided to draw up a master plan to help alleviate the uncertainty that is currently turning many investors away. Town planning concepts such as knowing which streets are to be widened to make major arterial roads in the future and where light and heavy industry may locate are key information.

In the coming years, there will be big opportunities for the construction industry will be residential housing. City officials estimate 60 per cent of the existing housing needs replacing for one reason or another. The majority of labourers have no proper housing or live in small inconvenient homes with a floor space of only two to three square metres per person.

The official population of HCMC is 4.5 million, but most officials believe it's closer to six million, with up to one million people entering the city every day. These migration flows are forcing city authorities to move on plans to relocate industry and people out of the city into the suburbs. 'We'll be moving all the manufacturers out of the city. When industry is outside, then people will follow the jobs,' Hai says. But workers cannot follow the jobs unless the infrastructure already exists. There is only one major bridge across the Saigon River and roads to the south and west are narrow and crowded.

Pham Si Liem, Vice Minister of Construction, explains that underground metro and light railway projects are being examined for the city with possible foreign involvement, while three joint venture public transit companies – North Star (Australia), Saigon Coach Company (Holland) and Indomobile (Indonesia) – have been licensed to develop bus services.

Development has to fit into the government's policy on urban expansion which bans construction on cultivable land, especially rice paddy. 'With the expansion of the cities we must plan ahead to spare land under cultivation,' says Mr Liem. 'At the moment land is given to people to build their own homes. But currently richer people are building three- to four-storey houses, while those with less money can only make do with one floor. This results in disorganization and causes land waste and unsightly architecture. So, we are establishing many housing development companies in Ho Chi Minh City that will take over the construction of people's homes and we are thinking about building tower blocks like those in Hong Kong or Singapore to save more land for factories. Such buildings are planned outside the city centres. Construction near industrial areas will be convenient for people wanting to near their workplace and housing development will be done through local projects.'

To solve the city's environmental problems, meanwhile, work is underway on rehabilitating the 16 km Nhieu Loc-Thi Nghe canal, which had become so filthy that water was no longer able to flow, becoming stagnant and creating severe pollution. The canal is now being dredged and occupants of slums along its bank relocated.

SAIGON SOUTH

But all the new construction outlined above will be of little use if it is not matched by development of the basic infrastructure. Electric power, for a start, cannot meet demand. A 500-kw power line from the north arrived in South Vietnam in 1994, but the city still tends to be plagued with power blackouts (depending on the district, from one to four times per week and from several minutes to a few hours). Promises of a 50 per cent decrease in the number of blackouts have not materialized. The 500-kw line has improved Saigon's power capabilities, but the problem now is that although power can reach Saigon there are not enough substations to distribute it.

This makes it difficult for large projects to become operational. The $65 million New World Hotel had to postpone its opening by about four months in 1994 due to unstable power supply. With this memory still fresh, the developers of Saigon South, a new satellite city being created on 2,600 hectares of land, took the initiative to instal their own infrastructure. Central Trading and Development Co. from Taiwan, which is involved in the establishment of an export proces- sing zone at Tan Thuan, took the precaution of including in its total $500 million investment funds for a $205 million power plant and $100 million for building an 18 km highway.

Despite this, Saigon South causes some concerns among develo- pers who wonder if it is one project too many at a time when the old South Vietnamese capital is trying to digest so much new development within its existing boundaries. The satellite town will be separated into five areas including a financial, manufacturing and educational centres. But with several hundred million more dollars needed to complete the basic infrastructure, will investors be lured away from the critical mass of jobs, services, and economic activity in the current city centre? Few developers will venture strong guesses. 'There's too much critical mass in the centre of the city now to look for office space out there. Why would you move there?' asks James Juers, General Manager, Vietnam Division of Colliers Jardine. 'Things like Saigon South and Thu Thiem do have a future, but it's way in the future.'

Saigon South's big challenge comes from Thu Thiem. The latter is an undeveloped area just across the Saigon River from the present downtown. Since the early 1970s, it has been destined as the natural extension of the central area and eventually becoming the city's new financial district. And there are certainly advantages. It is closer to the city's water source at the Dong Nai river and also closer to its power source at the Thu Doc power plant. The land of Thu Thiem is also apparently better for construction because it has a lower water table than in the area of Saigon South. It is also just across the national highway from An Phu, a residential area for foreigners.

All it lacks is a bridge across the Saigon River, although one has reached the stage of an architect's drawing. So when is it going to be built? 'That's hard to answer. We'll have to attract foreign investors,' says Luu Trong Hai. This would seem to involve a land swap deal (land in Thu Thiem for property development in return for building the bridge) or a Build, Operation and Transfer (BOT) project. A land swap deal is also economically possible, but politically sensitive as it would hand over a significant amount of prime location land to a foreign developer. Given Vietnam's reluctance to allow foreign investors into important areas such as telecommunications, media and distribution, it is likely to take some time before a land swap deal on the scale of a Thu Thiem project could take place.

For these reasons, Joe YC Chan, Vice President of Phu My Hung Corporation, which is developing Saigon South, is confident about his project. Even if a Thu Thiem bridge is constructed, it would take a long time and only one bridge would not be sufficient to develop the area, he argues. Several bridges would be needed and the land compensation costs for the bridge foundations and ramps on the city side of the river would make the project very expensive. Each bridge would have to be about 35 metres high to allow ships to reach Saigon's new port.

'In Hanoi they already have a law that there's to be no more building in the city centre. In the centre of Saigon, there's not enough infrastructure. We think they will follow Hanoi and not allow any more building in the centre,' says Chan. 'Saigon South appears to be well on its way to building a critical mass. The Tan Thuan EPZ has well over 100 companies signed up and they will need both office space and residential units for its workers. There is no more room in the city centre, so the auguries look good, says Chan.[6]

Tan Thuan is built on a finger of land created by a 180–degree turn in the Saigon River so that the north, east and west sides of the 300-hectare site are surrounded by water. This provides a natural outlet, but as yet it cannot be used because there are no port facilities on the peninsula. Berths eventually will be built on the southeast edge where a site has already been cleared, but as an official of the zone's management company explains, construction will not be carried out until all three phases of factory development are completed — and Tan Thuan is still far from filling its second phase.

For the moment, therefore, raw materials and equipment brought into the zone or finished goods being taken out for export, have to go on the back of a lorry through congested streets in a mixed residential/industrial area to reach the existing Ben Ngha Port. Admittedly, that is only a two-kilometre journey but a hazardous one.

Eventually, new roads will be built to ease this situation. The zone will be linked up to the steadily expanding Ho Chi Minh City ring road. The northern leg of this already exists, passing around the back of Tan Son Nhat Airport and linking up to Route 1 to the north. The next stage is for construction of the southern leg which will come close to Tan Thuan.

A close watch is being kept on Tan Thuan because of the difficulties experienced by other export processing zones around the country. Generally, it has done well in attracting investors[7] and keeping them relatively happy. The Tan Thuan Corporation offers a 'one stop' processing service, promising to evaluate investment applications within seven to 10 days and guaranteeing to get the applicant an operating licence in six weeks to three months, and then only a few more days to get the construction permit. Investors have to lease a minimum space of 1,500 square metres for 15 years, and be involved in an environmentally-clean manufacturing operation. Minimum start-up capital is $1 million. Trade unions are 'encouraged', but few companies have yet taken the hint.

Financial incentives include a four-year tax holiday and after that a reduced corporation tax rate (10 per cent). Equipment and raw materials brought in for processing are duty-free as long as the finished goods are exported. Should they be sold on the local market, the duties have to be paid. Some occupants of the zone have been lobbying for greater access to the domestic market, feeling this will make their operations more viable, but it is an issue that remains unresolved. To allow that on a major scale would destroy the whole concept of an 'export' processing zone.

HANOI TRANSFORMED

Forklifts clogging the narrow streets and cranes towering over the tree-lined avenues and lakes of Hanoi tell an unmistakable tale – the Vietnamese capital is changing fast. Conservationists are trying to preserve the best of the ancient old quarter of the 1,000-year-old city and the gems of the French colonial period. The small opera house built by the French in 1911 and still equipped with the original mouldings and red-plush seats, is closed for a $20 million renovation. Old French villas are coveted for renovation as up-market offices and residences. But in most of the city, concrete rules. And officials are having trouble regulating the growth. On many streets, a rash of new, tall, narrow 'mini-hotels' sit oddly alongside traditional Vietnamese houses. Big office blocks and new hotels are starting to sprout all over the city to meet demand for offices and homes from Asian and western executives doing business in the city. The trend is likely to intensify as American firms flock to Vietnam in the wake of the start of diplomatic relations.

Vietnamese who struck it rich after the Communist government opened up the economy in the late 1980s built houses near the picturesque West Lake, sometimes without permits. So bad was the chaos that the Government feared the main dyke protecting the city from Red River floods had been weakened by houses built on or alongside it. In early 1995, the authorities intervened to halt the building anarchy along the dyke and the city's deputy chief architect, Trinh Hong Trien, and two of his colleagues were suspended; some senior officials at the Water Resources Ministry were later indicted after an investigation.

The scandal came to light at the end of 1994 when it was revealed that 1,108 two- to six-storey buildings had been built illegally on three stretches of the dyke which runs along the river for several kilometres. About 220 of the dwellings were occupied by civil servants, including the families of servicemen and police. Experts warned that the thousands of tonnes of construction material had created cracks in parts of the dyke, posing a threat during the Red River's seasonal flooding – such as the devastating rise in water levels in 1971 which led to huge losses of life and of property. Thousands of people live in the illicit housing and the location of the buildings makes it impossible for Water Ministry workers to maintain and repair the levee. The Prime Minister's Office eventually forced owners of dozens of villas to demolish terraces and front rooms to clear a five metre path beside the dyke.

One unfortunate side effect of the scandal was to seriously delay approval for one of the largest and most ambitious property deals yet attempted in Vietnam. In March 1995, Singapore's Senior Minister (and former Prime Minister) Lee Kuan Yew led a ground-breaking ceremony for the $250 million Song Hong City joint venture between Antara Koh Development of Singapore and a development arm of the Hanoi People's Committee calling for the construction of office towers, apartment blocks, a five-star hotel and a commercial area. But then nothing happened for months as neither the Construction Ministry nor the Water Resources Ministry felt it wise to rush through the necessary approvals in the climate then prevailing — especially as the project comes within 20 metres of the undermined dyke.

The illegal building along the dyke is symptomatic of the construction frenzy which has gripped Hanoi. Owners were ready to pay fines imposed by local authorities in order to keep their homes or finish construction, according to local newspaper reports. There was widespread speculation that some owners had bribed officials in order to build on or expand their sites. Attracted by the fever of easy money, the capital's new rich increased investments in the dyke districts since the Government decided to make the area a tourist attraction in 1992.

The market economy has completely changed the landscape. Stalls and dilapidated housing in the district have given way to concrete blocks garlanded with electric lines which are the new tourist mini-hotels and which are pushing land prices skywards.

In 1995, the city of 3.2 million people only had a few hundred hotel rooms that can be considered of international standard, creating a pronounced shortage for the half a million visitors who arrived in Hanoi during the year and were forced engage in a something of a lottery, paying room rates generally higher than Southeast Asian regional averages to obtain decent lodgings. Hanoi had only one four-star hotel, the 109—room Metropole, and one even smaller modern three-star, the Hanoi Hotel.

But the shortage is now being corrected by a flood of new projects. According to Nguyen Tuan Nghia, general director of the Department of Tourism in the Hanoi People's Committee, 33 international standard hotels of between three and five stars providing a total of 5,023 rooms would be in place by 1998, but he wants still more. 'We intend to have 10,000 hotel rooms of international standard' by the year 2000, said Mr Nghia, whose department is responsible for Hanoi's hotel sector and advises the government on whether to approve hotel investment applications.

Hanoi's lakes are the focal points for many of the new hotels, in particular the shores of West Lake. The many hotel projects clustered around this large lake north-west of the city centre include 4/5 star properties such as the 375-room Lien Westlake and the 324-room Westlake International, both being developed by Singaporean companies, and the 278-room Malaysian-developed Sheraton.

But some property analysts feel 10,000 new rooms is a substantial overshoot. One hotelier commented: 'They need a maximum of 2,000 rooms in the four-star market, a couple of good three-star properties – and that's it. After all, Hanoi is not Hong Kong.'

Of interest to former American prisoners-of-war is that their old home, known by them as the 'Hanoi Hilton', is being replaced by a 22-storey hotel, service apartment and office block called Hanoi Towers. At an estimated cost of $45 million, the project is to be developed by Hanoi Tower Centre Co., a joint venture between Burton Engineering and Hanoi's Civil Construction Co.

Office space in Hanoi has also been in desperate supply. Many companies initially located themselves in hotels where power and telecommunications were already established, while they waited for other space to become available. Tired old French villas have responded well to loving restoration work and many now make impressive offices. This is not necessarily a cheap solution as renovation costs take time and may run as high as $100,000.

Quality office rental costs run at $30–50 per square metre in Ho Chi Minh and can be a little higher in Hanoi, tempting developers to build office blocks. Attracted to these are companies requiring more space than a single villa can provide or those without the time or inclination to renovate. New developments include the International Centre, a six-storey office complex in the city centre, a joint venture between Singapore's Fernland Investment, a subsidiary of Straits Steamship, and a Vietnamese government company; Singapore's Keppel Group is developing the Royal Park apartment complex of 20 villas, a business centre and a golf driving range at West Lake, where De Matteis is also building a 14-storey office tower. South Korea's Daewoo has an office and apartment complex, to be followed later by a hotel, some 15 minutes drive from the city centre. Although the office block of the Dae Ha commercial centre had attracted a number of tenants before its February 1996 scheduled opening, its attractiveness was not helped by an admission from project officials that the building, constructed on reclaimed swamp land, had sunk about 20 centimetres in a matter of months. Construction experts said a maximum of eight centimetres was acceptable in these sort of cases, forcing the company to rush in a team of international experts to establish what was happening and whether it presaged any structural damage in future.[8]

On the edge of the capital, work has begun on the largest domestic property investment so far — the $185 million Thang Long International Village. The project, not scheduled for completion until 2005 according to present plans, calls for the creation of 27 apartment blocks, villas, an office tower, hotel and shops in a self-contained village aimed at foreign investors. The first stage of work on the 10.2 hectare site calls for the construction of 53 detached villas and eight apartment buildings.

To avoid further congestion in the city centre, the Hanoi authorities have designated the suburb of Tu Liem, near the Noi Bai International Airport, as a future business district. Anticipating this, the first of three phases of the $90 million Schmidt Tower complex went on the market in late 1995, as the first wholly-foreign-investment licensed in the country. The Schmidt Group of Germany says the project is aimed at high-tech foreign companies and will include the 'Hanoi International Technology Centre'.[9]

Regarding the city's overall building plan, Pham Si Liem, the Vice Minister of Construction noted that Hanoi has more pressures on available land than its southern counterpart. In Ho Chi Minh City, the suburbs have been able to grow more extensively because the surrounding land is not good for cultivation. Hanoi has been inhibited in its expansion by lack of roads out of the city and the need to preserve agricultural land.

Despite the pressures, the government is determined to restrict the number of high rise buildings allowed in an effort to preserve the traditional character of the capital. The city has three distinct quarters. In the Old Quarter and the French Quarter, high-rise buildings will not be allowed. The third quarter, consisting of newly developed areas like the Hai Ba Trung district. high-rise construction will be permitted.

In March 1995, Prime Minister Vo Van Kiet caused palpitations among foreign investors when he announced a ban on the conversion of rice fields to industrial use — designed to ensure that the densely-populated north did not suffer from a rice shortage because of industrial development. Most alarmed were those investors who had already gained licences to build in farmland near Hanoi. By July, the prime minister had relented and ordered the Hanoi People's Committee to release 6,310 hectares of farmland for large investment projects, 2,350 hectares for infrastructure, 1,270 hectares for industrial zones and 600 hectares for housing. An additional 800 hectares was earmarked for 'unforeseen demands'.

Hanoi Mayor Hoang Van Nghien said seven per cent of the land would be converted to business uses by 2000 under the new regulations. Among the companies to benefit from the changes are vehicle manufacturers Toyota and Ford who will be granted greenfield sites for two planned factories.

Land issues have been among the most difficult problems facing foreign investors, many of which have had problems clearing sites of residents or getting land-use approvals. Some of these problems are perfectly illustrated by the bananas growing around the Schmidt Group's $20 million HITC Building in the Tu Liem district of Hanoi. Originally, the land was contracted to the local farmers to grow orchards and vegetables to increase their incomes. When the farmers heard about the clinching of the Schmidt deal they literally went bananas. Why? Land compensation can only be paid when trees are grown there. So they chose banana trees, which grow fastest.

Land compensation is just one more expense to be aware of for property developers who are constructing office and residential buildings outside the city centre. Satellite cities in both metropolizes are in promising development stages, but developers who build these new city centres will need to reach deep into their pockets for infrastructure costs, as already discussed in relation to Saigon South, as well as in the previous chapter.

The HITC building is a case in point. According to property consultant James Bargh of Richard Ellis International, the Schmidt Group took very little for granted and added basic infrastructure costs to their overall budget, including a private 2.4 km power cable. They also negotiated a separate fibre optic phone line installed by the Hanoi P & T. So far, water is not a problem as there are few consumers in the Tu Liem district. The developers also included two back-up generators to allow for full-time power. 'It wasn't a problem because we budgeted for everything,' said Bargh.

The Korean Daewoo and Hanil Corporations, constructing the Daeha Business Centre in neighbouring Ba Dinh district, faced a similar situation. Construction of the $135 million joint venture complex looked like being a white elephant when, nearing completion, it still had no guarantee of power, water or telecommunications. At the 11th hour, a deal was negotiated with the Ministry of Energy for a 2.5 km private power cable from the Nghia Do power sub-station to the complex for Daeha's use only. Other private deals were made with the water company and the post office.

WATER WORRIES

Do Van Toan recalls a common image from his first days as a water engineer in Hanoi: women hunching over wells, waiting patiently for their plastic tanks to fill up. Not much has changed. The wells are for the most part illegal — simple underground water tanks tapped into the ageing French-built water supply system. But they illustrate a bizarre set of decades-old circumstances which exemplify the problems facing city planners and engineers. These 1500 or so tanks in downtown Hanoi, once actually advocated by city officials, are now causing headaches for people like Toan, who as deputy director of the Hanoi Clean Water Business Company is trying to help modernize what is regarded by some as a disaster waiting to happen.

The Finnish government recognized the potential nightmare a decade ago. 1995 marked the tenth anniversary of the $90 million Hanoi Water Supply Programme managed by FINNIDA, Finland's international development agency. Since 1985, Vietnam's largest water system assistance programme to date has funded and helped lay over 300 km of new pipes into a primary supply network which links most of the city, coordinated the rehabilitation of four of the city's main water treatment plants, and increasing the working output of treated water from 165,000 cubic metres per day to 340,000 cu.m/d.

The Yen Phu plant, Hanoi's first water treatment facility built 100 years ago, showcases efforts to catch up with the city's growing demand. Equipped with French technology at its inception, then aided by the former Soviet Union, the plant is expanding its capacity with Finnish technology under a $4.5 million project funded by the United Nations Development Programme. The new water plant will double the daily production capacity to 80,000 cubic metres. The old plant is now unable to run at its full designed capacity of 40,000 cubic metres a day owing to the deteriorating condition of the wells, and only produces 35,000 cu.m.

But the rehabilitation of the old water supply system also poses fresh problems. According to Reijo Sarkkinen, programme coordinator for the programme: 'We still have an old network and a new network. The old one is weak, with so many leaks. It's the main reason pressure doesn't build up.' According to Toan, the new system, a state-of-the-art network with plastic and ductile cast iron pipes, reaches three-fifths of Hanoi but supplies only half the population. The older French-era system covers two-fifths of Hanoi yet also provides water to half the people. Sakkinen says the Finns have tried from the start to keep networks separate.

By late 1996, the Finnish programme will have run its course, leaving HWBC to negotiate a World Bank loan of about $50 million. Not to mention the establishment of commercial viability of the company. For years, Hanoi's water supply companies, now merged into HWBC, have operated at a loss. Water has been subsidized outrageously by the government, further compounding the company's woes and nurturing a wasteful attitude among citizens. 'As long as people don't have to pay for water, they'll still waste it,' says Toan. Until August 1994, Hanoi residents paid a water rate at only a quarter of cost; since then, the charge has risen to half.

City officials also have to ponder how to recoup money for the more than 60 per cent of the supplied water which is never paid for. Metering is the logical answer, but while nine of 10 Hanoi households do not have meters, the question remains: who will pay for the meters in the 300,000 homes using the system? HWBC has reminded citizens they can buy or rent meters from the government or private shops. Needless to say, few people are listening. So long as they are being charged a flat rate, residents are much more likely to spend the $20 or $30 on a new water pump to bring water up above ground level and into the upper floors of their houses and mini-hotels.

The whole metering dilemma has left the water supply company in a Catch 22: no meters, very little cash flow; no cash, therefore, to buy more meters, finance future repairs or pay off the foreign loans. While officials debate the issue, people continue to tap into the system, decreasing pressure throughout the network, causing costly leakage and perhaps most critically, further polluting an already dangerous water system.'The system is catastrophic,' warns a foreign doctor working in Hanoi who rattles off a dozen or so problems: 'Salinity is very high; treated water is mixed with sewer water; they're pumping too much ground water; the city is sinking; the property is not being tackled properly.'

Ultimately, his analysis is on target. Hanoi water is derived mostly from ground water 60 to 80 metres under the city, drawn from over 100 wells. This is funnelled into Hanoi's eight working treatment plants, where aeration and rapid sand filtration systems purge the water of iron and manganese, metals common in ground water sources.

Many officials claim this water is 'safe to drink when it leaves the treatment plants', but it is considered only a matter of time before the capital faces a major water pollution crisis. 'By far the biggest pollution problem in Hanoi is human waste — and it will be for many years,' says Gordon Johnson, an environmental consultant on water issues for the United Nations Development Programme. During flooding, when storm water, sewage and surface water mix in the streets, the entire city becomes a breeding ground for water–borne bacteria which enter the supply system through pavement wells, leaks, illegal taps and corroded pipes. Low pressure periods result in dangerous backwater siphonage of polluted groundwater into the system.

Studies funded by World Bank, ADB and FAO highlight the problem: the mortality profile in Vietnam is characterized heavily by diseases linked to the water supply and sanitation such as cholera, typhoid, dysentery and others; intestinal parasitic infection in the north runs as high as 90 per cent, consistent with high public exposure to water and soil contaminated with faecal matter.

Other factors double the trouble. Deep construction piling in the city could be puncturing the protective clay layer under Hanoi, further contaminating ground water. Industrial waste goes untreated into rivers and lakes, and though this affects all of Vietnam, the potential for such contamination in the north is particularly severe due to new industry centres being constructed. And perhaps more importantly, there is still no acceptable sewage or sewage treatment in Hanoi.

The 150 km or so of crumbling sewer pipes are woefully inadequate. Geographically speaking, the area has terrible drainage. Water canals that thread the city have nearly congealed, clogged with trash and waste. And pollutants with no way out of the city are now seeping into ground water supplies with dangerous regularity, says Finland's Sarkkinen. He also predicts that West Lake, the city's largest natural water filter, will soon reach its septic point and start to smell within six months. 'There is simply no existing sewage in Hanoi.'

Hanoi, of course, does not suffer these urban problems alone; water woes also plague Ho Chi Minh City. A third of the city's population does not have running water. And the city has been suffering from a chronic shortage of clean water, with demand rising rapidly due to new housing and industrial areas being built. Those Saigonese not connected to city water mains, typically the poorest areas, are supplied either by private wells or water vendors, whose price is six times higher than the public pipe price.

Of the 60 per cent who are tapped in, nearly half of those receive only an intermittent supply. Saigon's system — a mix of French pipes downtown and pre-1975 American pipes in the surrounding districts — produces 650,000 cu.m. per day, more than Hanoi but far from adequate. Nearly half of the city's water is lost, according to the ADB/World Bank reports. 'And at present,' writes Dominique Vasselin, project manager of French construction engineering firm Safege, which has published a survey of the Saigon system, 'non-revenue water is around 40 per cent'.

Today's urban domestic water demand is estimated at one billion cu.m. per year — 14 million city dwellers consuming 150–200 litres per capita per day. Additional water system costs for new city arrivals will be staggering: $100 for each additional person to the year 2000. This amounts to no less than $400 million in funds in addition to the approximately $500 million reckoned to be needed to rehabilitate the existing water supply systems in the two major cities.

As mentioned in the last chapter, Vietnam licensed its first BOT deal with two Malaysian companies to construct and run a water treatment plant in the south. Sadec Malaysian and Emas Utilities are building a $30 million water plant to supply the city with 100,00 cu.m. of water a day. The two firms will operate the company for 20 years before transferring it to the city government.

NOTES

1. Gray, D. 'Saigon battles back to its former glory', *South China Morning Post Weekly Edition*, 5 May 1995.
2. Pringle J. 'Tourist industry enjoys spoils of war', *London Times*, 26 April 1995.
3. Interview in Ho Chi Minh City, 22 April 1996.
4. In 1995, Ho Chi Minh City had a foreign business population of between 15,000 and 20,000, while Hanoi had about 8,000, according to official estimates.
5. A consortium of Singapore companies is building a 1000ha 'Vietnam–Singapore Industrial Park' (VSIP) about 45 minutes drive south of central Ho Chi Minh City, with highway links to Saigon port and Vung Tau, which will also include an export processing zone. The consortium comprises Sembawang Industrial, Sembawang Engineering, KMP Group, JTC International, LKN Construction, Temasek Holdings and United Overseas Bank. Its Vietnamese partner is Song be Import–Export Trading Company (Becamex), a state-owned enterprise that deals in agricultural and forestry products.
6. Agence France Press, 21 June 1995.
7. Of the 118 companies so far accepted, 58 have come from Taiwan and 40 from Japan. The remainder are split between Hong Kong, Singapopre, United States and Germany, along with three Vietnamese firms. Only 40 of these were in operation in April 1996, however.
8. *Vietnam Investment Review*, 22–28 January 1996.
9. *Bangkok Post*, 30 May 1995.

7 Provincial Tour

HAIPHONG: GATEWAY TO CHINA

When the governor of China's southern Yunnan Province visited Haiphong in 1993 shortly after the ground-breaking visit to Vietnam by President Jiang Zemin, local officials knew the Chinese were on to something. The economy of landlocked Yunnan is growing rapidly but the province has no easy access to sea ports in the region. With the thawing of relations between China and Vietnam, the port of Haiphong offered a tantalizing solution to their problem. 'When I asked the governor how many tonnes of cargo he could bring through the port annually, he said "40 million tonnes a year",' recalled Hoang Van Dinh, Director of the Foreign Affairs Office of the Haiphong People's Committee.[1] As was discussed briefly in Chapter 5 on infrastructure, this is far beyond Haiphong's current handling capacity. Since the visit, Yunnan has opened a trade office in Haiphong. Whether its governor's target is realistic or not, the Vietnamese are clearly hoping Chinese trade will boost the port's economic development.

The city's ambitions mesh with government plans to develop a dynamic 'growth triangle' linking Haiphong with Hanoi and the former's closest neighbour, Quang Ninh Province. The idea is to kick-start rapid economic growth in the north of Vietnam to balance growth with the rapidly developing south.

However, Haiphong has no head start. During the Vietnam War, the bulk of its industry was obliterated by heavy aerial bombing. Soviet hand-outs helped rebuild much of it in the following years, but today it is in such a state of disrepair that the only alternative is a complete overhaul. A huge cement factory in the city centre still feeds the construction industry but it belches dangerous levels of noxious fumes and the authorities have decided to close it down unless it can find investors to modernize its Romanian kilns soon.

In foreign investment, Haiphong has not fared much better. Despite a decade of *Doi Moi*, most foreign funds have skirted Haiphong and other peripheral areas in favour of Ho Chi Minh City and Hanoi. Total commitments by early 1996 totalled $900 million in 48 projects, the largest of which is a joint venture cement factory, capitalized at $488 million, in which Taiwanese interests have a 70 per cent stake. Taking advantage of large limestone deposits in the delta area, the factory has an initial capacity of 1.4 million tonnes a year, but this is due to be raised to four million tonnes by the turn of the century. The plant has its own port facilities which form part of a shipyard that was developed some 15 years ago with Finnish assistance.

Other major projects include a $120 million industrial zone by Nomura of Japan, which will be reserved largely for Japanese companies,[2] a $100 million brewery being built by the French brewer BGI, a $40 million rolled steel plant joint venture between Posco of South Korea and Vinasteel, a $25 million Australian steel venture.

One of the problems in attracting large amounts of investment is Haiphong's geographical location, which is both a strength and a weakness. The city proper, with about 600,000 residents, is actually only a small part of Haiphong administrative area, which straddles six major and numerous minor channels of the Red River delta and has a total population of 1.6 million.[3] It is estimated that each year the Red River carries away about four million tonnes of effluvium from its mountainous upper reaches, all of which it deposits in the delta.

Thus, Haiphong is steadily gaining more land for development purposes,[4] but is also being strangled by the silting up of its port. When this was established by the French in the nineteenth century, the wharves abutted the sea. Now, they are some 18 kilometres up river. In the mid-1980s, ships of 15,000dwt could get up the channel to the port, but further silting reduced this to 8,000 dwt. With Japanese and Belgian assistance, dredging has nudged the maximum handling tonnage up to 10,000. Concrete walls have also been built along the lower reaches of the river to encourage an additional scouring effect by an increased current.

But Haiphong is now pinning its hopes on developing a new deep sea port in the estuary at Dinh Vu. A consortium including IPEM of Belgium, American International Group (AIG) and Thailand's Asian Infrastructure Development Co. is to invest $185 million in the first phase of a long-term development, beginning with the creation of an industrial zone covering about 300 hectares and a wharf with an annual handling capacity of 1.2 million tonnes in ships up to 10,000 dwt. In the longer term, ships of 30,000 dwt will be able to berth and handling capacity will reach an estimated 12 million tonnes a year.

This cannot come soon enough for foreign shipping companies who see Haiphong close to being overwhelmed by the rapid growth of Vietnam's trade. The port managed to handle over four million tonnes of cargo in 1995, but with Vietnamese trade growing annually by an average 30 per cent, the time may not be far off when congestion becomes too much.

'Haiphong is hopeless,' says Kazuki Fukuda, local head of Mitsui OSK Lines. 'Even if they renovate, they can never solve the dredging problem that will inevitably limit the size of vessels that can dock. There has been a huge increase in container traffic which has created a severe shortage of storage space and causing a back-up all the way down the line to the ships waiting to dock.' The Japanese International Cooperation Agency (JICA) has estimated that Haiphong needs at least $170 million more than has already been committed for renovation, but at the time of writing there was no sign of the money being forthcoming.

The only road at present linking the port with Hanoi 105 kilometres away is the congested Highway 15, which is mostly two lanes (and occasionally even one), apart from a 13-kilometre stretch on the outskirts of Hanoi where there are four lanes. Work is going ahead to try and eliminate some of the bottlenecks, but it will be a long time before the entire road can be upgraded and by then the traffic demands could have grown beyond even the capacity of a four-lane highway.[5]

A railway which runs parallel to the road is an old narrow-gauge link. Britain's Balfour Beatty is studying possible rehabilitation of the railway in order to facilitate the movement of goods to and from Haiphong but is awaiting a firm commitment from Hanoi to give the project priority before it invests any more.[6]

Apart from industry, Haiphong also has ambitions to enhance its tourism industry, taking advantage of the natural wonders available in Ha Long Bay – home to thousands of small rocky islets twisted into fantastic shapes by primeval forces during the earth's cooling billions of years ago – to the north in Quang Ninh Province, and the golden sand of Do Son beach within its own administrative area on a small promontory to the south. In a joint venture with Hong Kong business interests, the city is building up a major tourist resort which will include Vietnam's only casino. 'The [national] leadership wasn't too happy with this, but we will ensure that only foreigners can use it and all Vietnamese will be barred. We have to prove that the casino can be a good and not a bad influence now,' explains Mr Dinh.

HANDS ACROSS THE BORDER

The two southern Chinese provinces of Yunnan and Guangxi border six provinces of Vietnam providing a mostly mountainous land border of 2,373 kilometres. On both sides of this frontier are communities who have the same ethnic origin, language and customs. Close relations go back a long way and contacts between these trans-border communities have never really stopped despite war or hostile bilateral relations between the two countries.[7]

In modern times, China and Vietnam started promoting trans-border trade by signing their first agreement in 1953 and economic exchanges grew steadily until the military clashes in 1979 led to frontier markets being closed. However, the trans-border communities continued a reduced form of secret trade. At first it took the form of relatives living on either side exchanging their goods at appointed spots. Gradually as government-level hostility lessened, these secret informal points became regular markets for exchanging goods. They were called the 'Sod Market' or 'Dew Market' for the trade was usually underway on the sod before sunrise. As the security situation on the frontiers improved, China opened more than 30 trading posts along the frontier and cross-border traffic became increasingly unobstructed.

The frontier trade has developed rapidly since the mid-1980s. According to Chinese statistics, the annual total volume of Sino-Vietnamese frontier trade rose from about $83 million (at the then official rate of exchange between the Yuan and the US dollar) in 1988 to $439 million in 1990, and then hovered around this level for the next three years. The early 1990s marked the beginning of official efforts to re-open old transport lines. For instance, Guangxi's 'Sino-Vietnamese Friendship Pass' railway bridge was reopened in 1991, followed by Yunnan's 'Sino-Vietnamese Friendship Bridge' the following year. But the rail link from Yunnan was only reopened in 1995.

The main Chinese exports along this border are diesel engines, cement, steel, bicycles, sewing machines, textiles, daily necessities and medicines, while those from Vietnam are agricultural products, coal, cotton, yarn, rubber, grain, herbs and fruit. The methods of payment are varied. Chinese currency has been habitually accepted for settling accounts, although barter is also practised. Nowadays, both national currencies and the US dollar are freely exchanged. Trading has usually been by the 'cash on delivery' method, but a more sophisticated trading environment is emerging with the introduction of credit.

The participants in this growing market are also getting more varied. No longer is trading only done by border inhabitants on an individual basis; trade has drawn to this border the state-owned companies, the collectives and the private enterprises on both sides. And the firms no longer just belong to border counties but also from the inner provinces. However, between 70 and 80 per cent of the trade is done by private enterprises. Frontier tourism and economic-technological cooperation have also come into being. Industry and the construction of trading towns is appearing on both sides of the border.

The factors that have contributed to the growing border trade have been the geographical proximity of market places, similar political-cultural background, and the complementarity of commodities and industrial needs of China and Vietnam. Since the normalization of relations in November 1991, there have also been a series of agreements to promote economic cooperation which have provided the legal basis for the frontier trade and there is room for growth.

However, there are also factors which have or will be hampering the growth of this trans-border commerce. First, although the Sino-Vietnamese relationship has been normalized, age-old suspicions plus unresolved territorial disputes on land and at sea still exist. As a result of which, Sino-Vietnamese relations have had their ups and downs. Vietnam has also complained that the smuggling along the border causes it to lose vast sums of revenue from taxes. At the same time, imports from China have also put tremendous pressure on Vietnam's own light industries. The second potentially restrictive factor is the availability of other sources of goods to the Vietnamese, especially through the auspices of Asean, while the third is the lack of physical and bureaucratic infrastructure along the border to handle trade properly. This is in terms of communication facilities as well as banking and other institutional conditions to settle trading accounts properly.

POVERTY IN HA GIANG

Ha Giang is the poorest province in Vietnam, yet a cup of coffee costs twice as much as in Hanoi and is a luxury most locals forego. Soaring prices for food, goods and services are being felt acutely in the mountainous area, which has to rely on food, including coffee, and building materials from lowland provinces. Ha Giang has a 270 kilometre-long frontier with the Chinese province of Yunnan. Yet this sleepy, scenic area, home of the H'mong ethnic minority, has a long way to go to match the bustling cross-border trade and smuggling volumes of Lang Son, Lao Cai and Quang Ninh, the other provinces that border China.

'Inflation in our province reflects the country's overall trend. Prices are higher here owing to high transport costs for all essential commodities brought from Hanoi and the deltas,' provincial governor Trieu Duc Thanh explains. About 30 per cent of all rice consumed in Ha Giang comes from the lowlands because the province is only 70 per cent self-sufficient in food production. 'At the peak of the cement shortage season, when prices shoot up to 1.4 million dong per ton, transport costs add 200,000 Dong to each ton of cement arriving here,' the governor says. Ha Giang generates minimal revenue, has poor farming ability and no industry to help it pay for the expensive goods it needs. At least one worry — cement supply — should be solved with the opening at the beginning of 1996 of its own plant with annual capacity of 300,000 tonnes.

The 320-kilometre journey from Hanoi to Ha Giang along National Highway 2 takes seven hours. The road is relatively smooth from Hanoi to the former industrial town of Vinh Phu, which is a third of the distance. The backbreaking stages begin in Tuyen Quang province. The Kinh [Vietnamese] account for 10 per cent of the provincial population of more than 400,000. The others are 22 groups of ethnic minorities dominated by the H'mong, Tay, Dao and Nung. Ha Giang is also home to two rare ethnic groups, the Pupeo and Phula, whose dwindling population of 400 each makes them off-limits to the government's family planning campaigns.

Ha Giang faces an uphill battle to introduce a 'green revolution' because of its geographical characteristics and lack of capital. Even in places where soil and water are kinder, making cash crops possible, a lack of roads hampers marketing and distribution. A Taiwanese company is experimenting with tea plantations and a Japanese company is running a pilot scheme for sedge, a material used to produce mattresses. Ha Giang wants to develop commercial planta-tions of tea, pine, eucalyptus, cinnamon, oranges, corn, tapioca and coffee. Slash and burn cultivation in the past has led to depletion of natural forest resources. At the beginning of the 1990s, forestry cover was down to 24 per cent. But by the end of 1994 it had risen to 36 per cent. Plantations of bamboo and eucalyptus on previously denuded hills are counted as 'forest cover' and Vietnam's reforestation schemes are usually commercial forests of a single species.

Ha Giang's development picture is bleak. In 1994, several state-owned enterprises managed by the provincial authority were dissolved, resulting in 1000 lay-offs, said Do Ngoc Thuy, chief labour officer for the province;. Away from the town, the province faces under-employment. Growing one crop of corn a year provides the only work for the highland population in almost all districts. Provincial officials hope to succeed with an ongoing experiment that will enable two corn crops a year. They also want to develop the quality of high-value cash crops, including apples and pears, which Vietnam imports in large quantities from China. Apples and pears were grown in the province before, but this came to a halt when the province became the scene of fierce fighting with China in 1979.

The Vietnamese-Chinese border crossing at Thanh Thuy lacks the human drama of the endless cat-and-mouse chases involving police and smugglers that are common at Mong Cai in Quang Ninh Province. Also missing are countless porters straining their muscles to balance baskets of piglets, bottled beer and fruit while scaling the difficult slope in Lang Son Province; and the busy traffic of traders and porters peddling their goods across the bridge in Lao Cai Province. Since the checkpoint's official opening in June 1993, trade with Yunnan Province has declined on the already-small level that existed before customs and immigration formalities were imposed. 'Petty traders said they could not make good money if they had to pay tax,' said a border guard.

The provincial governor has no illusions or grand ambitions for Thanh Thuy, which is about 25 kilometres from Ha Giang town. 'Lang Son, Quang Ninh and Lao Cai border Guangxi and Guangdong which have huge economic potential. Ha Giang is opposite the Yunnan hinterland where the economy is not so developed,' he says. 'Economic cooperation between two poor provinces of China and Vietnam is therefore less than between those richer provinces.'

In Thanh Thuy, the Vietnamese have built a market. Across the border at Thien Bao, the Chinese stopped work on the foundations of a four-storey hotel because they could see no immediate business potential. A few stalls manned by Chinese on the Yunnan side sell snacks and soft drinks from China and cigarettes from Cambodia that arrived through Vietnam. Lang Son, Mong Cai and Lao Cai have better land access than Thanh Thuy to Hanoi. Larger volumes of trade give these areas an edge in wholesale prices.

Province officers of Ha Giang and Yunnan met in June 1995 to try and find ways to promote the movement of goods and people across the border. Upgrading of the roads between Ha Giang town and Thanh Thuy is underway. The two provinces hope to persuade their central governments to make the Thanh Thuy crossing international so that it can be used by other nationalities than Vietnamese and Chinese. At present, only three to five Chinese tourists and businessmen cross into Ha Giang each day.

TRADE NOT WAR AT TINH BIEN

All is definitely not quiet on Vietnam's south-western front, but it is the bustle of business that has replaced the vacuum created by war.

Cross-border trade is picking up in areas of An Giang province which had no civilian population for many years after alleged atrocities committed by the Khmer Rouge in the late 1970s — the trigger for Vietnam's invasion of its neighbour in 1979. But all that is now largely forgotten. Rice farming has returned to normal. Khmer traders, petty and wholesale, from Takeo province travel back and forth for daily business with their Vietnamese counterparts at the checkpoint called Tinh Bien by the Vietnamese and Phnom Den by the Cambodians, which opens daily from 6am to 6pm.

Vietnamese customs authorities estimate the value of trade at 1.2 billion dong a day, which is small in comparison with trade along the Chinese frontier with China, but a reasonable start. Vietnam sells rice, fertilizer, instant noodles, bananas, coconuts, jackfruit and construction materials including steel rods. Goods transported from the Cambodian side mostly originate from Thailand, key items being ceramic toilets and canned soft drinks. 'Thai goods used to pour in at the height of smuggling, when Vietnamese traders bribed Cambodian officials. Now smuggling has subsided as Vietnam has developed the quality of its local products,' An Giang province deputy chief Nguyen Minh Nhi says.

About 10 kms from Tinh Bien checkpoint is the Southwest's most active smuggling route — Cho Choi (the daylight market) at Chau Doc on the bank of the Bassac River that flows through Cambodia. At Vietnamese checkpoints with China, the trade surplus tilts in favour of the Chinese. But at Tien Binh, Vietnam has a rare trade surplus. 'Vietnam sells a lot more than it buys, because Cambodia can produce very little,' explains a customs officer. He recalled days when 5,000 cases of canned Seven-Up from Thailand passed through his territory.

But Tinh Bien's cross-border trade is relatively new and has a long way to go to catch up with business at Moc Bai checkpoint in Tay Ninh province opposite Svay Rieng in Cambodia. Moc Bai has better road transport links and goods take less time to reach Phnom Penh than from Tinh Bien. But Tinh Bien is catching up fast as the Vietnamese in 1995 finally repaired a three kilometre portion of Route 91 that runs to the border checkpoint (previously goods had to be carried by boat). Goods passing through Tinh Bien still have to rattle a further 60 kilometres along a bumpy road that is either muddy or submerged during the wet season to get to the provincial seat of Takeo.

Vietnamese security authorities banned foreigners other than officials from the United Nations High Commissioner for Refugees from visiting this area until recently. Like several other spots in An Giang province, Tinh Bien provided refuge for ethnic Vietnamese in Cambodia who fled threats of serial killings by the Khmer Rouge. These threats emerged soon after the general election in Cambodia in May 1993 and continued for almost a year. Tinh Bien remains one of the very few places in Vietnam where clearance from security authorities is required before journalists can enter. Another is the area where the borders of Laos, Cambodia and Vietnam converge in Kontum province in the central highlands.

Deputy Mayor Nhi said the authorities had no plan to promote or expand cross-border trade with Cambodia in this area. 'We just let it carry on spontaneously because the private sector is the main force of these current exchanges. There's very little official trade, if any at all,' he said, adding that whether or not stability is sustainable depended on the situation in Cambodia.

HAVEN IN DONG NAI/SONG BE

Australia's BHP Steel had some clear criteria it wanted to see met before moving on a $4.7 million investment in a construction materials steel mill. They needed good industrial land and they wanted to retain 100 per cent ownership. In Ho Chi Minh City, much of the industrial land is owned by state companies or ministries, which means joint ventures are usually necessary. So, BHP turned to the provinces.

In the Bien Hoa industrial district of Dong Nai province, about 25 km from the Saigon Port, the company found all their conditions being accepted. With plenty of inexpensive industrial land available and a local People's Committee willing to help companies slice through the red tape, Dong Nai has become a haven for 100 per cent foreign-owned ventures. And although provincial development has been dominated by offshore oil developments — creating an onshore support industry in the Ba Ria–Vung Tau area — officials are looking for more than just oil revenues for its future growth.

Local People's Committee Vice Chairman Dang Van Tiep says: 'According to the Ho Chi Minh City plan, 14,000 hectares of land are set aside for industry. In Dong Nai, we have 12,000 ha. The time needed to get the land [in HCMC] is long. Here it's quicker' With the price of land continuing to climb in the industrial suburbs of former Saigon, its neighbour is scrambling to build industrial parks to attract investors. At present, the province is the third biggest magnet for foreign investment after the two big cities. There are four industrial parks either up and running or being built. The Bien Hoa Industrial Zone, which had 65 companies operating in it at the end of 1995, was former South Vietnam's manufacturing powerhouse. The zone, in fact, opened as far back as 1968 and housed some of the largest factories of the former southern regime.

These days, the People's Committee is looking to replicate the industrial park's former success by providing investors with solid infrastructure and convenient access to roads as well as one-stop service for licensing. Provincial officials have organized exhibitions abroad ro promote the parks, and have worked hard to speed up procedures to make them as free from bureaucracy as possible.

However, the high number of 100 per cent foreign owned ventures is still a cause for concern. Blessed with lower land prices than Ho Chi Minh City, the Vietnamese side cannot contribute much in the way of legal capital since they can generally only offer the value of the land into a joint venture. 'We want to try and have more joint ventures,' says Tiep, while admitting they have no money.

For manufacturers, highly skilled labour could be a problem, stresses Nguyen Van Giang, deputy general manager of Dana Bochang International Co.Ltd, a towel manufacturing joint venture between Taiwan, Dong Nai province and Textimex, a national textile company. 'We have them [workers] in Dong Nai, but fewer,' says Giang, adding that many skilled engineers and managers have to commute to and from Ho Chi Minh City.

The province of Song Be also forms part of the core of industrial development around the old southern capital. At the time of writing, the government had just approved in principle the establishment of an industrial park there involving Singaporean investment. This will be very much along the lines of new industrial towns that consortia involving Singaporean state-owned and private companies are developing in Suzhou in China and Bangalore in India, for example.[8]

The project partners, Song Be Trading and Import/Export Company (Becamex) and Singapore Industrial Park Pte — a consortium led by Sembawang Corporation — plan to develop the park on a 500 hectare site in Thuan An District, about 17 kilometres from Saigon Port and 14 kilometres from Tan Son Nhat International

Airport. The investment capital for the first phase, totalling $53 million, will be broken up into 49 per cent provided by the Vietnamese side in the form of land use rights for 50 years and relocation costs, while the Singaporeans will contribute their 51 per cent in cash.

The park is intended to house mainly factories producing consumer electronics, auto components and processing food, and provide an estimated 50,000 jobs. Construction of the first phase was expected to take three years, with the entire park completed in eight.[9]

VUNG TAU: OIL CAPITAL

Taiwanese investors are also heavily involved in the Ba Ria–Vung Tau. area abutting the South China Sea. After long delays to settle land compensation issues, the $97 million Fairyland resort is under way. This resort is located on a 200 hectare area of land next to the sea and will include a 27–hole golf course, luxury hotels and an amusement park.

'Oil, tourism and ports. This is what we will develop,' says Nguyen Van Chinh, vice chairman of the provincial planning committee. It has its eyes on the $636 million Sao Mao port development, which will be the biggest in Vietnam. There are several other ports planned as the province gears up for what it hopes will be an oil rich future, even if many industry analysts feel this remains somewhat uncertain.

Like Ho Chi Minh City, there are construction sites on nearly every street as large villas and hotels are being quickly built up to cash in on either oil or a likely solid alternative, tourism. The People's Committee has published a glossy portfolio of 57 investment projects calling for investment and well over half the projects are either oil or tourism related. 'In all the country we are the biggest oil centre. We have all the services to meet the oil sector's needs,' said Chinh. But he was quick to point out that the province was not putting all its eggs into the oil basket. 'We have over 100 kilometres of beach front. We have many foreign investors coming for tourism,' says Chinh.[10]

Vung Tau in French times was known as Cap St Jacques and was a popular weekend retreat for foreign residents of Saigon wishing to escape the steamy heat of the capital for more balmy parts. It was a pleasant drive of no more than 100 kilometres to loll on the golden sands and contemplate a delightful dinner of freshly–caught lobster or other sea food to be found just off the coast. During the Second Indochina War, the resort was a popular in-country r & r (rest and recreation) centre for American and Australian troops, and its port was a key logistics channel for the vast amounts of equipment and food needed to keep the respective armies in the field.

Today, those lolling up against the beach umbrellas tend to be local, while the port has been taken over largely by Russian ships supporting the vast offshore oil drilling programme being undertaken by the VietSovPetro joint venture [see Chapter 4]. Under the former regime, the port was part of Phuoc Tuy Province, of which the inland town of Baria was the provincial capital. Now, they have been combined to form Baria-Vung Tau Province with some realignment of provincial boundaries.

Tourism will surely be in future years an important foreign exchange earner for the province. But the moment it is the offshore oil and gas that provides the key source of income. As already discussed, the pipelines are now in operation to bring ashore the oil and gas from beneath the sea to feed existing and planned power stations in both Baria and Vung Tau. A shipyard has been created in the old port area to turn out the drilling platforms for further exploration which are then floated out to their allotted positions at sea. Much of the piping for the platforms comes from a Vietnamese-Korean steel plant just outside the city. These activities, along with ship repair, and the overall provision of support services for the energy industry will be a key area for foreign investment for the foreseeable future.

To provide a home for an expected rush of investors, the province plans to establish six industrial zones. These will include one at Dong Xuyen in Vung Tau, where a 160-hectare site was being prepared in mid-1996 mainly to house the growing oil and gas industry support services. Meanwhile, a 130-hectare site at Phuoc Thang will become a 'clean industry zone', offering a home to high-tech and non-polluting industries such as electronics and garment manufacturing.

From the turn of the century, the province plans to switch the development emphasis the light industry in the more remote rural areas especially in the processing of agricultural, aquatic and forestry products which grow in abundance.

One of the problems for both Vung Tau and Baria is access from Ho Chi Minh City. The existing road is a nightmare as it first struggles

out of the old southern capital through the industrial strip development that has sprung up on either side of Route 1 to Hanoi, and
then turns right for the bulk of the journey along Route 51, a road
hardly wide enough for two lorries, where overtaking oncoming
vehicles are a constant menace to the nervous driver. The good news
is that the central government has approved a plan to turn the road
into a four-lane highway. At the same time, a feasibility study has
been approved for an expressway from Phu My to Baria.

There are no railways in the province at present, but after finishing
the proposed roads, the provincial authorities are hoping to turn their
attention to a railway to link Baria with the growing industrial base
around Bien Hoa [see above]. At the same time, the small airport at
Vung Tau, now used mostly by helicopters serving the oil industry, is
due to be enlarged under an infrastructure master plan although
primarily to handle cargo rather than passengers — the international
tourist expected to land in Ho Chi Minh City and then drive to the coast.

Mr Si says foreign investors will have to bear most of the burden if
the province is to achieve its objective. 'Every one of these tasks is
an urgent one, because we need to build up both our industrial
capability and the supporting infrastructure side by side. But our
own resources are very limited. For the oil and gas industry we need
to procure an estimated $400 million every year for vital equipment,
and this is bound to grow larger as more discoveries are made. But
I would estimate that by ourselves we will be able to fund only about
five per cent of this, and the total from the Vietnamese side can only
be about 15 per cent. That means we have got to find 85 per cent
of the funding from foreign investors. And the same applies to the
big infrastructure projects. Here we can rely more on ODA. but we
will still need a lot of foreign help in funds, expertise and equipment
to meet our goals.'[11]

QUANG NGAI-DA NANG: CENTRAL ECONOMIC NUCLEUS

There are numerous small altars built at each end of the notorious Hai
Van Pass (1,172 metres), testimony to the horrific traffic accidents that
have occurred there ever since the road, Route 1, was built there at
the turn of the century. Appalling weather conditions, with snap
flooding and landslides, add to the hazards of an extremely difficult
road covering some 20 kilometres on each side of the 'Pass In The

Clouds' that separates the central coast provinces of Thua Thien-Hue in the north and Quang Nam-Da Nang to the south. Many truck drivers find it obligatory to present flower and incense offerings on the altars and pray to the mountain god for safe passage before proceeding on their journey. Even in the best of conditions, it takes more than four hours to cover the 80 kilometres between Da Nang and Hue at present.

Soon, that will be only a memory. At the time of writing, a World Bank-financed feasibility study was in progress for the construction of a series of three tunnels carving out a straight route under Hai Van Pass, and opening up areas on both sides of the mountain. There will be three separate tunnels, the longest of 4.5 kilometres, and two others of 1.5 kilometres each. Four lanes are planned, the inner two for motorized traffic, the outer two for more rudimentary means of traffic such as ox carts. Construction was scheduled to begin in the first half of 1997. When completed, this section of Route 1 will become a toll road to help recover the costs.

The Hanoi-Ho Chi Minh City rail link has long passed under Hai Van pass in a series of tunnels which took four decades to complete. But little maintenance has been carried out so that these are in fairly poor condition. Phan Ngoc Thuy, project director, is confident the planned tolls will ensure that there is sufficient money to ensure so such deterioration happens to his tunnels.

Thuy sees his project closely linked to the development of several ports on both sides of the mountains, along with planned industrial development to the south, and the prospects for increased trade and transportation links with land-locked Laos to the west.

Just below Da Nang, Dung Quat in Quang Ngai Province, is to be the home of the country's largest petroleum processing and heavy industrial centre, as well as the economic nucleus of central Vietnam. The plan calls for the expenditure of around $500 million in the next five years to begin creating an industrial complex covering almost 14,000 hectares, with petroleum processing and petrochemical plants, fed by crude oil pumped from Dung Quat Port. The country's first oil refinery, as mentioned earlier in this book, is to be established on a 200 hectare site south of Nam Tram Cape with a total annual processing capacity of 6.5 million tonnes when in full operation. A second refinery is now on the drawing board in the same area. The proposed petrochemical zone will have various plants with a total handling capacity of 10 million tonnes of oil a year.

Dung Quat Port is being upgraded to give it a cargo handling capacity of up to 30 million tonnes a year, serving primarily the petroleum and metallurgy industries as well as for inland freight transport. Meanwhile Chu Lai, an important American military base during the war, about three kilometres from Dung Quat is to be developed into an international airport with an initial annual handling capacity of 500,000 passengers, but doubling in subsequent years. Areas in the industrial zone have also been set aside for the development of a significant ship building and ship repair yard, along with a steel rolling mill, a vehicle assembly plant, and various oil industry service establishments.

MEKONG DELTA DIVERSIFIES

The Mekong Delta produces over half of Vietnam's rice and contributes more than a quarter of its gross domestic product. But the region of some four million hectares is is no longer content with its role as the country's rice bowl. Officials in the region have high hopes they can draw off some of the investors who currently don't venture further south than Ho Chi Minh City. So far, few have been tempted. Throughout the entire delta comprising 11 provinces, there were by 1995 only 51 licensed foreign investment projects with total investment capital of $500 million.[12]

The lack of a processing industrial base as well as the absence of a financial services infrastructure, has meant that everything has to be provided by Ho Chi Minh City. Now, provincial officials are looking at ways to develop the delta as an economic centre with a distinct personality of its own. 'The issue we're facing is how to unite the southern provinces to match Ho Chi Minh City-Bien Hoa-Ba Ria-Vung Tau,' says Vo Van Luy, chairman of the State Planning Committee of Can Tho province.

Can Tho Province, located at the heart of the immense fertile plain, is already one of the fastest-growing areas among the 11 delta provinces, but this has been built solely on agriculture like all the others. Now it would like to diversify. 'One can live on agriculture, but one cannot get rich. Only with industrialization can people here become rich. So, we have got to have foreign investment,' said Buu Hui Tri, vice-president of the local People's Committee.

Eight years after the first joint venture was launched, there were by the end of 1995 only 10 foreign-funded projects in the province.

One-third of the $53 million invested came from a single joint venture involving the American agribusiness company American Rice. 'We are way behind. Our infrastructure is not good; we don't have adequate water or electricity, and our transport links with Ho Chi Minh City are difficult,' said Vo.

Dilapidated ferries are the only way to cross two important branches of the Mekong River to reach the former southern capital. It takes at least five hours under the best conditions to cover the 170 kilometres on a road that also needs serious upgrading. Can Tho planned to get rid of the ferries, however, with the start of work on construction of bridges in 1997.

For the moment, Can Tho is the only province in the delta to have been authorized to establish a free trade zone. This will cover 500 hectares north of the provincial capital, close to the port and airport, both of which were to be upgraded. Apart from the processing of the area's rice, sugar and fruit output into various food products, it is hoped to attract foreign investment in the areas of electronics and construction materials. Sme 8.3 billion Dong has been earmarked to rebuild and extend Can Tho port. At present it can handle vessels of up to 5,000 dwt, but this will be doubled.

The French group Rhone-Poulenc opened a representative office in Can Tho in 1995, while three hours away by road in My Tho on the Mekong River, a French-Vietnamese brewing joint venture has set up shop. The firm BGI has invested $43 million, which represents the largest foreign presence in Tien Giang Province, some 70 kilometres south of Ho Chi Minh City, and is the country's third largest brewer. The bad state of the roads does not pose a problem. 'nearly all our production goes by boat to Ho Chi Minh City or Cambodia. It's much cheaper,' said a company spokesman.

Can Tho apart, the government has a Mekong Delta Master Plan which sets out to develop the region as a 'growth pole' to balance advances in other parts of the country. The emphasis remains on the primary sector of agriculture and fisheries. These include large-scale water resource projects that will allow farmers to control flooding during the wet season and obtain water during the dry — together creating an environment where it should be possible to move from the present one rice crop a year to two and possibly three.

Shrimp farming is another promising area. The master plan calls for two semi-intensive shrimp-raising pilot projects of 1,000 hectares each in Ben Tre and Minh Hai provinces. In the long term, local officials have identified around 75,000 hectares of land which they consider would be suitable for shrimp raising.[13]

NOTES

1. Interview 27 April 1996.
2. A dozen Japanese language classes were started by the enterprising Haiphong authorities in late 1995 in anticipation of an influx of Japanese companies seeking labour.
3. Politically, it is one of three special cities which are not part of any province that form the second tier of Vietnam's four-tier administrative structure, but instead are autonomous governing units (the other two being Hanoi and Ho Chi Minh City). This allows Haiphong to handle all the processing of foreign investment licence applications, although referring a project to the central government for final approval.
4. In 1983, for example, a new dyke was built in the Kien Thuy area to enclose some 2,000 hectares of hardened silt that had built up outside the existing dyke. The area is now being developed for both residential and industrial purposes.
5. I cannot over-emphasize just what a nightmare the road is at present. On a weekend drive to Haiphong, which took around four hours, it was impossible to get up any sort of speed. The road is jammed with cycles and motorcyles moving from one village to the next, and through these the rest of the traffic somehow has to weave its way. It is unnerving to see a juggernaut loaded with containers or a bus packed to the seams and tilting alarmingly, overtaking a gaggle of cyclists oblivious to the chaos around them, and bearing down on you with seemingly no room to pass. Time after time this happened, but somehow, at the very last moment, the onrushing vehicle would swerve to the right to allow just enough room for my car to carry on unscathed. The worst bottleneck is a river bridge which is not only restricted to one lane, but also shares the space with the main railway line. If one is unlucky with the direction of the regulated traffic flow, or if there is a train due, waits of up to 45 minutes are common, I was told. Happily, a new bridge was being built nearby to carry the road traffic. At the same time, Route 18, which comes off Route 15 near Hai Druong, and proceeds via the stunningly beautiful Ha Long Bay resort area, to the Chinese border, is also being upgraded to cope with a huge increase in traffic as drivers seek to avoid having to go via Haiphong, where two of the river channels have to be crossed on very slow ferries – although the northernmost one will eventually be replaced by a bridge.
6. *Financial Times,* 13 November 1995.
7. Some of the information in this sub-section is based on an article submitted to the Straits Times, Singapore, in August 1995 by Liu Zhi, Associate Research Fellow, Institute of Southeast Asia Studies.
8. Interested readers can obtain more details of these developments in the two previous volumes in this Pacific Rim Business Series – *China: The Last Great Market* and *Singapore: Global City State.*
9. *Vietnam Commerce and Industry,* a monthly magazine published by the Chamber of Commerce and Industry of Vietnam, Hanoi, March 1996 issue.
10. *Vietnam Economic Times.* December 1994/January 1995.
11. Interview in Vung Tau 23 April 1996.
12. *Vietnam Economic Times,* May 1995.
13. Ibid.

8 Banking and Finance

KEY POINTS

- Vietnam rediscovers banking
- Banking reforms of 1987
- An under or overbanked country?
- Foreign branches and joint venture banks
- Getting a bank loan
- Prospects for a stock exchange
- Foreign involvement
- Upgrading accountancy practice
- Insurance

VIETNAM REDISCOVERS BANKING

FOR A while in 1995, large queues were forming early under the huge glass atrium of what was once the French colonial Banque Francaise de L'Asie but is now the state-owned Bank for Foreign Trade of Vietnam (known for short as Vietcombank) in central Ho Chi Minh City. The depositors waiting patiently with passbooks and small bundles of cash might not have known it, but they were taking part in a minor revolution. After decades of suspicion, however, southern Vietnamese were beginning to trust banks with their money. Banks like Vietcombank are polishing their images, taking out advertisements in local newspapers and offering basic banking products for the first time.

The government is as pleased as the banks at the new-found trust in the banking system. It is struggling to mobilize capital for public investment. It also helps soothe World Bank concerns that the country's domestic savings rate by East Asian standards, is still relatively low.[1] 'For the first time ever, the customer is being wooed by retail banks, and the banks are beginning to develop a range of products,' says John Brinsden of Standard Chartered Bank.

But it was not always this way. Many residents have painful memories of the Communist take-over in 1975, when savings evaporated as banks, including branches of US institutions such as Chase Manhattan, Bank of America and Citibank, were taken over by the government. This prompted a rush to hoard gold, which is still used for many property transactions. Foreign currencies were stored at home, as the lack of confidence in the dong matched that of the banking system.

Banks in Ho Chi Minh City have been more aggressive than those in Hanoi in courting customers, offering credit cards and cheque books. In one corner of the Vietcombank lobby is an experimental automated teller machine. Nevertheless, by the end of 1996, it was estimated that there would still only be about 40 ATMs at maximum throughout the country.

However, the banks were also helped by the collapse of an underground financial system called 'credit circles'. These were local networks of citizens who each put up a set amount of principal and then were able in turn to use of the total raised. Stung by losses, thousands of depositors lost confidence in the credit circles, prompting the central bank to reorganize what was left of the system into a more formal network of cooperative banks.

This came as the government was liberalizing the banking system by encouraging the establishment of joint stock, or shareholding banks, as part of economic reforms. There are 26 Vietnamese state and joint stock banks but many more smaller, shareholding banks in HCMC. The major shareholders in joint stock banks are often state-run companies.

Vietcombank — marketing slogan: 'Always For Your Everlasting Success' — started its transformation from faceless monolith to customer-friendly lender by launching new products in January 1995. Among them are local currency deposit accounts paying 20 per cent in interest. Truong Van Phuoc, the bank's deputy director, said some $50 million in deposits was attracted in the first 10 months. 'It's crazy for people to put money under the pillow. We don't have a stock exchange yet, but domestic investors can still choose between competitive savings rates at the banks.'

This seemed somewhat debatable, however, when, at the end of 1995, the state-owned banks were ordered to cut interest rates on short-term loans in the national currency to a maximum of 21 per cent per annum (a reduction of 2.4 percentage points), in order to alleviate some of the debt repayment burden on state-run firms and also try to entice them away from borrowing dollars (available from the private sector at rates as low as nine per cent) to help hold down inflation. The immediate result of this was that the banks had to lower the rates they offered depositors to a maximum of 16.8 per cent.

Banking analysts said this was getting perilously close to the existing inflation rate, and could discourage the nascent national effort to mobilize savings. 'The biggest problem in Vietnam is attracting capital, particularly from domestic sources, into the banking system,' says economist Dennis McCornac. 'If you decrease the return, it's not much of an incentive.'

In a major policy speech in January 1996, Communist Party Secretary General Do Muoi said Vietnam's main concern had to be 'capital, capital and more capital' to build up the basic infrastructure and develop business. Foreign money was important, he conceded, but it often came with strings attached. Therefore, the country had to concentrate on mobilizing domestic capital.

At the end of 1995, only about five per cent of the population was using banking services of some sort — and the majority of those are said to be bank or government employees — although the industry was hoping to double this figure by the end of 1996. Most people so far have been interested in savings accounts alone, and at the time of writing there were only about 10,000 individual cheque accounts in the whole country. The banking industry, however, is optimistic that with the gradual growth of ATMs and the use and acceptance of personal cheques, this sector will become popular by the turn of the century.[2]

Introduction of an information technology infrastructure has been assisted by a $50 million loan from the World Bank, and most of this will go towards developing a national system of electronic fund transfers. There is no interbank transfer system at present, although there is a limited intrabank arrangement (transfers between different branches of Vietcombank, for instance).

All this will help bring Vietnam into the modern banking world. Yet the intervention by the government to force banks to lower their rates, rather than leave it to the dictates of supply and demand, seems to confirm the general feeling in Vietnam that there is still a long way to go before the banking and financial sector can play its full role in economic development, as has happened in most other parts of Asia, starting with Japan, with spectacular success. Before considering what else needs to be done, it is necessary to take the story back a few years to the mid-1980s.

BANKING REFORMS OF 1987

The subservient position of the State (Central) Bank vis-à-vis the ruling Council of Ministers, and hence the lack of appropriate administrative and professional autonomy in monetary affairs — being no more than a disbursing/receiving agent of the Ministry of Finance — effectively shut out the banking system from the process of monetary and fiscal policy formulation. The Council of Ministers approved both the credit and cash plans for the entire economy. The credit plan allocated all government expenditure to all production units for the entire year, with clearly determined quarterly guidelines, by pruning and combining the requests from the ground level upwards. The State Bank then administered the plans through its branches in each of the 37 provinces and four autonomous cities.

But in 1987, the banking system underwent fundamental reform. Basic banking functions were delineated clearly between the State Bank and the commercial banks. The former was entrusted with responsibility for regulating the monetary supply and credit, this safeguarding the value of the national currency. The provision of cash and credit to both producers and consumers was handed over to the commercial and specialized banks.

Two of the latter already existed, and two more were newly created, all state-owned. The Bank of Foreign Trade, as its name implies, took over commercial transactions and operations for the foreign sector. The Construction and Investment Bank became responsible for the transfer of budgetary appropriations for basic infrastructure projects. The Bank for Agricultural Development and the Vietnam Industrial and Commercial Bank were given broader commercial functions in their related fields. At the same time as they concentrate on their specialities, however, all four are now being developed into what the government calls 'universal banks' — offering a wide range of services similar to those of the West.

Below these is a rather extensive network of credit cooperatives, which had operated since the early years of independence in the north. Of rather modest scope in terms of credit facilities and scale of operation, the cooperatives catered essentially for the limited credit needs of the rural community.

But what was essentially omitted from the equation were the needs of the non-governmental sector, especially if these enterprises were to respond to market signals. Both short and medium-term loans were not readily available from the banking system; private entrepreneurs were often forced to resort to non-banking sources at exorbitant rates of interest that undermined the sector's ability to make a rapid contribution to economic growth.

The banking reforms, therefore, were not as fundamental as they should have been, or implemented to the fullest extent. By failing to perform its proper function as the 'bank of last resort' by inter-bank lending and through other regular central bank practices as discounting and rediscounting commercial papers etc., the State Bank could not provide the economy with adequate working liquidity when the banking system was stretched to its loan capacity.

Some of the burden was taken over by the credit cooperatives which in the late 1980s extended an exceptionally large amount of private loans, often indiscriminately, and paid the price when many of these turned out to be non-performing. According to some reports at the time, close to one trillion Dong may have been granted essentially on the basis of personal, friendly or family trust. The result was a widespread credit crisis which saw prices and the exchange rate in 1990 more than double from the level of 1989.

Further reforms in 1990 included legislation providing the first tentative moves towards a limited private sector banking through the establishment of shareholding joint venture banks. Apart from, nearly 50 joint stock banks now operating, there are also four foreign joint venture banks, which will be discussed in more detail later in this chapter. More than 60 foreign financial institutions have also been allowed to establish either a branch or representative office.

Other aspects of the financial sector are limited. A limited treasury bond market was launched in June 1995. But the establishment of a stock market, originally planned for 1995, was postponed due to ideological unwillingness on the part of some in authority to sell off state enterprises, a lack of proper financial market laws and a deficiency in accounting methods. As will be made clear later in this chapter, repeated delays have raised considerable doubts as to when a stock market will eventually appear.

AN UNDER OR OVERBANKED COUNTRY?

According to the World Bank, Vietnam is an 'underbanked' country, with total assets in the banking system equivalent to just over 20 per cent of the gdp, a level well below that of most other Asian countries. Conversely, Vietnam may also be 'overbanked' in that there are too many financial institutions chasing too few assets in the system. Most analysts feel a shake-out among the banks is inevitable at some stage. Many of the new joint stock banks are seriously undercapitalized or insolvent. The state banks lack proper audit controls.

Foreign bankers who rushed to Vietnam in anticipation of big business are rethinking their strategy. It is likely some will decide that operating costs are too high to justify staying any longer. One foreign fund manager says the problem in Vietnam is not a truly monetized economy. 'More than 70 per cent of the labour force is involved in agriculture where barter is more important than cash. There is still a considerable mistrust of banks. What is often seen as a grasping and unfair tax regime and general suspicion of the government's often contradictory policies have tended to weaken public confidence in entrusting their hard-won savings to the banks. There is also a lot of ignorance about what banking services. So substantial savings tend to exist outside the banking system.'

The banking system is still dominated by the state rather than the market, attuned to serving large public conglomerates rather than the needs of the private sector. According to World Bank figures, the four state-owned commercial banks accounted for nearly 90 per cent of total assets held by deposit money banks at the end of 1994. Private sector lending has tripled in the previous three years, most of it in the form of short-term loans — mainly to the agriculture and commerce sectors.

But sources in the private sector say there is a lot of resentment at the way the banks manipulate their loans. The tendency is to ensure that the term is so short, say four months, that is hard for the borrower to gain sufficient return on investment in time to meet the repayment schedule. That enables the banks to bring in penalty clauses and recoup a bigger profit than ever.

Being so heavily geared towards the public sector in their loan policies — as well as in their deposits base — the major banks face problems when it comes to assessing the degree of risk involved.

And many a bad guess has cost them dearly in recent years. Analysing the financial affairs of the state-owned enterprises is difficult as auditing methods do not conform to international standards and there is little transparency in company operations.

The government says only nine per cent of the state companies are losing money. This is viewed as a serious underestimate. While the number of state companies has been reduced by nearly 50 per cent in recent years, many are still believed to be either insolvent or in a precarious financial situation. 'The state banks are dangerously over-exposed to bad debts in the state sector,' says a resident foreign banker.'The government has pushed through reforms in some areas but is still stopping short of dismantling the numerous state firms that are inefficient and a drain on precious resources.'

There are other handicaps to the developing of the bank sector and ancillary financial services. The legal framework governing the sector is still inadequate. Borrowers are unable to use land as collateral to raise loans as the government has declared all land to be the property of the state. Recent legal changes might bring some improvement, but analysts say several grey areas in the law need to be cleared before any real progress in financial services is made. For years Vietnam devoted its educational energies to producing engineers and technicians rather than bankers and financial managers. There is now a serious shortage of financial sector expertise.

Former government economic adviser Nguyen Xuan Oanh[3] says: 'There is an acute shortage of qualified financial managers, bankers, bank supervision and control staff. A new class of 'socialist bankers' are needed to be trained in financial management, credit evaluation, foreign exchange management, asset-liability management, maturity gap management, hedging strategies, underwriting and a host of other technical and specialized operations. Financial specialists are desperately needed who can evaluate corporate financial performance and provide an independent opinion on financial status.'

Prime Minister Vo Van Kiet takes a dim view of his country's financial sector. 'The financial system is not keeping pace with the development of the economy,' he told the National Assembly. 'Our capital markets are still too primitive. We have been too slow in the equitization of state companies as well as the establishment of a stock market.' Vietnam's economic progress would be in jeopardy if the financial system was not modernized. 'To perpetuate this situation is to perpetuate the backward, ineffective nature of the economy,' the prime minister declared.[4]

Mr Oanh expands on this: 'The financial system still cannot play much more than a subservient role. Most financial instruments, which are supposed to constitute major weapons for direct control, cannot be effective not because they don't exist, but because some the remaining rigidities of the old mode of operation leave these instruments little scope for effective action.'

Answering all these criticisms, a senior official of the State Bank of Vietnam, Dr Nguyen Toan Thang,[5] says, in essence, that certainly things are not as they should be, with many key deficiencies. At the same time, look how far Vietnam has gone in a short time. 'There was no financial market of any sort under the old command economy. We've had to create everything from scratch in order to cope with the change to the market mechanism. When we began this shift, we didn't have the commodities to deal in; there were no buyers and sellers; the supporting legal system was totally lacking; and we didn't have any experience whatsoever.

'We have had to change people's habits, their way of thinking. we have had to educate them in economic theory. We are, therefore, a developing country in a very special category. Take the example of Bangladesh, which in many respects is at a similar economic level to us. But Bangladesh at least had the basic structures in place – a proper banking industry and the concepts that support it – so that it is at least 10 years ahead of us in this regard.'

But, he argued, things are changing rapidly, citing the policy move towards corporate equitization, the creation of a commercial code, a law on trading in commodities, a law on land use in financial dealings, and new policies and laws on the operations of state-owned enterprises. 'With the legal environment in place, we can then move on to create the material conditions for the development of a fully-fledged financial services sector. We have to modernize banking, introducing better management ideas from abroad and taking full advantage of the developments in information technology.'

Above all, the official stressed, however, the State Bank had to assert its rights as a true central bank, exercising more control over fiscal and monetary policy – through various instruments such as interest rate adjustments, reserve requirements and open market operations – and strengthening its control and supervision of all banking activities. But this can only come about if that is part of the government's overall economic policy and there are no 'territorial disputes' with other ministries over who has the final say.

Ultimately, the biggest challenge for all the banks is going to be how to mobilize savings and utilize these for economic development. The banks, as briefly discussed earlier, face the dilemma of financially-strapped businesses requiring loans at a modest rate of interest, and potential savings demanding high, inflation–proof interest rates to make it worth their while putting the money in the bank. In fact, claimed Dr Thang, many banks are actually awash with cash and simply do not know what to do with it. They have experienced so many problems with bad loans that have proved unclaimable that bankers are now reluctant to lend any of their money at all.

International borrowing has been an importance source of finance for Vietnam, but the government has become worried that it is building up a foreign debt burden that will undermine its ability to achieve future economic targets. There are billions of dollars of outstanding old debts that remain the subject of difficult international negotiations to achieve some sort of rescheduling, along with the partial writing off (figures of around 30 per cent have been talked about, but so far rejected by the international financial community).

FOREIGN BRANCHES AND JOINT VENTURE BANKS

Foreign banks have not been able to operate in Vietnam for very long, but already the sector is beginning to look crowded. Take the example of a few days in January 1995. During that period, Citibank became the first American bank to open a branch in Vietnam since the war ended in 1975, while Bank of America also received a branch licence. Both, however, had representative offices in Hanoi from 1993. Asahi Bank, meanwhile, opened a representative office in Ho Chi Minh City, the seventh Japanese bank to do so, and Germany's Dresdener Bank announced it would soon open offices in both cities.[6]

Citibank country manager Bradley C.Lalonde said the branch was not planning a full line of retail products, reflecting a general view of foreign bankers here that checking accounts, changing travellers' cheques for tourists and other forms of 'high street' banking were not the way to go. The American bank quickly made its mark, when it became the first foreign institution to participate in the secondary market for treasury bonds. It bought T-bills worth 20 billion dong ($1.8 million) from the Bank for Foreign Trade of Vietnam in the first transaction on a secondary market in securities in mid-1995. The latter had acquired 60 billion dong worth of six-month T-bills and then sold a 20 billion tranche to Citibank at an interest rate of 17.5 per cent per year.

Most foreign banks prefer inconspicuous premises — a couple of small rooms where businessmen can meet in private and discuss their financial needs. According to one diplomatic source, this is because 'the banks want to avoid the impression that they are going to come in and overwhelm the domestic banking sector given the latter's lack of experience in operating full banking services. The image is one of being supportive and operating in a specific niche.' But there is one foreign bank that does have a flourishing 'retail' business in Hanoi — the Australia and New Zealand Banking Group (ANZ). Its branch in the city centre has all the trappings of an ordinary high street bank in the West where the average man or woman in the street is made to feel welcome — even if there has not yet been such a public response.

In addition to the various branches and representative offices, there are four 'joint venture banks', which are a curious hybrid of foreign capital and local expertise that actually pre-dates the arrival of most foreign banks in Vietnam. These are: Indovina Bank (Industrial and Commercial Bank of Vietnam and Bank Dagang National, Indonesia (1990), VID Public Bank (Bank for Investment and Development of Vietnam and Public Bank Berhad, Malaysia, 1991), Firstvina Bank (Bank for Foreign Trade of Vietnam and Korea First Bank, 1993), and Vinasiam Bank (Vietnam Bank for Agriculture and Siam Commercial Bank and Charoen Pokphand Group of Thailand, May 1995). The first three were among the top five foreign banks as rated by the State Bank of Vietnam, along with Bangkok Bank and BNP of France.

There are unlikely to be any more such joint ventures. Foreign Banks now will either wait for upgrading from representative licences or sign up as shareholders in one of the 46 joint-stock banks in the country. Opportunities for this option are growing as the State Bank of Vietnam encourages the joint stock banks to increase their share capital as a means of strengthening their financial base.

Niche markets for the four joint ventures are obviously businessmen from the foreign partners' home countries. A South Korean banker says the reason for the approach is that 'we can have better access to information about our local customers, and current credit assessment can be done with assistance from our local partners'.

For Indovina, Noel Bintac, head of the international banking department, said his bank has focused on import-export financing at an average of $500,000 loans for each project. 'Basically, we have medium-sized customers, and not only Indonesian joint ventures with Vietnamese, state-owned enterprises are also our clients.' It has offices in Hanoi and Haiphong and plans to expand. VID Public Bank has branches in Ho Chi Minh City and Da Nang offering a range of banking services like trade financing, foreign exchange services, credit facilities, bank guarantees and remittances.

But there may only be a limited number of customers. Many foreign joint ventures tend to use their own country's banks. That has been the case at First Vina where 80 per cent of its deposits are from Korean companies and individuals. But it is in this reliance on their own foreign nationals and the Vietnamese private sector that the joint venture banks are limited, says one European banker. 'The JVs may not have access to the major clients like the state banks will have,' he says. This potentially could lock them into the high risk private sector supplemented by some joint venture clients while the state bank serves state companies and foreign branches serve foreign corporate clients.'

Access to corporate clients is likely to become more competitive due to the issuance of branch licences for Hanoi to Bank of America and Citibank. Banking industry sources say it is only a matter of time before other major international banks follow suit, bringing with them their lists of corporate, blue chip clients.

The question was raised at the beginning of this section as to whether the foreign banking sector was becoming overcrowded, given the limited opportunities to make profit it present. Certainly, many foreign bankers think so, pointing to Vietnam's poor profit-to-risk ratio. 'High risk naturally means high reward, but here in Vietnam, though we have high risk given the shaky legal system and low-level infrastructure, the reward is small due to the severe competition,' said one foreign banker who requested anonymity.

The government is not too sympathetic. Dang Thanh Binh, director of the state Bank's Financial Institution Department, observed that 'they are complaining because they don't want to see any more competition. But it depends on your perspective. Vietnam is registering high growth rates, foreign trade is growing at high speed, so it seems simple for the foreign banks to find more opportunities to expand their business. So you can't say the market is too small.' In addition, said Mr Binh, foreign banks enjoyed big advantages over their local rivals, including a profit tax of 25 per cent, compared to the domestic banks' level of 45 per cent, given them immense opportunities to expand if they were prepared to take some risks.[7]

GETTING A BANK LOAN

From the general let us now turn to the specifics of what the foreign businessman can expect from the banking sector in Vietnam. According to the prevailing regulations in Vietnam, an enterprise with foreign capital which invests in Vietnam according to the Law on Foreign Investment is entitled to borrow money from credit institutions in foreign countries as well as institutions in Vietnam, including foreign bank branches and joint venture banks. These activities are regulated by the State Bank and the Ministry of Finance. As will be seen, there remain substantial areas of doubt as to the circumstances in which, and the terms under which loans — particularly medium and long-term loans — can be obtained in Vietnam.

The borrowing of capital from abroad by enterprises may take two forms: (1) direct borrowing with the enterprise borrowing directly from and repaying institutions in foreign countries, and (2) reborrowing, with the enterprise borrowing from a wholly Vietnamese-owned bank (either a commercial bank or one of the banks for investment and development) which bank usually has obtained the foreign capital from foreign loans taken out, or foreign currency reserves held, by the Government or State Bank. Re-borrowing of capital by the enterprise from the foreign loan funds of the Government or State Bank can be effected only through those banks approved for that purpose by the State Bank.

1 **Direct Borrowing.** The borrowing of capital directly by enterprises from lenders in foreign countries must meet a number of conditions imposed by the Vietnamese authorities depending on the purpose of the loan. Significant among these is the requirement that the loan amount comply with the overall level of foreign loans already

approved by the Prime Minister in the annual and five-year plans. Furthermore, the terms of the foreign loans must be approved by the State Bank and, in certain circumstances, the Ministry of Finance.

2 **Re-borrowing.** The re-borrowing of capital by enterprises through the commercial banks or the banks for investment and development must meet the following conditions:

(i) The investment project must be in the fields of production, trading, or the provision of services;

(ii) It must be capable of repaying the full debt when due;

(iii) the financial situation of the enterprise must be healthy and the enterprise must not owe taxes or duties, or have any overdue debt; and,

(iv) the enterprise must use the borrowed money according to the aims and plans submitted by the borrower as approved by the lending bank. The borrowing and repayment must be in the same currency.

Subject to State Bank approval, the enterprise can open an offshore loan account if requested by the lender (as is often the case) in order to borrow from abroad, so long as the value of the loan contract is at least $3 million. Any offshore income stream can be directed to this loan account in order to pay principal, interest and any associated costs of the loan and will be closed after the enterprise repays the debt in full. Each quarter, the enterprise is required to submit a report of its borrowing and repayment to the State Bank. Of course, as a matter of practice, this option is open only where the enterprise seeking the loan will earn foreign currency.

Domestic Loans: The enterprise can borrow money in Vietnamese and foreign currencies at any credit institution in Vietnam (wholly Vietnamese-owned banks, credit organizations and credit cooperatives and joint venture banks and foreign bank branches) in order to finance industrial transactions. However, it should be noted that not withstanding the general scope of the bulk of the provisions regarding banking operations in Vietnam, these provisions have been applied differently depending on whether the bank, or borrower, is Vietnamese or foreign-owned (e.g. the time period over which the loan may be permitted to be repaid can vary depending on the parties).

Domestic loans can be obtained in either the form of short or medium/long-term credit. **Short Term Credit** is generally intended to provide working capital and may be arranged subject to the following conditions:

(i)   The enterprise must be a Vietnamese legal person, which would include joint ventures and wholly-owned foreign enterprises formed the Foreign Investment Law and operating in accordance with Vietnamese law;

(ii) the enterprise must have no overdue debt;

(iii) The legal capital (long term and current assets) of the enterprise must be sufficient, in the lender's judgement, to cover any eventual liability;

(iv) The enterprise must carry the account activities in accordance with the Ordinance on Accounting and Statistics;

(v)   The enterprise must mortgage its property, which might include real estate property, to the lender, or the loan must be guaranteed by a competent entity, including foreign bank branches.

Short-term borrowings may be for a particular transaction or for an ongoing production need. The enterprise is entitled to borrow from any credit organization in Vietnam. However, the State Bank requires that when borrowing capital from a lender for the first time, the enterprise must disclose all its debts owed to other credit organizations, the terms of such loans, and commit to repay them when due. The bank must base its decision on the amount to lend by reference to the amounts involved in the underlying contractual documents of the enterprise. The repayment term for short-term credit may not exceed 12 months.

If the enterprise violates the State Bank's regulations established by the relevant credit organization, the latter can terminate the extension of the credit temporarily, transfer the debt to an overdue debt account (incurring default interest of 150 per cent of the applicable rate), foreclose on the mortgaged property and liquidate it at an auction in order to collect the debt, or bring the matter to the Economic Court for adjudication.

Medium or long-term credit. In practice, most domestic loans are short term, as lending organizations are often reluctant to provide medium or long-term credit because of the lack of clear regulations ensuring repayment. Moreover, the absence of any effective means of enforcing such loans, as well as the unrealistic ceilings on interest rates for medium and long-term credit — in view of the credit risks involved and possible adverse inflationary impact on borrowers generating significant amounts of the revenues in dong — have discouraged banks from providing such finance.

It is generally the case that foreign bank branches establish their own conditions for the provision of such finance (which the Vietnamese authorities have permitted to date) which will almost inevitably require the provision of security offshore, usually in the form of a parent company guarantee or a pledge of offshore assets.

Mortgages. The loans by any bank in Vietnam, whether a domestic bank, foreign bank branch or joint venture bank, to an enterprise generally will be characterized as an 'economic contract' under the Ordinance on Economic Contracts in Vietnam, which allows security for such a loan to be given by way of mortgage or a pledge over the borrower's assets. The possibility of granting or obtaining a mortgage over land has, however, been complicated by a fairly bewildering series of enactments in 1995 which have all but removed the possibility from the statute books. It is clear that this matter will be the subject of further legislation some time in the near future.

Under a decree issued in January 1995, land-use rights could be mortgaged by enterprises, although the circumstances under which such right could be so secured was not clear. Land in Vietnam is deemed to be owned by the people and administered by the State, and individuals and entities can own only land-use rights akin to long-term leaseholds. The Land Decree provided that Vietnamese banks and credit institutions may obtain a mortgage over land-use rights, but did not provide any guidance to the rights of their foreign counterparts. More detailed implementing guidelines regarding the Land Decree were expected, but what followed was a decree which in fact emasculated the system under which mortgages could be secured. However, it was considered likely that certain rights would be restored.

The Land Decree, while allowing a mortgage over land-use rights, has clouded the issue where the land-use rights were contributed by a local partner to a joint venture (which is nearly always the form of contribution). Some consider that the local partner remains the holder of the rights, and under the terms of the Ordinance, it is the only holder which can mortgage the relevant land-use rights (notwithstanding the fact that in a joint venture such rights should be the assets of the joint venture). The foreign joint venture partner might therefore find itself having little or no control over the mortgaging of such rights by the local partner (which might, for example, mortgage the land use rights for purposes independent of their joint venture). This needs further clarification by the authorities.

The Land Decree provides as follows with regard to mortgages:

1 The underlying loan must be concluded between the lender and the mortgagor/borrower;
2 If the mortgagor cannot repay the debt when due, the bank/mortgagee has the right to ask the Economic Court to foreclose on and sell the mortgaged property in order to recover the debt; or the bank can simply benefit from its pro rata right to ownership in the property and transfer its interest, presumably subject to the approval of the foreign investment regulatory body, and the other joint venture partners, in order to collect its debt.
3 The mortgage contract has to be in writing and signed by both parties. The mortgagor must register the mortgage of land use rights at the Land Department and attend to the release and discharge once the loan is repaid.[8]

PROSPECTS FOR A STOCK EXCHANGE

It is generally agreed that in order to raise the substantial amounts of money Vietnam needs for its industrial development, one key element will be the establishment of a stock market. When this might occur remains a subject of considerable debate. According to government officials, many of the pre-conditions have now been satisfied in the shape of the establishment of a public bank deposit system, a foreign exchange market and the issuance of treasury bonds. State Bank Vice Governor Chu Van Nguyen, told a monthly magazine:[9] "The way the Vietnamese economy is going we will need a stock market soon. However, [the country] does not have any experience with this rather specific industry so we need time. We are looking for ways in which to build a stock market, operating it safely and efficiently from the beginning.'

A committee was established in mid-1995 to draft the necessary legal documents and government decrees on issues related to the establishment. But among the biggest obstacles quickly identified were the lack of potential securities to be traded. Privatization and incorporation of state enterprises is proceeding slowly, while most local foreign-invested joint venture companies remain small and do not issue shares. Hence, the exchange was always likely to start on a very small scale, trading in bonds issued by the central government, provincial authorities, commercial banks and state-run companies, with trading in shares of privatized state companies, to follow much later.

According to a government analysis, in order to raise money for industrialization while avoiding speculation in shares, the model to be followed will be a state-managed, tightly-controlled market. A report said small bourses would be formed in Hanoi and Ho Chi Minh City opening only two days a week. Licences to deal in stocks would be granted to Vietnamese only, although foreign individuals and companies would be allowed to buy into domestic securities companies as minority shareholders in joint ventures. As for investors, 'Vietnam should allow and encourage foreign investors to buy bonds and shares issued by the Vietnamese Government and companies.' To ensure that companies remain under close control, investment funds would be allowed to take only passive stakes in listed companies, the report said.

'Once there is enough management experience, the state can apply many measures to expand Vietnam's stock exchange into the orbit of the international financial markets,' the report said. After studying stock markets in China, Thailand, India and South Korea, Vietnam chose South Korea as its model because it developed its stock market slowly with a long period of state management. The case of China, where stock markets were started quickly and where in their early stages were plagued by rioting share buyers, is cited as an example to avoid.

Nguyen Dinh Hung, Vice Minister of Finance,[10] argued that given Vietnam's lack of capital and experience in business management, foreign security companies certainly should be allowed to take part in the future stock exchange. The questions to be answered are how and when. 'Other countries generally limit the number of shares held by foreign security companies operating in their stock exchanges. This gives their domestic companies a helping hand and also keeps strict controls on foreign security companies in the market.

'In the proposal "Capital Market Development and the Establishment of a Stock Exchange in Vietnam" submitted to the government, the committee responsible for setting up a stock exchange has suggested that foreign security companies should be allowed to set up their representative offices in Vietnam and establish joint venture security companies. Vietnam needs to have a policy of mobilizing money through investment in stock. But we should limit the share of foreign securities companies.

'The rate should meet two demands: to encourage foreign investment in stock and ensure the safe operation of the stock exchange. There is one question, however, that may be raised by foreign stock investors: what industry will they be allowed to invest in? Personally, I think the industries they are currently flowing their investments into should also be open for their stock investment in the future. But Vietnam should be careful to avoid risk. The financial crisis in Mexico shows what can happen when there are no effective measures to control the foreign capital source. Foreign investors simultaneously sold their shares, converting their money into hard currency, causing a devaluation of the peso and so pushing the country into an economic and political crisis.'

To avoid a repeat in Vietnam, the official said, the government would have to:

- Maintain political and economic stability (such as controlling inflation) so foreign investors can make long-term investment;
- carefully choose the foreign capital source; and
- control issue the rate of shares foreign investors are allowed to hold which will limit the consequences of sudden simultaneous withdrawal of cash.

The key issue in the formation of any stock exchange, of course, is whether it has anything to buy and sell. Foreign analysts have pointed to the slow progress of the 'equitization' policy in the state sector — with only five companies having gone public by early 1996 — as an indication that conditions simply are not yet right for a stock market to have any meaningful role. This problem may be in the process of being solved, however.

By the end of the year, the Ministry of Finance said it wanted to see at least 100 state-owned enterprises issuing shares. Each of the country's 53 provinces was asked to put forward between one and four candidates for consideration. In many cases, the government would seek to retain a minority share, somewhere between 20 and 30 per cent. At the same time, the ministry was engaged in drawing up a list of companies which 'played a decisive role in the country's cultural and material life' which would remain entirely in state hands. The best estimate was that about one-fifth of the companies would fall into this category.

In May 1996, a government decree was issued offering tax reductions of 50 per cent for two years for any company that sold its shares to their workers and the public. The decree also said that the shares could be sold through commercial banks pending the establishment of a stock market. This could also prove to be an attractive route for small and medium-sized private companies to raise capital as the government said that any that accepted 'equitization' would be able to gain access to bank loans on the same basis and terms as state-run companies. Heads of provincial and city governments will be able to approve the sale of shares in companies with capital of less than three billion Dong ($272,000). Larger companies will have to obtain central government approval.

The trouble in achieving equitization, a senior ministry official[11] admitted, was that 'leaders of state-owned enterprises and of local authorities don't have much understanding of the benefits. Directors have an easier job working for the government than when they have the burden of responsibility for their activities in a stock company.' At the same time, managers of some of the better state-run firms have seen the opportunity offered by equitization to two and offload only the unprofitable parts of their business, according to reports in the official media.

Another question raised by the government plan is: who is going to manage these newly-equitized firms? Why should an inefficient manager of a state-run enterprise suddenly become a highly efficient manager of a stock company? Vietnam does not, as yet, seem to have the necessary management skills. Entrepreneurs exist, of course, and there are quite a few in the private sector. But if private companies cannot issue shares the stock market is going to be formed on a rather narrow base. And there is also the question of putting in place the necessary accounting procedures so that potential shareholders can see what they are getting — especially with most Vietnamese unfamiliar with the whole concept of share trading. According to the Finance Ministry, only about five per cent of firms in the country are properly audited. Most see it as an expensive and unnecessary procedure.[12]

Given all these difficulties, then, it came as no surprise when the Finance Ministry abruptly announced in mid-1996 that the stock market plan was being put on hold once again for an indefinite period.[13] There were some within the local and international finance communities who thought this was a mistake. Better, they argued, to get something going which would provide an incentive for more rapid equitization. State Bank official Nguyen Toan Thang supports this argument: 'The sooner we can get it going the better, because only then will be have a weapon to motivate enterprises to increase efficiency.'

But John Pike, chief investment officer for Vietnamese fund managers Finansa Thai has a blunt rejoinder: 'When they kept talking about target dates such as 1995 or 1996, it was quite clear to us that this was all "pie in the sky". I would always reply: "Introduce me to the first Vietnamese stock broker." These people have got to be found, trained and the system put in place first. Even getting a market off the ground by 1999 won't be easy. But if they are serious it can be done.'

And Dennis McCornac is one who feels the government is right to be cautious: 'It is much better to be a little late in starting a market and make sure everything is properly in place than to start one too early. My big fear is that if a stock market is started before all the necessary rules, regulations and institutions are properly put into place it will turn into a legalized form of gambling. While some may win in the short term there is a good chance that most will lose. Once this happens people will lose confidence in the stock market and there will be no place to raise that capital that is so vital to development.'[14]

UPGRADING ACCOUNTANCY PRACTICE

In preparation for the stock market, Vietnam undoubtedly needs to upgrade its accountancy practice to international standards. It is estimated that Vietnam needs several thousand more certified public accountants to meet demand for accounting and auditing business. By mid-1995, however, the country only had 60 CPAs in five local firms, along with six foreign companies.

The Law on Foreign Investment includes a requirement for all enterprises with foreign invested capital to be subjected to an annual external audit. As independent audits had not been required since 1975, a number of auditing companies required to be established and when the law was introduced to provide such a service.

The first auditing company to be established following the introduction of *Doi Moi* was the Vietnam Auditing Company (VACO), under the auspices of the Ministry Finance, followed shortly after the Accounting Services Company, later licensed to provide auditing services when it changed its name to the Auditing and Accounting Services Company (AASC).

Whilst these entities were created to satisfy the needs of the growing base of companies with foreign invested capital, their level of experience of dealing with international organizations was limited. Of equal concern at that time was their limited experience and understanding of auditing techniques. For this reason, assistance was provided by certain international accounting firms in the form of training courses for local auditing companies and representatives of government bodies.

In the early training courses held by Price Waterhouse in 1992, a considerable amount of time was devoted to explaining the fundamental accounting and auditing principles accepted internationally. In view of the absence of any prior auditing experience, the external audit was viewed initially by many Vietnamese as requiring a verification of substantially all of the transactions of a company. As a consequence, the concept of random and judgmental testing to ensure only that the financial statements present a 'true and fair' view was a key area of initial training.

As the first local auditing companies were established under the auspices of the Ministry of Finance, audits by such bodies generally involved an increased attention on the company's compliance with prevailing tax laws rather than a wider review of all aspects of the company's accounts.

By early 1994, with an increased understanding of the role of accounting firms in Vietnam, the accounting profession was expanded to include three domestic accounting firms and three international ones with full licence to provide these services. These were followed by two other international accounting firms establishing joint ventures with local entities. Many other developing countries have sought to protect the local accounting profession by requiring foreign accounting firms to establish joint ventures. Vietnam has, however, adopted a more liberal and progressive approach by permitting international accounting firms to establish wholly foreign-owned enterprises as well as joint ventures.

Having been subject to an external audit as required by law, a foreign investor might believe that the examination of the company's financial records will be complete. However, further inspections of the accounts are permitted to be made by the local tax authorities, the General Department of Taxes and State Committee for Cooperation and Investments. These latter inspections appear not to have been anticipated by many foreign investors and has resulted in a number of problems and unforeseen costs.

All companies with foreign invested capital are required to submit their audited financial statements to the local Department of Taxes and to the Ministry of Planning and Investment on an annual basis. The Department of Taxes will not place direct reliance on the fact that the financial statements have been audited and will inspect most of the companies on a regular basis. Whilst tax audits are also a feature of the regulatory environment in many other countries, the degree of reliance by the Department of Taxes on the external audit is lower in Vietnam, and therefore the frequency and the depth of tax audits here is generally greater. These inspections will focus on many aspects of the company's compliance with tax laws, following which a notice of assessment will be issued for additional or reduced taxes based on the findings.

The General Department of Taxes in Hanoi is also permitted to inspect companies with foreign invested capital. This visit is likely to occur at a later date than the original inspection and the findings might differ from those of the local Department of Taxes. It should also be noted that there is no statute of limitations in respect of tax audits and in theory, any tax years in the life of the joint venture can be reassessed at any time.

There are a number of issues which have frequently been identified during audits by the tax department. In particular, many companies have been assessed for additional withholding taxes in respect of payments to foreign contractors, errors in the calculation of personal income taxes, additional turnover taxes and expenses not allowed as deductions for profits tax purposes. These assessments are likely to result in additional tax payments which cannot be recovered at that time from other parties representing a real cost of the business.

When a company disputes the finding of the inspection, appeals can be made to the General Department of Taxes in Hanoi and thereafter to the Ministry of Finance. In view of the complexity of the tax laws, the potential ambiguity regarding their application and unclear procedures for tax administration, investors are naturally advised to seek professional advice regarding tax matters at an early stage.[15]

INSURANCE

Before leaving the issue of financial services, a brief word about insurance. The sector has certainly developed rapidly since 1995 with the establishment of several local companies breaking the monopoly of Bao Viet, and the introduction of several international insurance companies cooperating with it. But insurance remains the last financial service that is not open to 100 per cent foreign-owned companies.

Speaking at an industry seminar, Pham Chi Lan, General Secretary of the Vietnam Chamber of Commerce and Industry, said that although four new local insurance companies had been formed, Bao Viet still held a 84 per cent market share. Foreign insurers are, in theory, allowed to set up joint ventures, but the lack of choice of a strong local partner limit their activities. 'So many foreign insurers want to set up joint ventures, but Bao Viet cannot join with all of them,' she said.

Vietnamese experts believe the country should have at least 10 qualified local insurers in order to integrate into the global insurance market. But, in fact, Bao Viet reinsures up to 94 per cent of its policies with foreign companies due to its inability to underwrite many of the risks it insures.[16] So, in practice, many international companies already have a toehold in the market.

The fastest growing sectors are automobile, fire, engineering, and oil and gas insurance. Large foreign investment in construction also offers good opportunities.

At the time of writing, the government had granted only one insurance operating licence – to Inchinbrok – a $250,000 joint venture between Bao Viet and Inchcape Insurance Holdings of Hong Kong. Bao Viet was also waiting for approval from the Ministry of Planning and Investment for a $6 million joint venture with Britain's Commercial Union Assurance Co. and Japan's Tokyo Marine and Fire Insurance Co.

NOTES

1. At an estimated 17 per cent of gdp, this is only half the rate in China, for example.
2. Vietcombank planned to open the first 'do-it-yourself' branch in Hanoi in 1997, in which customers would handle most of their transactions through ATMs, including foreign exchange. The main motivation was to try and move the Vietnamese public away from cash and into a more card-orientated money society, an official spokesman said. [*Vietnam Investment Review* 22–28 January 1996].
3. See notes to Chapter 2 for details of his career.
4. *Financial Times*, 13 November 1995.
5. Deputy Director, Economics Research Department, interviewed 3 May 1996.
6. Reuters news agency 19 January 1995.
7. *Vietnam Investment Review*, 1–7 April 1996.
8. This section is based on an analysis of the loans regulations contributed by lawyers Michael A.Polkighorne and David L.Weller to *Vietnam Business Journal*, August 1995.
9. *Vietnam Economic Times*, October 1995.
10. Interview, 2 May 1996.
11. Nguyen Duy Truoc, deputy director of the General Department for Management and State Funds and Assets at Enterprises, speaking to the *Vietnam Investment Review*, 19–25 February 1996.
12. *Vietnam Investment Review*, 26 February–3 March 1996.
13. An original target date was 1993, put back to 1994, and then to 1995, and finally the end of 1996. There are some suggestions now that the market may not be up and running before 1999.
14. *Vietnam Investment Review*, 18–24 March 1996.
15. This section is based on an analysis by Ian Wilson, Senior Country Manager of Price Waterhouse in Ho Chi Minh City.
16. In 1995, Bao Viet said it settled over 400,000 claims, the biggest being an oil well blow-out which caused an estimated $60 million in damage. [*Vietnam Investment Review*, 22–28 April 1996]

9 Marketing and Distribution

GROWING CONSUMER POWER

M&M, A POPULAR type of sweet (candy) from the Mars Corporation of the United States has found its way into Vietnamese consumer tastes. The firm shipped one container of M&M in August 1994, but by the end of the year was shipping five a month. It is not the only one. Brisk sales of Black & Decker power tools, fashionable clothes and Lego toys in Hanoi and Ho Chi Minh City reveal that many urban Vietnamese have well-defined consumer tastes and some spending power to match.

'Most of our clients underestimate the number of sales they will do,' says Matt Godfrey of the advertising company Bates Vietnam. Their American client is one of a growing number of Western companies profiting from Vietnamese interest in their products and the quality and fashion-status that is associated with them. 'The major change in recent years is that the Vietnamese consumer is growing up very rapidly,' says Andy Miller, Indochina Business Development Director at Ogilvy and Mather in Bangkok.

After years of drab, Comecon-standard consumer durables, Vietnamese are looking for a change and keeping their eye open for quality. 'All the research we do to measure quality says it is American number one, European number two and Asian countries, number three, except in automobiles/transportation where Japan is number one,' says Godfrey. Mai Ba Thien, director of the Saigon Advertising Company, says: 'Japanese products are the most popular. Vietnamese are used to them since these products have been here for a long time. Their quality is known while American products have not been here long enough for people to get to know them well.'

Some Western companies offering more expensive items have established quite a presence. Black & Decker, for example, moved in at the start of the 1990s to create a network of nearly 100 dealers nationwide. According to marketing executive Bach Ngoc Giao, his office will sell on average $50,000 worth of power tools per month to dealers and individual customers. 'Month to month it's growing. In 1991, 1992 and 1993 we sold little. In 1994, we sold a lot,' he said. The majority of sales have been to state construction companies, but the number of smaller private construction companies is growing. To prime that market, the company spends $2,000 per month on advertising.

Eurovision, a trendy eyewear shop in Hanoi and Ho Chi Minh City did a brisk $100,000 in frame and lens business in 1994. One year later, turnover had doubled. American, European and Japanese cosmetics companies are locked in a furious battle for domination of the fast-rising make-up market among trendy Saigonese youth.

Denim jeans, perhaps the ultimate casual Western fashion statement of all, are now officially made in Vietnam. Though bogus versions of Levi's and Calvin Klein jeans have been sold here for years, a Singaporean joint venture is now manufacturing the goods locally. 'Jeans are the fashion of the century,' boasts Nguyen Phuong Thao, an owner of the first Jackball! jeans store in Hanoi. Once priced out of reach for Vietnamese, 3,000 pairs of Jackball and 'authentic' Levi's and Calvin's are sold each month at Thao's shop at a minimum of 180,000 dong per pair.

Since 1994, a number of Western clothes shops have opened in Ho Chi Minh City. Their products are not cheap. One clothes shop that imports American women's clothes sells full outfits for about $100 a piece. Yet they claim to have many customers.

That is no surprise, says Thien from Saigon Advertising. 'The first thing Vietnamese consumers will buy is clothes,' he says. Thien estimates that an average family will spend about 50 per cent of their income on food with an additional 30 per cent on other expenses. This leaves roughly 20 per cent as disposable income. Twenty per cent of how much, is the real question.

Tuoi Tre (Youth) newspaper used government statistics to estimate the average income of Saigonese for 1994 at $810 per year, 2.8 times higher than the national average. The paper also said the consumption of consumer goods rose 10 per cent over 1993. According to research data compiled by the Vietnam Living Standards survey done by the General Department of Statistics and the State Planing Committee, Ho Chi Minh City household expenditures totalled roughly $70 per year, while in Hanoi expenditures were about $50.

But it is also estimated that a further 50 per cent of family income comes in unofficial forms that are not reported, while up to 30 per cent more flows in from overseas subsidies in either money and/or consumer goods from the almost two million first-generation Vietnamese living overseas. Purchasing power is also boosted by the fact that most Vietnamese own their own houses, usually do not go on vacations, do not pay for superannuation and have hardly any tax or insurance payments to fulfil. In addition, the majority live as extended families – average households contain six persons – where income is pooled for major purchases.[1]

Go through any magazine on Vietnam, however, and you tend to find that much of the coverage is devoted to infrastructure development, with little said about the dynamics of the consumer market. Yet about 10 per cent of the population now has enough disposable income to upgrade their living standard by surrounding themselves with newly available luxuries.

NORTH/SOUTH PURCHASING DIVIDE

But companies hoping to make their mark have to keep in mind Vietnam's cultural, historical, geographical and religious differences which has different influences than those of modern western markets. When launching a new product, one has to take note of the five major population segmentations within Vietnamese society. These are geography, age, sex, religion and income. Each of these segments have shown differences in opinion on advertisements, purchase, intent, cost and place of purchase. The most notable differences have been identified to be geographical. 'They are like two completely different countries,' says market researcher Michael Potter. 'In general, North Vietnamese consumers are driven by other forces than are the South Vietnamese.'

Why these differences exist and what they actually are have equal importance in understanding how to launch a product in Vietnam. The North Vietnamese consumer, more specifically those in Hanoi, firstly do not have as much disposable income as their southern counterparts in Ho Chi Minh City. Jan Standaert, of the market research company Nielsen SRG Vietnam, says: 'Saigonese have more to spend and are apt to buy more sophisticated and expensive products.' Since Hanoians have less money to spend, it also stands to reason that they have fewer trappings of a modern life. Generally, Hanoians are purchasing cheaper, but essential consumer goods, while Saigonese are already begin to purchase 'big ticket' items such as motorcycles, cars and cellular phones.

According to the National Statistical Office, out of every 100 households in Ho Chi Minh City, 64.7 owned a television set, 19.7 had video cassette recorders, 54.3 per cent possessed motorcycles and 23.5 per cent had refrigerators. Later figures update motorcycle ownership to 73 per cent of Saigonese households, compared to the Hanoi rate of 55 per cent.

Such difference in economic purchasing power influences Vietnamese consumers greatly within and between Northern and Southern Vietnam. If a Saigonese won a lottery jackpot of $1000, he or she would most probably buy presents for their families, purchase clothing, foodstuffs and other luxury items, while Hanoians feel that the money should be spent on necessities like 'fixing the roof' and 'buying new kitchen utensils.'

Chinese influence has also created differences between the two regions. A look at the current demographics reveal that there are no significant ethnic Chinese groups in the north, but half of Ho Chi Minh City's inhabitants are reckoned to be Chinese or have Chinese ancestry. On the whole, according to market researchers, Hanoians are more talkative and philosophical, but also more elusive when answering questions. Northern Vietnamese are also somewhat more traditional and still hold the family and the longevity of old age in high respect. Thus, advertisements must not attack but embrace these values more in the North than in the South. Hanoians are also said to be a little more laid back and calmer than their somewhat frenetic Southern counterparts.

One of the most noticeable differences between Hanoians and Saigonese consumers is their perception of advertisements. For example, if a television commercial is not directly product related, the Saigonese tend to dismiss it, saying, 'What does this commercial have to do with the product?' Any unrealistic portrayal of a product will raise doubts as to the sincerity and quality of the market and thus jeopardize its marketability. In contrast, Hanoians seem to enjoy television commercials for their sheer entertainment value. This could be due to the poor variety of entertainment available in the North. So long as a commercial does not attack their family values, the commercial will be seen on the whole as suitable.

One aspect of commercials aired in the two cities is production value. Both Hanoians and Saigonese appreciate the high quality of foreign ads. The higher the production value, the more likely the viewer will be impressed by the ad, regardless of the portrayal of the product. Advertising will be discussed again in more detail later in this chapter.

Ho Chi Minh City is by far the most economically and thriving centre of Vietnam, as was discussed in Chapter 6. The presence of the French and then the Americans played a significant role in altering Southern Vietnamese desires, expectations and purchasing habits. Branding of product names into the consciousness of the Saigonese seems to have achieved much greater penetration than in Hanoi. Saigonese are aware of branding and have already made the association of brand name with high quality — such as having a Sony or Honda Dream II motorcycle. As a whole, Saigonese have more exposure to foreign products than the rest of the country.

The North has only just begun to understanding branding. For example, they identify a Sony product with top quality but are still largely unaware of other brand names. Today, branding in Vietnam is not so much a question of purchasing a product because of its name or manufacturer but rather where the products come from, as already noted.

Hanoians still predominantly shop in markets, largely because agriculture still compromises well over 40 per cent of Hanoi's work force, while only about 14 per cent of Saigonese work on the land.

With the influx of mini-marts and bigger state-run shopping centres, southerners are getting more and more exposure to new products and choices for the moment. Finally, a poor transportation infrastructure makes it difficult for goods to flow easily between the two main urban centres, which further encourages the tendency to treat them as two completely separate markets.

NARROW TRADING CHANNELS

Egon Heldner, country manager of Dietholm Vietnam, believes businessmen hearing about,about Vietnam's 'open market' policies have in some cases taken the word 'open' too literally. Little do they know, he says, that there are certain obstacles put in place to control foreign trading firms. 'Pure trading is not allowed to foreign companies. There is considerable reluctance on the part of the Vietnamese government to allow foreign trading firms to operate in the country. This protectionist attitude is to safeguard local enterprises.'

In the past, only one state-controlled firm was allowed to import goods. This changed when the government decided to loosen the regulations to allow more state agencies into the picture. Today, thanks to this deregulation, a large number of state-owned enterprises are import agents. According to trade official Hoang Ngoc Cu,[2] there are about 1,500 companies which have been given the right to deal directly in foreign trade, mostly in the state-sector but including 120 private firms. The former are designated as Government Trading Companies (GTCs), while the latter as Foreign Trading Companies (FTCs) who have a marketing agreement with a foreign company. There are also about 1,500 foreign-invested companies who also have rights to import and export directly, although there are some restrictions depending on the type of product.[3]

But this proliferation of channels can cause confusion. Mr Heldner cites pharmaceuticals, where as many as 30 state agents have import rights. Representatives who come to Vietnam often find their products coming from three to five different countries, such as the United States and from parts of Europe and Asia, all at the same time. The consequences of such a market structure are irregular supply, quality problems, inflated and widely fluctuating prices. 'The local distribution network is there, but they are not at the level of sophistication we would like to deal with. It is a problem to organize distribution for anyone. There are a lot of different elements involved.'

The reason for this situation can be attributed to the unpredictable regulatory environment that is shrouded in bureaucracy. Many a time, goods imported into Vietnam are stuck at customs because of overnight changes in import regulations. The mass of government red tape has to be negotiated virtually ensures that the time spent in waiting for approvals and licences can be daunting and tedious. For instance, import licences are granted only for goods that appear not to compete directly with those made locally so as to protect the country's manufacturers, which can allow a literal-minded bureaucrat considerable leeway to obstruct. Another condition is that they must be deemed necessary for the well-being of the society. Therefore, 'capitalist' products such as luxury goods could be caught in the official net.

This probably explains why an estimated 70 per cent of the goods sold in Ho Chi Minh City are smuggled in from abroad, mostly foreign-made electrical and electronic products, much coveted and prized by the locals. The government is struggling to tackle the problem, but illegal trade is so strongly entrenched that it may be many years before it can be wiped out. It is perhaps somewhat ironic that a vital contribution to the North's victory in the Vietnam War — the porous border with Cambodia and Laos, which provided a key logistics channel via the 'Ho Chi Minh Trail' — is now undermining the government's efforts to stamp out unregistered trade.

Due to the complex distribution channels, it is hardly surprising that price mark-ups occur to a significant extent, creating consumer prices generally 10 or 20 per cent dearer than Thailand. Prices tend to be more expensive for goods brought in through the official channels than the more informal routes, especially as the government has to impose heavy taxes on such items as spirits and cigarettes to try and offset the revenue losses from smuggling.

RUDIMENTARY RETAILING

Most Vietnamese dollar millionaires probably will not be listed in *Who's Who In Asia*. But if you are looking for one, you might want to visit Binh Tay market in the Cholon district of Ho Chi Minh City. Look for small, four-by-12-metre stalls that have piles of consumer goods cluttering the entrance. The successful shops will probably offer goods ranging from American make-up to Australian pharmaceuticals to Japanese televisions. If a steady stream of buyers from the provinces arrive in trucks, buses or cyclos to cut a deal with the shop owner, you have probably found your millionaire.

For electrical and electronic goods in particular, however, everyone heads for An Duong Vuong and Hung Vuong in the city. In 1989, research indicates that there were about 40 such establishments around An Duong Vuong. By 1995, there were over 200.

For foreign manufacturers who want to sell their products in Vietnam, traders say 90 per cent of the distribution and retail goes through private hands. As noted already, as the law now stands, foreign trading and distribution companies cannot distribute in Vietnam so it is almost entirely up to the private sector to get your goods into the market. For the foreign trader, this means standing in line to negotiate a price deal with a Chinatown wholesale trader – just like the other buyers and sellers.

'They [private companies] are faster and have more customers. We can bring down the logistics' costs which are frightening, especially with consumer goods, because your margin is only about 10 per cent,' says Nguyen Trung Truc, Managing Director of Peregrine Capital Vietnam Ltd. He distributes his clients' products 100 per cent via the private sector, including big names such as Johnson & Johnson, Ciba-Geigy, and Hewlett Packard.

Costs can add up when there is limited freedom to import and distribute. For most goods, even though the state companies have a monopoly on importing they actually lack the facilities and incentive to set up distribution networks to push foreign products onto the market. Traders say private companies will import goods through a licensed state importer and pay the latter a flat fee of one to three per cent of the invoice value. In fact, because this is such easy money the state companies have much more incentive to work with private wholesalers and distributors rather than compete with them. Private wholesalers will then distribute the goods through their own retail networks to get the goods to the end user. Only 10 per cent will eventually go through state wholesale and distribution companies to cooperatives and state stores. Foreign and local traders say the same channels are used for high-price items such as computers and automobiles as for cheaper goods such as consumer products.

In some cases, the private sector company may be an offshoot or a subsidiary of the state importing company. With connections to state importers, some private companies will be able to bring in higher volumes than others. 'I would say there are very few fully 100 per cent private companies here,' says D.J. Jones, Chief Representative for Connell Brothers, a US trading company that distributes Kraft products.

The major hurdle for foreign trading companies and representative offices based in Vietnam is to deal effectively with private wholesalers. According to Vietnamese law, foreign trading companies are only allowed to consult on distribution; they cannot legally take an active part in a private company's operations in order to develop sales and marketing strategies. The level of activity and cooperation allowed is not at all clear, says Jones. For example, Vietnamese employees of a foreign trading company may have legal problems if they try to work directly with private distributors on behalf of their foreign employer.[4]

Aside from the legal issues involved, most private wholesalers are very secretive about their distribution network. 'We're still reliant on those wholesalers and we'll never be involved in the network they set up,' says Jones. Industry sources say most of the best wholesalers and distributors have come out of the smuggling rings and that is the reason they are able to move products much more efficiently than the state. It is also the reason they can be difficult to contact and deal with. 'You have to give them some kind of freedom to work within the price margins. In our strategy, we try to be the sole exclusive distributor,' says Mr Truc of Peregrine.

For the foreign manufacturer, therefore, the lesson to be learned seems to be: find the most efficient wholesaler you can, and continually supply him or her with the hot foreign products in demand. Vietnamese wholesalers and distributors are pure capitalists, after all.

But if most Vietnamese are indeed 'brand and image' conscious, for many retailers, there is no such thing as brand loyalty. Shops selling electronic goods in particular are normally very reluctant to be locked into selling goods from just one manufacturer. Essentially they are free agents who are interested primarily in the final price on offer above all else. If the importer is able to source the same product cheaper, sometimes through an illegal channel, then chances are it will use that channel.

This mentality has caused some problems for sole agents. In order to win retailers over, incentives have to be offered. These might include bearing the cost of redecorating the showrooms and providing credit facilities to the shop owners. But it is too soon to say whether this will sway retailers to give up some of their freedom in what is an extremely price sensitive market.

Summing up, one source says: 'There is no such thing as a national distribution network as is seen in other countries. Instead, it is a network of wholesalers and sub-wholesalers that move the goods from producer or importer to consumer. Essentially, they are passive rather than active. If there is an established demand for a product then they will fill this demand. But at present they are doing very little to develop the market. For established brands, this is less of an issue, as demand will pull the product through the system. But for new brands that need effective distribution as part of their entry strategy, this remains a crucial concern.'[5] The channels are further confused by the fact that it is often not clear who is a wholesaler and who a retailer. Many of the major consumer goods wholesalers, who shift several hundred cases of soft drink a day, for example, are often just as happy selling a single can. Many of these wholesale/retail firms, on investigation, turn out to be family concerns operating out of a home. With overheads minimal, large profit margins are not a major concern. A profit of $100 a month would probably justify a family setting up a distribution channel, creating further proliferation.

The distribution infrastructure if plainly under-capitalized, and in terms of warehousing and distribution, it is extremely basic if almost non-existent. Goods tend to be piled up in the living room, and then delivered on the back of a motorbike.

But the good news is that a new generation of Vietnamese are beginning to graduate from western universities with marketing degrees which should gradually produce a shift away from passive wholesaling into more proactive distribution. Alternatively, for those who do not want to wait there are some possibilities now for setting up one's own distribution channel. But for the moment that is probably an option only open to a few household names like Pepsi and Coca Cola in the beverage field.

At the moment, the retail scene is rudimentary. The industry consists of small, state-run shop outlets and family businesses which sell local products such as lacquerware, handicraft, silk, furniture and antiques that appeal to foreigners. There are also black markets that offer electrical and electronic goods. Finally, the ubiquitous wet and dry markets cater to the daily needs of the locals. Currently, supermarkets and shopping centres are rarely even in the main cities.

As already mentioned, the journey from the warehouse to the

consumer is a complex maze. Electronic goods in particular tend to go through five or six different distribution layers before eventually reaching the end user. Some shops in Ho Chi Minh City also have special links with the countryside. People from rural areas may not have the same buying power as their city counterparts. So, a retailer may be inclined to allow a general instalment plan, but only to people with whom they are familiar — perhaps being from their native village, for example. If one bought a colour television on a cash basis, the shop might allow the purchase of a VCR by instalments, interest varying widely from individual to individual.

But although the retail scene is still dominated by the tiny market stall, big shopping centres are beginning to appear. For example, the Saigon Superbowl, a $10 million two-storey shopping and entertainment centre complex in Ho Chi Minh City opened at the end of 1995. The project featured Ho Chi Minh City's first bowling alley, an amusement centre, fast food outlet and a host of shops, catering mainly to the expatriate community and tourists. It aims to attract well-to-do locals with its unique entertainment facilities and quality goods.

DISTRIBUTION DIFFICULTIES

Vietnam's geography, as a long, thin country with population concentrations at either end — like the long balancing pole with baskets on each end widely used by peasants for the carrying of goods — tends to dictate a company's distribution policy. First, crack the market in Ho Chi Minh City and then perhaps Hanoi; then, perhaps, begin to look at key provincial cities such as Da Nang.

But the question then becomes how to get the goods out to the market given some of the rudimentary infrastructure in place outside the two main urban centres, as was discussed in Chapter 5. Rail offers some possibilities as the existing line does go all the way from Ho Chi Minh City through the main coastal cities to Hanoi and on to China. Some beverage companies have played with the idea of shifting their products this way, but what looks good on paper doesn't look the same when on the ground.

Apart from the rail network being in a bad state of repair, there are other difficulties. For example, at Hanoi station, goods can only be loaded and unloaded at night because of a ban on trucks in urban areas during the day. Unfortunately, by then the customs and inspection offices have closed.

In terms of both goods and passengers, road is the most widely used, not so much in terms of cost effectiveness but simply because the alternatives tend to be worse. There is actually quite a high density of roads by regional standards if one looks at the map, but most are in an advanced state of disrepair and many bridges are in an even worst state. During the rainy season, the main North-South highway can often be impassable for larger vehicles for days at a time.

The main plus is that the road haulage sector is highly competitive. But the low profit margins have also led to severe under-investment in new vehicles so that most of the transport fleet is old and inefficient. The bad state of the roads also does not help poorly-maintained vehicles to survive. Broken-down lorries blocking a narrow road with the driver lying underneath desperately trying to work out what has gone wrong is a common sight. Still, as mentioned in Chapter 5, something is at least being done about the roads.

Vietnam is a country with a very extensive river network, particularly in the two delta areas of the Red River in the north and Mekong River in the south. The two areas account for 38 per cent of the total population so that as the economy grows river transport could be an attractive proposition. Many local wholesalers are already beginning to use this route for some goods.

In theory at least, the country's long coastline also offers strong possibilities of moving goods by sea along the coast. Certainly, with the port upgrading programmes discussed in Chapter 5, there should be no problem in physically moving the goods around. But there are problems, mainly legal. One key area is that under present regulations, goods shipped out of Ho Chi Minh City's port are deemed for export and taxed accordingly. Then, all cargo brought into Haiphong, the main port for Hanoi and the Red River delta, are treated as imports and also taxed accordingly. One brewery that investigated the sea route concluded that a can of beer sent by sea from south to north would more than double in price at the end of the 2,000 kilometre journey.

But if this administrative issue can be solved, sea transportation certainly looks a cost effective solution for the future.

CULTURAL ISSUES

You could call them Vuppies on a Honda. They are young, urban and certainly eager to be taken seriously in the world. The new generation of Vietnamese is determined to develop the country their parents fought for, and they may well match their mothers and fathers in perseverance. For these baby-boomers, born in a united country, the war is a rarely discussed phenomenon of the past. The pragmatic and materialistic new generation tends to be devoted to the dollar rather than driven by idealistic ideas. With more money to spend each year, they form raw and ready material for capitalist consumer giants.

Marketers trying to win over Vietnam's young consumers are facilitated by a homogenous age structure. With 55 per cent of the population under 25 years old — and an under 45 population of 85 per cent — advertisers are automatically addressing young people. One problem, however, is the fragmentation of the youth segment because sub-cultures have not yet formed in this market-in-the-making.

'There is no Vietnamese Michael Jackson yet,' says Paul Cushman, account service director of McCann-Erickson Vietnam. 'The country is not united by mega-star role models or certain fashion trends. Most role models are historical personalities, such as the Vietnamese king Nguyen Hue, the communist general [Vo Nguyen] Giap and also contemporary figures like Prime Minister Vo Van Kiet.' Images of political or military leaders, however, are off limits to advertisers.

An explanation of this heroism can be found in the country's martial past, but the post-war generation bears no grudges and welcomes foreigners, who are seen as bringing in capital, technology and a hint of the West. In 1994 alone, more than one million foreign visitors — the so-called 'walking dollars' — visited Vietnam, affecting life-styles all over the country, but especially in the cities. Viet Kieu, overseas Vietnamese, who are now returning with investment dollars and also introducing new ideas as well as a fair amount of envy.

'Increased exposure to Western media influences their thought process, even if they don't have purchasing power yet,' says Neville Barker, country manager of Australian firm Optel Media. 'The Vietnamese have a competitive streak anyway, and television offers them ideas of what they could achieve; it triggers their aspirations.' New ideas are affecting Vietnam's urban life more than the traditional rural population, and tend to gain a foothold in the south faster than in the rest of the country. It is Ho Chi Minh City that sets the trends for the rest of the country. Though, as Cushman predicts, the two parts will become more alike as the country develops.

The increasing power of television was demonstrated in 1995 when 'Maria madness' swept the country for a while. The lady in question was the young Latina heroine of a highly popular Mexican soap opera 'Simply Maria' which became the cultural event of the season and gave its star temporary icon status. In Hanoi, beauty salons specializing in the 'Maria look' seemed to be on every street. Maria restaurants tried in vain to reproduce the show's sultry aura. Maria hair. Maria clothing. Maria madness. Then one day, Maria vanished as urban youth grew tired and looked around for some new sensation.

Undoubtedly, Vietnam is undergoing a Western cultural blitz that turns many heads at least temporarily. But there are those who still feel that Western culture appeals only superficially, as it is dimmed by a strong pride the Vietnamese youth take in their country. 'It is an attraction rather than an influence, mainly in fashion and lifestyle,' emphasizes Cushman. 'Foreign advertisers have to avoid an approach that is unpatriotic or against the culture of Vietnam.' Traditional clothes such as the *ao dai* dress is considered fashionable and on the rise again. The conical leaf hats are enjoying a similar renewed appreciation, being considered as a sign of virtue, though the rural connotations of the peasant hat make it unsuitable for trendy city teens.

Hau Ngoc a self-described 'importer and exporter of culture,' who is chairman of the Advisory Council of Vietnamese Studies, has strong views on issue of cultural influence. He tackles it with a dignity and a perseverance that is astonishing, having written 50 books on Vietnam and the cultures waiting on the doorstep. 'The first Indochinese war against the French, and the second against the Americans, saved our national identity,' he asserts. 'Now, we find ourselves waging the third war of resistance. It is not a military but a cultural war even harder than the previous two. But if we lose this third war, the gains we have made from the first two will be of no use, because we would have lost our cultural and national identity. That is our soul.'

He is uncomfortable with this Western–style consumerism. 'It's difficult, because there's a conflict between economy and ethics, between cultural and morals. What we particularly fear is the introduction of a materialistic concept of life. This is the danger, and it's a trend. The Western modus operandi is a consumer society. Materialism is their way of life. Moral and spiritual values are degrading. It's out deepest concern.'

Others believe that recent modernization is the first sign that Vietnam is losing its cultural bearings. 'Vietnamese today are making huge sacrifices [in order to buy into] modern technology and trends,' says an economic researcher who did not want to be identified. 'People will eat poor food for six months straight to save extra money for a cordless phone or a pager. They think that anything from the West is better. These goods, like Honda Dreams and Ray Bans, have status. This younger generation has never had strict socialism. And there's information coming in fresh from abroad. People are losing respect for elders. Information is decadent. Socialism is breaking down.'

But is this image a rather superficial one? Even modern-thinking teens have traditional ideas when it comes to family ties and caring for the elders is still perceived to be a child's duty. An in-house youth report of McCann-Erickson states that authority derives from parents, elders and peers as well as the government and military. Money is an authoritative element that makes independent decision-making possible. With a yearly growth of eight per cent, there is more money to go round every year, much of it earned by the new generation. In Vietnam, children may well earn more money than their parents, who lack their education and opportunities, but according to Michael Potter, operations manager of Market Behaviour Vietnam, this is perceived to be family money, which they hand over to their parents. 'Financial independence generally triggers rebellion in youngsters, but Vietnamese want to maintain harmony within the family more than anything else. A generation gap is emerging, but at a very low level. Children deeply respect their parents,' he said.

Andy Miller, chief representative of Ogilvy & Mather, Vietnam takes it one step further, suggesting that parental pressure is stronger than peer pressure. 'Like anywhere in the world, Vietnamese kids don't want to be different than their peers, but parental advice guides every step a Vietnamese kid takes, even in brand choice. Not for small consumer goods but major purchases. It is a partnership, which is a normal part of life for the children,' he says. Parents tend to take pride in their offspring who, as a whole, are conforming to the role they are expected to play. 'Kids like to do their own thing, but indoors they face a lot of family control,' says Cushman. 'Living in a Communist country means that they are used to control anyway, but the youth is not tied to the past.'

At the Hanoi Economics University Student Club, there does not seem too much cause for concern. Nguyen Hong, 18, is pragmatic about the 'foreign cultural influence' which assaults his senses. 'Look, we are young. We must learn about the new stuff all over the world. I like Vietnamese culture, but we want to know about other people's culture, too.' Hong speaks excellent English, like many of his colleagues. But like them, he lives with his parents — a tradition still widely observed in Vietnam — and expects to until he gets married. Vietnam's traditions remain important to him and his friends. His friend Do Hoai Nam, 16, adds: 'Cultural influence will not be dangerous if we can still keep our national identity. We know the choice. Every country must accept things from other cultures. That's unavoidable.'

But Hong is quick to point out where their cultural allegiance lies. 'We always think about the past. We must remember what our ancestors have been through. We do not want to waste the effort of previous generations.' This exploration of a haunting Vietnamese dilemma re-inforces Huu Ngoc's faith in his young countrymen., whom he sees as torn between the West's materialistic allure and the traditions of their community-oriented ancestors.

ADVERTISING CONSTRAINTS

How are these cultural concerns reflected in the advertising world? Many local campaigns portray family values, but tend to lack focus and do not carry a clear message, while foreign advertisers merely adapt their regional campaigns for the Vietnamese market. The Dutch-Singaporean beer giant Asia Pacific Brewery would only consider a local campaign if it is clear that the regional approach would not fit in Vietnam.

Its joint venture beers, Heineken and Tiger, are not actively promoted among young consumers in Vietnam. 'Already there is a sensitivity in the market about promoting youth and alcohol,' explains marketing manager Michael van der Poel. 'As an industry leader and corporate citizen we don't want to push the boundaries.'

But the managing director of the local ad agency Vietnam Advertising, Dinh Ba Thanh, has noticed that family values are losing ground in favour of individualism among teenagers. 'Today's youth has lost direction in the sudden economic boom. Young people are more dynamic and want it big,big,big. They love earlier, play harder and display escape behaviour. Advertising can play a role in educating young people to more community and family-minded.'

The current rise in juvenile crime may be a signal of growing uncertainties among the young Vietnamese. According to the Vietnamese Investment Review, crimes committed by youngsters have been rising by 150 per cent a year since 1991. Juvenile crime may also be accelerated by impatience to succeed, as McCann's youth report points out that career and product aspirations are enormous, but generally unreachable.

In February 1996, some of the government's concerns about 'social evils and cultural poisons'[6] were channelled into a campaign against foreign products and the advertising of them. In Hanoi, for example, police dismantled billboards and painted over advertisements for Sony, Kodak and other well-known foreign goods. The owners of a Hanoi convenience store stocking British breakfast cereals and French wine strung a blanket over a 'Euro foods' sign they had previously displayed in some prominence. Other retailers were reported to have followed suit in removing or covering up signs for imported goods.

Rules passed at the end of 1995 called for the enhancement of the 'Vietnamese characteristics' of advertising. Thus, English names on billboards had to be smaller than Vietnamese lettering. The new regulations [Decree 87/CP] that the advertisements on public transport and sales promotion in the form of attachments to goods for sale are to be licensed by the local Department of Culture & Information, although approval will be valid throughout the country.

Billboards are supposed to display the full name of the company in Vietnamese even though many imported goods are sold by joint ventures with long names. In northern Vietnam, Coca Cola, for example, is bottled by the Coca Cola Ngio Hoi Soft Drinks Co. Ltd.[7] – which does not exactly roll off the tongue.

In an attempt to allay widespread concerns that brand names and logos will lose their impact if they are translated, assuming that this is possible. Minister of Culture and Information Tran Hoan said that names, labels and abbreviations which cannot be turned into comprehensible Vietnamese could still be used.[8] The minister insists the government is not engaged in an anti-foreign campaign. 'You could see an Australian film last night on television and a foreign ballet group today. But we have to fight against immoral things that may cause negative influences.'[9]

One poster stuck to the back of a lorry in Hanoi said: 'Protection against poisonous cultural items is the duty of all society.' However, Vietnamese officials have trouble defining negative influences, a fact acknowledged by the official Vietnam News in commenting on another government crackdown against pirated video tapes: 'What is unclear to the sceptics is what exactly constitutes, in the eyes of the Ministry of Culture and Information, culturally harmful, pirated and illegally imported videos.'

TRADEMARK AND COPYRIGHT PROTECTION

With Vietnam's market-oriented economy still in its initial development stage, many private enterprises have been licensed up to now without the necessary strick controls on their operations. One of the key areas of concern is trademark and other copyright infringement which the government fears may be scaring away potential foreigner investors.

Many products, intentionally or otherwise, are often produced under the trademark of foreign companies without the necessary licence from their legitimate owner. This not only causes consumers difficulty in distinguishing the real thing from the fakes, but can also damage the prestige of the trademark. It is readily admitted by the authorities that trademark abuse is on the rise. In the past, only cursory attention was paid to the problem, which tended to encourage even more abuse. Now, however, closer attention is being paid to dealing with the issue through such organs as the National Office on Industrial Property, the Ministry of Science and Technology and the Environment, the Market Control Department, the Economic Police and the Customs Office.

As long ago as 1976, Vietnam joined the World Industrial Property Organization, and also later signed the Paris Agreement on the Protection of Industrial Property and the Madrid Agreement on International Trademark Registration. In 1993, it signed the Patent Cooperation Treaty. From 1982, these steps were supported since 1982 by a series of legal documents. The Ordinance on the Protection of Industrial Property, for example, was corrected and amended many times. To this have been added regulations on inventions, utility solutions, industrial design, trademarks, licensing and technology transfer. All these measures have now been largely incorporated into, and thus superseded by, the new Civil Code which went into effect on 1 July, 1996.

Trademark abuse occurs in many different fields, but soft drinks, clothing, shampoos and medicines are the areas most often targeted. Many are made in Vietnam using a well-known foreign trademark. But there are other products made abroad which are either imported illegally or smuggled in, and which also violate the trademark regulations. New regulations were introduced during 1996 to try and stop smuggling, as well as the manufacture and sale of fake products, as well as the circulation of products regarded as being of 'low quality'. Regulations on the import and export of products with foreign trademarks have also been strengthened, including a requirement that importers and exporters now have to prove the legal status of the trademarks on their products before obtaining permission for the trade to take place.

The National Office on Industrial Property, which received a record 5,465 applications for the protection of foreign trademarks in 1995, recommends that foreign companies hire a good local lawyer who can then negotiate with the relevant authorities for a quick settlement of any case of abuse. Often, it says, this can be achieved without the necessity of a costly court case – especially as the resultant publicity might damage the foreign brand's image.

But it should also be stressed that Vietnam still has some way to go in providing a watertight legal framework for protecting foreign trademark and copyright holders wanting to do business in the country.

NOTES

1. *Vietnam Today*, Issue 4 1995, and Issue 7 1994.
2. Deputy General Director of the Foreign Investment Department, Ministry of Trade, interviewed 29 April 1996.
3. For instance, there are restrictions on the import of fuels, raw materials for industry and imputs for agriculture such as fertilizer, sugar, automobiles and motorcycles.
4. *Vietnam Economic Times*. August 1995.
5. 'Marketing and Distribution in Vietnam'. *Vietnam Today*, February 1996.
6. Including prostitution, gambling, karoake and advertising signs encouraging consumption of popular foreign brand products.
7. *Financial Times*, 2 February 1996.
8. *Vietnam Today*, February 1996.
9. *Financial Times*, op.cit.

10 Coping with Vietnam

KEY POINTS

- Confucius plus Marx
- Creating a management culture
- Overcoming the culture of secrecy
- Strategies for business survival
- Do Asians have an inside track?
- Avoiding labour problems
- Labour recruitment
- Negotiating rules

CONFUCIUS PLUS MARX

SOME 2,300 years ago, the great Chinese military strategist Sun Zi wrote: 'Know yourself and know others well and you can go through one hundred battles without danger. But if you do not know the other, but only know yourself, there will be only half a chance of victory.' In business anywhere in the world that is good advice: know yourself, know the market and know your partner. And it's definitely sound advice when it comes to establishing a business presence in Vietnam.

Above all, everyone — and that includes the Vietnamese side — has to learn to wait, to be patient. 'It's just like the war with the United States,' says one American businessman in the bar of Hanoi hotel. '[The Vietnamese] can wait and wait and wait. Their sense of time is very different from Westerners. We always expect action now. They're willing to stick it out.' But that is not an exclusive Vietnamese trait. Business personnel learnt this valuable lesson a long time ago in Japan. I can recall writing books in the 1970s about doing business in Japan which extolled the need for patience and more patience.

And, those foreign businesses taking advantage of China's open door from the early 1980s onwards have found exactly the same situation. So, if you have experience of either of these countries, there is no reason why you cannot succeed in Vietnam — except for the fact that as far as a business culture is concerned it is still in its infancy, still low on the learning curve.

Mind you, there is a danger that Vietnamese negotiators will allow their belief in an ability to outlast other players at the negotiating table to damage the induction of vitally needed funds. One foreign banker, helping a client work out a joint venture with a hotel in Hanoi, recalls: 'Every time we returned to pick up where negotiations left off in the previous round, there was always a new demand for an extra inch from the Vietnamese. It was almost if they felt they had to do this to show their toughness and business acumen. What happened, however, was that after a year of pointless negotiations my client scrapped its plan to invest in Vietnam.' Other examples of this problem were mentioned in Chapter 1.

To help understand Vietnamese thinking and behaviour at the present time, Mai Nguyen, representative of ING Bank, offers the following advice:

'To understand Vietnam's business culture, one must first consider the culture of the country. Vietnam's history is littered with foreign influences from the French to the Russians, but perhaps the greatest influence has been Confucianism from China. This permeates many aspects of the country's daily life and consequently its business practices. Confucianism is characterized by unconditional obedience to the figurehead of the family. In a business setting this translates into respect for the boss often favouring seniority over merit. Vietnam also shares with other Asian societies the importance of saving face, avoiding confrontation and maintaining harmony.

'After 1975, a reunified Vietnam followed the socialist model of the former Soviet Union. Indeed, this continues to exert a strong influence. The result has been a business culture characterized by extreme caution with drawn out decision-making process. The demise of a socialism in Eastern Europe as a commercial model and the switch to the market economy has resulted in a kind of split personality; some managers cling to socialist practices while others energetically forge ahead. Also, there is now emerging a young entrepreneurial class whose methods are firmly rooted in the capitalist system. This group is often self-assertive and aggressive, and is predominantly concerned with short-term goals rather than long-term growth.

'The Vietnamese are proud, disciplined and independent, and foreign business people often complain that their Vietnamese counterparts are suspicious and tough to deal with. This is not simply a result of centuries of foreign involvement, but also of the influence of Asian business practices where relationships are important precursors to business negotiations. Since Vietnam has only recently opened its doors to the outside world, it is too early to make any concrete predictions about the direction its business culture will take. However, Vietnam's Latinized alphabet and fascination with the West sets the stage for a migration towards Western business practices. The country has a remarkable ability to absorb foreign influence while retaining its character and the people are pragmatic – using what works and discarding what does not. The result will be a business culture uniquely Vietnamese.'[1]

CREATING A MANAGEMENT CULTURE

Sticking it out is complicated in today's Vietnam. The investment game is more mature than a few years ago, but that does not mean it has become easier to do business. Government policy concerning foreign investment is more voluminous, if not more detailed, and these policies need to be pored over by Vietnamese and foreign business partners to discern current thinking – with an awareness always that things may change tomorrow. One good thing is that rogue traders and entrepreneurs of the early 1990s are finding it harder to survive. Some trading companies and representative offices who had been operating in grey areas are slowly being accounted for, and in some cases, are having difficulties setting up official offices because of past transgressions. These recent times, however, may turn out to have been the easy part compared to the current day-to-day job of management and seeing new investment projects over numerous hurdles. Undoubtedly, foreign investors who are not committed to the long term are not only out of touch with the business reality of Vietnam, but will likely find bureaucratic life extremely difficult to cope with.

The management culture that emerges will have to take into account a number of factors related to political road the country is following. According to Le Dang Doanh, President of the Central

Institute for Economic Management, Vietnamese business practice will have to take account of:

- **Wealth redistribution.** 'State control over people's incomes is considered necessary in order to redistribute wealth to improve social welfare. This is a prerequisite for the development of any management culture. Countries such as Brazil and Zaire, for example, show that extreme differences in income block the path to economic progress for the majority of the population and also cause unrest.' But the present investment structure, with its heavy emphasis on the two strong growth areas surrounding Hanoi and Ho Chi Minh City are actually creating greater income disparities at present; in addition, the government does not have the resources to narrow this gap.
- **Improvement of equal opportunities** in education, health care and culture. 'Taiwan is a good example. For a long time, the country has maintained a high growth rate and reigned in big income differentials. The education system and social welfare are also well developed.' The same problems exist here as have just been mentioned in regard to wealth redistribution.
- **Decentralizing decision-making.** 'Decision-makers should have a clear perception of responsibilities and interests. The decentralizing principle is based on assigning responsibility to all areas of decision-making'. But this will not be easy given the strong grip the central bureaucracy has over the economy which is its only source of power and opportunity for enrichment.
- **Access to information.** 'This is an important part of any society and is crucial to management culture. Decisions that are made public from the beginning will have more public support and participation. Lack of information sometimes leads to misunderstandings and causes biased predictions and rumours.'

Reliable statistics on the Vietnamese economy have never been easy to obtain. The Trade Ministry has routinely required businessmen and journalists to pay for data on imports and exports, for example. Vietnam is in many ways behaving in the same way as China has done for many years — treating even the most basic data as a 'state secret' and covered by the most stringent 'need-to-know' requirements; this is, however, beginning to change. Secondly, is the difficulty of obtaining accurate and detailed figures when no sophisticated mechanism for gathering, processing and analyzing raw data is in place. China is now tackling this problem, but Vietnam remains far behind.

Basic facts give companies the edge in doing business in Vietnam as does locating the right contacts, because information is usually secured through personal connections and by computing data from different agencies which often contain discrepancies. But it should be stressed that this is not just a problem for foreigners. Even the country's own government agencies do not share information among themselves! 'We have been through many decades of war; it will take some time before we can overcome the wartime culture of secrecy,' a senior Trade Ministry official says by way of mitigation.

An example of the difficulties foreigners can encounter comes from a team of consultants under contract to the Japanese government who visited Hanoi in mid-1995 to draw up a country report on the direction of Japanese aid to Vietnam. Despite official sponsorship and an introductory letter from the Japanese Embassy in Hanoi, the team encountered uncooperative state agencies which refused them access to perfunctory gross domestic product data. The State Planning Committee, which coordinates all official foreign aid and loans, was called in to use its clout to make those agencies release the information. Japan, it should be pointed out, is Vietnam's largest aid donor so that one would have thought that cooperation with the consultancy team would be have been fairly obvious to even the most obtuse bureaucrat.

However, its commitment to share trade-related data with fellow ASEAN members, following its admission to the regional organization, is a big leap forward in prying open the secrecy phobia about information. By becoming the seventh member of ASEAN, however, Vietnam is committed to keeping the other six countries fully informed of all the changes in its trade regulations and laws, and to ensure its trade relations are open and harmonious. If implemented seriously, the commitment will be a boon not only for ASEAN but also for the foreign business community operating in the country.

In keeping its regional partners informed of all changes in laws affecting trade ties, however, Vietnam has committed itself to a demanding task given the frequency with which its regulations and bylaws fluctuate. Vietnam-based foreign businessmen can barely keep up with figuring how changes will affect their interests. There was, for example, the wild variations in rice export regulations which created during a four-month period in mid-1995 a situation in which the government allowed, banned and then re-approved rice exports. Another example is Prime Minister Vo Van Kiet's order banning the conversion of rice fields to other commercial uses. The order came out in March, but on 11 July Kiet endorsed the Hanoi People's Committee's proposal to set aside 6,310 hectares of farmland for industrial, technical and residential use, making outsiders wonder whether the ban really existed or not.[2]

STRATEGIES FOR BUSINESS SURVIVAL

If Vietnam is the next Asian dragon, why is it that so few foreign companies seem able to make a profit? That was the question Malaysia Borneo Finance Indochina Ltd, the Vietnam business development arm of the MBf Group, asked itself in 1994. The largest financial services and construction company in Malaysia began operating in Vietnam in 1991 offering Mastercard services in cooperation with Vietcombank. It entered Vietnam, according to Hanoi manager Jeff Swiatek, because the country was considered of strategic importance to its plans for international expansion.

Representative offices were set up in early 1993 in Hanoi and Ho Chi Minh City. The initial objective was to gain expertise in the market and to pursue large-scale projects in finance and property developments. After the first 18 months of operation, the management identified several obstacles to profitable operations inherent in the business environment: unclear and rapidly changing legal structure; low disposable income/lack of capital; lack of expertise and training; smuggling; lack of exposure to high quality products; and protracted and costly development period.

'Considering a one minute phone call to the United States priced at $4.60 and asking prices for residential and commercial space at $8 per square foot, the cost of doing business in Vietnam was surprisingly high. Even the cost of office staff was higher than would be expected in light of the low per capita GDP,' Mr Swatiak says. To minimize the obstacles and take advantage of the opportunities created by them, therefore, MBf Indochina developed a strategy for the market comprising two key elements.

1 **Finding the niche**. 'Identify sectors which will attract foreign capital. Provide services and products which will be demanded by the sector without getting involved in project development work.

The strategy is the cornerstone to our plans in this market. We know, for instance, that resorts will be built in Vietnam, but we don't want to incur the risk and expense of developing the project. Instead, we provide goods and services we know are required by already licensed resort projects such as property management services, building materials and equipment.'

This approach, claims Mr Swatiak, has the following advantages:

- **Self-reliance.** 'We are able to organize a business structure which depends mainly on internal competence for success. Business transactions which require the company to wade through bureaucracy are avoided.'
- **Reduced development cost.** 'Although day-to-day operating expenses are still high, overall development costs are lower because costs do not need to be incurred while waiting for project licensing and other formalities.
- **No competition with smuggling.**
- **Less subject to risk of legislative change.** 'Since much of our business will be done on a trading basis, the chance that a relevant law will change in the middle of a transaction is slim. Furthermore, our obligations are based mainly on international laws which are comprehensive and stable.'

2 **Adding Value.** 'Vietnam has strategic importance to our business and we need to position ourselves to contribute to its economic growth over the next few decades,' says the MBf manager. 'To add value beyond that of a normal trading company, we will need to incur development costs. However, this is done with long-term positioning considerations in mind, rather than a project-to-project basis.' To that end the company focused on the following programmes:

- **Training and education.** 'This is the most important aspect of our in-country operations. The dearth of local expertise and training provides one of our greatest opportunities to distinguish ourselves from our competitors. We invest in training programmes for our staff, seminars to promote awareness and understanding of our products within the relevant community, and identify and support competent local companies with which to cooperate. Showrooms sponsored by selected local companies are used to introduce new products and systems to the public at large and to expand our activities in the retail market.

- **Information.** 'Our office has developed a database which includes every major foreign-funded infrastructure and construction project in Vietnam. Contact information for the developer, architect, contractor and consultant is included. Ongoing discussions with contractors, architects and quantity surveyors enable us to package our goods and services to meet market demands.'
- **Tactical partnerships with suppliers.** 'We find foreign suppliers which have a superior product and support service. Preferably, the supplier also has a strategic commitment to Vietnam. These companies assist us in our training programmes, seminars, advertising campaigns and marketing, and in future may assist us in identifying and researching manufacturing opportunities.[3]

DO ASIANS HAVE AN INSIDE TRACK?

Many executives say that previous experience of Asia and its developing economies is of considerable help in adjusting to the challenges of doing business in Vietnam. Many aspects of the market, as has been mentioned already, are similar to those prevailing elsewhere in the region. So, if having Asian experience is helpful, does that mean Asian enterprises have an inherent advantage over Western ones? Should multinationals, therefore, then send in their Asian manager from Hong Kong, Singapore or Bangkok rather than someone from their European or American offices?

On the surface, says a Foreign Ministry official, this would seem to be true. 'At the very least [an Asian] is eating rice and using chopsticks. He doesn't turn his nose up at *nuoc mam* [the pungent fish-based sauce that relishes most Vietnamese meals as soy sauce does in, say, Japan or chilli sauce in Singapore and Malaysia]'. But this ignores the fact that many Westerners are now thoroughly familiar with using chopsticks and rice is often just as much a fixture on Western dining tables as those in Asia. And, in addition, Asians are just as faddy about food, the Japanese, for instance, unable to travel without their own local delicacies and often refusing to eat local food on the basis it is unclean or too exotic.

But if you scratch beneath this surface referred to by the Foreign Ministry official, will you find a deeper understanding of Vietnam among, say, Japanese, Koreans or Taiwanese? Asian countries may share a long list of traits, but in the end they are still different cultures. The Vietnamese press often carry articles criticizing certain Asian companies, in particular joint ventures and 100 per cent foreign-invested manufacturers accused of abusing Vietnamese labourers. Charges of bribery, false invoicing and tax evasion are routine.

Confucian values may be shared by many Asians, but this can be a double-edged sword in Vietnam. A Japanese diplomat says, for example, that while there may be a common understanding of how to behave and how Confucian societies work, there are different interpretations. Confucianism, he argues, can imply authoritarianism or at the very least a hierarchical structure. This could lead to the Asian business executive looking down on the Vietnamese partner during business negotiations. This is especially relevant in Vietnam, where in almost every joint venture, the local partner is in a substantially weaker financial position.

Vietnam's brief free market history clearly shows one thing: if foreigners start business relationships off this way, they will quickly wish they had never boarded the plane.'[The foreign partners] have to respect us. They cannot impose their rules and methods on the Vietnamese.' says a local representative of a Vietnamese-American office service joint venture.

Certain culture clashes always depend on circumstance and the particular individuals involved. But experience is the best yardstick, says the Japanese diplomat, pointing out that Japanese companies have been dealing in emerging markets in Asia for many years and, having experienced many problems in dealing with their neighbours, have finally gained some helpful knowledge from some bad experiences. Many of the labour problems, and accusations of labour abuse that the local press levies against Korean and Taiwanese companies, also happened to Japanese enterprises in the past, the diplomat pointed out. But the companies had since learnt how to deal with these potentially explosive issues.

What it comes down to is that on a certain level, Asian business executives may understand the Vietnamese, as fellow Asians, better and instinctively some of the rules by which the business game is played in this part of the world. But Western businessmen also have their strengths, and if they take an effort to learn about Vietnam and its people and demonstrate their understanding they can be just as successful. In China, for example, I have found Japanese businessmen just as frustrated and expressing exactly the same sort of irritation at the slow pace of negotiations or the complex maze of regulatory channels to be negotiated, as their Western counterparts.

AVOIDING LABOUR PROBLEMS

Foreign investors are facing a strong trade union drive for more laws, higher wages and better conditions. According to speakers at a national trade union review meeting in 1995, many workers in foreign-run enterprises face little more than three months' job security, with few contracts, minimal safety and health insurance. Complaints were minimal, however, because potential complainants knew there were long queues of applicants outside the factory literally waiting to take their jobs.

The official Vietnam News commented: 'It is easy to fire employees who want to try their luck in these joint ventures. Most trainees who want to join work very hard at first. After a while their productivity declines, because of low salary. Applications pile high on employers' tables, enabling them to dismiss the previous trainees. Shop unions, where they existed, are hampered by lack of contracts, meaning any attempt to strike would lead to workers losing their jobs.'

Only about 100 strikes were reported in Vietnam between 1990 and 1995 and most of those were illegal. The 1995 figure was 46, against 28 the previous year, all but eight involving foreign companies. But this would seem to be a serious underestimate, ignoring the numerous wildcat strikes and disputes of short duration that did not attract official attention through the arbitration process. Low wages appears to be the main cause. Other reasons cited include strict working regimes, long hours without overtime pay, management refusal to grant medical and other social benefits as stipulated by law, and direct physical abuse by employers.

The worst offenders were not identified by the government, but union officials have previously singled out South Korean and Taiwanese investors in particular for having bad relations with workers. Certainly, 11 of the 1994 strikes occurred in South Korean factories, according to various official sources. Of eight industrial disputes recorded in the first quarter of 1996, six were in South Korean-owned firms. Among these, about 970 workers at a footwear factory in Ho Chi Minh City walked out after a Korean technician allegedly beat 15 employees around the head and face with unfinished shoes. Two of them required hospital treatment. Negative press treatment of various problems at Korean enterprises became such a source of concern that the country's ambassador to Hanoi warned the government this might result in less Korean investment in future.[4]

A Labour code went into operation on January 1,1995, giving workers the right to form trade unions and to strike for the first time. It also provided for the formation of labour courts, a mechanism for tripartite arbitration involving business, unions and government.

'The operation of trade unions and the inspection of and management of labour problems in enterprises, especially in the private sector, is still too weak to force employers to follow the regulations,' complained Hoang Minh Chuc, deputy president of the Vietnam General Confederation of Labour. In the state-run sector, these were often a legacy of decades of bureaucracy and the inability, in some cases, of companies to pay their work-force. 'But as many state-run enterprises are becoming more stable and profitable, the number of strikes is likely to decrease.' He also admitted, however, that on occasions disputes could be solved through negotiations, '... if Vietnamese workers were not so hasty in over-reacting to what they see as violations of their rights'.[5]

To push for more regulation, unionists cited recent trouble at a Taiwanese garment joint venture, Da Nang Valley View, with more than 1,000 employees. The Vietnam News said staff petitioned the government with complaints of unfair dismissals, low pay and 'high-handed' management – a move followed by a stiff Confederation of Labour report demanding unions and changes at the company. But just days after a union was created, the company announced that half the staff would have to leave because of 'production cutbacks'. The newspaper said: 'This is seen as a trick that the management board played on those who wanted to protect their own legal rights.'

The Ministry of Labour estimates that around 90,000 Vietnamese are now directly employed by foreign-invested joint ventures or wholly-owned companies, not to mention several hundred thousand labourers who find temporary employment especially in the construction industry. But while around 90 per cent of state enterprises are said to have trade unions, the figure in the private sector and for foreign companies is only about 30 per cent.[6]

In the industrial zones of Dong Nai on the northern outskirts of Ho Chi Minh City, one of the fastest growing areas for foreign investment, there have been a number of major disputes, prompting the provincial labour organization to step up its efforts to persuade employers to sign labour contracts with their work force. But it admitted it did not have the resources to monitor all labour violations nor the muscle to overcome managemnt resistance. The Vietnam General Confederation of Labour submitted proposals to the National Assembly calling for harsh punishment for those who violated the labour laws, including having their operating licence revoked. A watchdog body should be set up with powers to bring to court foreign investors who repeatedly violated the laws, and after being punished the specific managers should be expelled, it argued. It also called on the government to only license those foreign investments projects that agreed to recognize an in-house union. Whether these far-reaching steps would be accepted remains unclear, especially as Vietnam needs to balance the protection of workers' rights without discouraging foreign investment.

LABOUR RECRUITMENT

Labour recruitment is covered by Decree No.72/CP issued on 31 October 1995.[7] It states:

1 The foreign-invested enterprise shall give recruitment priority to Vietnamese. In cases where the work requires certain technical or managerial skills for which Vietnamese are not qualified, the enterprise can recruit foreigners for a specific period of time, but must demonstrate a commitment to providing training so that Vietnamese personnel can acquire the necessary skills. Foreigners recruited to work long-term in Vietnam must obtain a labour permit from the Ministry of Labour, War Invalids and Social Affairs.
2 Workers have the right to work for any employer and in any place not prohibited by law.
3 The normal minimum recruitment age is 18. However, employment of those aged 15 to 17 is permitted in certain sectors, such as textiles, subject to permission from the ministry. Under-age workers, however, are not allowed to do heavy or dangerous work or handle toxic chemicals. Enterprises who are employing under-age workers have to maintain a special record of such employees subject to regular checks by labour inspectors.
4 Companies have to report to the ministry on their labour recruitment in January and July each year.

5   The normal (although not obligatory route) for finding workers is through A Labour service Centre established in each province and major city by the local People's Committee.

A minimum wage for workers in foreign-invested joint ventures and wholly-owned enterprises was set at $35 for Hanoi and Ho Chi Minh City, and $30 in other localities, on 5 May 1992. From early 1995, however, there were many complaints on the Vietnamese side that this was far too low, especially as successful domestic firms were paying a higher rate, sometimes as high as $80–90, while inflation had actually eroded the spending power of the minimum wage by at least 30 per cent. In addition, as Labour Minister Tran Dinh Hoan, pointed out, 'employees in foreign enterprises have to work harder [than their state counterparts] in order to meet the higher productivity demands set by their employers to justify the investment'.[8]

From 1 July 1996, therefore, a new four-tier minimum wage structure was applied. The top rate was $45 in Hanoi and Ho Chi Minh City, $40 in the cities of Haiphong, Vinh, Hue Da Nang, Bien Hoa and Can Tho, and $35 in other localities. A fourth category was also created to apply to what the minister described as 'enterprises with outdated infrastructure and employing a large work-force,' or in areas where facilities were poor but foreign investment was desperately needed. In these cases, with ministry approval, the minimum wage level can remain at $30–35. Mr Hoan stressed, however, that even with the increases, Vietnam's wage levels would still be below those of other Southeast Asian countries, enabling its labour-intensive industries to remain competitive.[9]

NEGOTIATING RULES

Business rituals in Vietnam are much the same as anywhere else, so that a basic combination of politeness and common-sense should see the business executive through a negotiating process without serious etiquette difficulties. Vietnamese business meetings tend to relaxed affairs with less of the formality that one encounters particularly in Japan and to a lesser extent in China. Exchanges of gifts common in China do not seem to be part of the Vietnamese culture.

Meetings are an integral part of doing business in Vietnam, face-to-face contact being considered vital; few, if any, negotiations are possible by phone, fax or letter. Businessmen with a lot of experience on the ground warn that meetings tend to take a lot longer than you might anticipate, so it is not considered wise to fill the day with too many tight appointments, some of which might eventually have to be cancelled amid much embarrassment. Business cards should be exchanged with everyone in the room on the initial encounter before any discussions have taken place. But unlike Japan, it is not necessary to be terribly formal (i.e. handing over the card with two hands accompanied by a deep bow). But politeness suggests it is better not to sit down until the opposite principal has done so.

Tea drinking is an essential business ritual as in other parts of Asia. Again, it is usually considered polite to wait for the senior member on the other side to begin drinking before doing so oneself. A few sips will be quite sufficient for politeness sake, especially if you do not find the tea to your liking. You may be offered a cigarette, and although smoking is prevalent in Vietnam it is not obligatory to light up and a polite refusal will not be taken amiss!

Good communication is obviously of paramount importance. For a long-term commitment, it would be advisable to learn the language. Patrick Aronson, Market Development Manager for Motorola, after five years in the country, says: 'Successful business people in Vietnam should have every intention of planning to learn Vietnam's culture, take lessons in Vietnamese and make a concerted effort to have Vietnamese friends. Nine out of 10 people who come here planning to learn Vietnamese end up by dropping it. People need the personal contact to stick to it. It makes your life so much easier.'

Alan Head, Managing Director for Procter and Gamble Vietnam Ltd, is a perfect example. After a three-day trip to Vietnam in 1993, he knew he wanted to work in the country and immediately put in an application to his company. A year later his assignment was confirmed and that summer he studied Vietnamese at the Southeast Asian Summer Studies Institute, an American academic programme offering intensive courses which squeezes a full academic year into 10 weeks. In August, he arrived in Vietnam to set up the P & G office and move towards a project with a previously identified local partner. But after only one night in a hotel by personal choice he moved in with a Vietnamese family to continue language study and learn more about the language and culture.

If, however, you are forced to use a translator, in conversation always face the person you are addressing and try not to talk to the interpreter all the time. It is considered a good idea to let your Vietnamese counterpart speak uninterruptedly for a stretch. The advice is not to question him or her immediately on points you think ought to be dealt with there and then. It is far more polite, and effective, to make notes, bringing up queries when it is your turn to speak. One can be direct, without being *too* firm, even though the other side may not be. There may be many reasons why your Vietnamese counterpart cannot give a straight answer — including the need to check with his or her political masters — other than sheer negotiating deviousness.

Finally, entertaining is, as elsewhere in Asia, an important part of the business ritual, although it may not necessarily occur at the first encounter. However, at some stage, an opportunity will arrive to unwind and get to know each other better. Vietnamese banquets can be fairly riotous affairs, with a great deal of drinking, so it helps to have a strong head and stomach. It starts to get serious when the words 'Tram Phan Tram' (100 per cent) are spoken, indicating that you are being urged to down the entire contents of the glass at one go. Readers with experience of the Chinese *'Gambei'* (bottoms up) will know what this entails.

NOTES

1. *Vietnam Economic Times*, September 1995.
2. *Bangkok Post*, 8 August 1995.
3. *Vietnam Business Journal*, August 1995.
4. *The Nation*, Bangkok, 3 May 1996.
5. *Vietnam Investment Review*, 29 January, 4 February 1996.
6. Estimate of Pham Gia Thieu, deputy director of the Vietnam General Confederation of Labour's Foreign Department.
7. English translation courtesy of the Vietnam Chamber of Commerce and Industry.
8. *Vietnam Economic Times*, March 1996.
9. Announcement made in *The Saigon Times Daily*, 22 April 1996

11 The Challenges Ahead

KEY POINTS

- Faint hearts, profiteers stay away
- Weeding out the dodgy dealers
- Is Vietnam investor-friendly?
- Possibility of a U-turn
- Problem areas identified – and solved
- MPI's promises
- The Fifth Tiger?
- Vietnam's regional focus

FAINTS HEARTS, PROFITEERS STAY AWAY

IT IS now time to sum up and look ahead. There are two points that should be made right away. Firstly, faint hearts should stay away. Vietnam is no place for those of a delicate constitution or expecting an easy life. Secondly, short-term profiteers may want to give Vietnam a miss. The Vietnamese do not want them, and, anyway short-term profits are hard to come by.

'Vietnam remains an acquired taste for many investors,' is the assessment of Dr Nick Freeman, a research fellow at the Institute for Southeast Asian Studies in Singapore. While considerable investment opportunities may exist, there is likely to be a high cost in terms and dollars which only long-term visionaries may be able to sustain, or stomach.

It may be no coincidence that Asian investors dominate the market at present. People like the Japanese, Koreans and Taiwanese have experienced the subtleties and policies of their own relatively recently

227

developed economies. In addition, they have learnt hard lessons from doing business in other Asian countries — especially, China — and thus have been able to adapt their strategies to cope with challenging conditions that western businessmen may not be accustomed to. The former's notable strength has been is diversifying investments across several sectors, identifying early on which are likely to be the growth areas of the future and getting a toehold now for later expansion. They are prepared to wait patiently for a good return on their money, in the meantime building up experience and goodwill.

What is very clear from my research, and that of other experts, is that the honeymoon between Vietnam and the international investment community is probably over. I have written in various chapters about many of the problems that have produced something of a sour mood for some investors. The stayers are now talking in terms of 20 years before Vietnam can expect to move to the status of a fully industrialized nation. Those who came in full of optimism that there was a pot of gold just waiting to be dug up at the end of the rainbow have quickly woken up to the reality.

And that, according to the Hong Kong-based Political and Economic Risk Consultancy Ltd, is that businessmen now rate Vietnam as the most stressful country in Asia in which to live and work. The main cause seems to be an inability of the two sides to clearly understand each other's specific business and economic goals.

The organization also made the following evaluations about Vietnam:

- It is the riskiest place in Asia in which to do business. The country now heads the annual 'systematic and socio-political risk table'.
- It is ranked the worst in Asia in terms of physical infrastructure and red tape.
- It is one of Asia's most corrupt countries.

However, on the other side, one has to understand some of Vietnam's concerns. It has, for example, been unhappy at some of the quality of the early investment and now wants to working more in harmony with the country's long-term socio-economic goals. Officials questioned about the withdrawal of some investors tend to dismiss these as 'cowboys, just out for a quick profit and not interested in developing a long-term mutually beneficial relationship with us'. As one official told me: 'We're better off without those people. It's good to lost interest and stopped wasting our time and resources.'

One foreign economic analyst, who declined to be named, suggests that: 'Having learnt some of the tricks employed by less scrupulous foreign investors, issues of quality and ability will become more prominent in the foreign investment inflows from now on. [The Vietnamese] are fast learners. You can expect to see the investment authorities paying increasing attention to the degree of technology transfer involved in proposed projects, the way investment proposals are structured and the financial capabilities of the sponsors to enact and develop projects.'

An official with the Ministry of Planning and Investment concurs. 'Of course, the quantity of investment projects is important for the development of the country. But from now on the government will be paying more attention to the quality of the projects. We feel we have a perfect right to pick and choose what is best for us and not just what is best for the potential foreign investor.'

There is a pattern in foreign investment when a new sector opens up. At first, the atmosphere is fairly relaxed. It looks as if anything is possible. Then, as the sector begins to fill up, the government starts to get more careful. It looks at each application with a sharper eye. According to analyst Le Van Tan:[1] 'When Vietnam opened the economic floodgates eight years ago, investors often rushed in with the cavalier attitude that Vietnam was a frontier where rules didn't matter and the opportunities were there for the taking. Like the excessive era that symbolized Wall Street in the 1980s, the free-wheeling days are over. Vietnam's investment environment is maturing and changes in government policy mean that investors often have to make inconvenient adjustments to new regulation or existing laws that are only now being enforced.'

As part of a crackdown on dodgy deals, the government in late 1995 named 12 foreign companies which were said to be seeking vast deals with domestic partners despite having no apparent means. Official reports paraded a range of apparent scams, including one man who could not pay a $700 hotel bill despite offering a $700 million 30–year loan to officials of three different provinces. The Laotian businessman's office was a Hanoi flop-house and no company was found at the London address he supplied.

Another businessman offered Communist Party General Secretary Du Muoi and other leaders a loan of up to $2 billion at four per cent interest. Investigations showed the California-based man had less than $100,000 bank accounts which he used to run a tiny fruit export company. The investigations were carried out by foreign banks and US researcher Dun and Bradstreet — the first time international firms had been used for such work by the State Bank. More probes are underway.

'This investigation is part of a drive by the State Bank to remove cowboys from the Vietnamese financing arena,' an official report said. 'Most of the foreign companies investigated came to Vietnam and offered sizeable loans to government entities over long duration and with low interest rates to gain State Bank guarantees and commissions from lenders.'

The first probe involved concerns from California, Italy, New Zealand, Liechtenstein and Britain. Six probes involved multi-million dollar loans to provincial governments to finance infrastructure projects and cement plants. Some were found to be in serious debt while others could not provide documents or did not exist. News of the investigations was seen by foreign businessmen as part of a wider campaign to keep official control of foreigners and overseas-funded developments.

Seeking to attract good quality foreign investors, Vietnam is now stopping foreigners on tourist visas from conducting business. Those running operations without licences — which can take more than a year to obtain — face fines of up to $50,000 and house arrest.

Finally, it must be stressed that Vietnam is a poor, underdeveloped country. Prime Minister Vo Van Kiet says: 'Vietnam is following a policy of industrialization and modernization with the aim of alleviating poverty and under-development in order to have a strong country and a just and civilized country. We are trying to have dynamic and sustainable economic development, harmoniously combining them with economic and social welfare development, while *preserving national identify at the same time.*'

I have emphasized the last few words because they are crucial to understanding the Vietnamese approach. This is a people who fought for 100 years for a united, independent country — along with memories of previous battles for independence hundreds of years before. They won that fight, and have no intention now of surrendering any of their hard-won independence and sense of national identity. Self-reliance is the name of the game. Foreign investment is vital in order to cut some of the corners, and shorten the development process, but the money and know-how will be accepted on Vietnamese terms.

That is not to say the Vietnamese do not realize the foreigner's need to make a profit. But that profit has to come under conditions set by the Vietnamese to guarantee that foreign domination will not lead to any significant dilution of Vietnamese culture, the undermining of the dominant role of the state (in the shape of the Communist Party) or the destruction of fledgling domestic industries before they have had a chance to develop a competitive edge.

Vietnam is determined not to allow itself to be 'anybody's fool' as its doors swing open. In essence the state must find new ways to ensure it will not grow captive to foreign capital. It wants to continue to welcome offshore funds and widen international ties — to be friends with everyone. But at the same time, it is being emphasized this must be done to tune the economy to 'new socialism' through a more rigorous state-sector and more control of joint ventures. One is constantly reminded in Vietnam of the comment once said to have been made by Lenin to the effect that 'we are not afraid of capitalist enterprises, but of not being able to control them'.

IS VIETNAM INVESTOR-FRIENDLY?

But a serious question remains whether Vietnam can be considered an 'investor-friendly' country? Some anti-foreign and anti-foreign investment statements by senior government officials and important local newspapers in 1996 were certainly cause for concern.

Take this extract from a column on security issues by the army newspaper *Quang Doi Nhan Dan*, which complained that 'foreign executives and scientists attending seminars in Vietnam are gaining access to state secrets and are a threat to national security'. Seminars, particularly those funded by foreigners, were being managed in an anarchic fashion allowing overseas companies to gather information from Vietnamese, the newspaper reported, Foreigners were particularly eager to get hold of 'information that helps them work out their investments, calculate prices and put pressure on their Vietnamese partners'. Nobody seems to have told the army that foreign companies were hardly likely to want to invest in Vietnam unless they had access to basic information on their potential partners, along with the ground rules for cooperation and a market analysis.

Nhan Dan has been in the forefront of the fight against foreign influences. On another occasion[2] it bitterly attacked the government's open door policy with a warning that every foreigner was a potential spy. 'It is a serious matter if we mistake enemies for friends in the current era of information, flow and civilization. Many foreign organizations and individuals in Vietnam have been exposed as reactionaries and anti-revolutionaries. They label themselves as tourists, visitors, representative offices and survey groups seeking investment opportunities. There have been hundreds of cases in which foreigners have tried to take our military, national scientific and technological secrets.'[3]

Some analysts link such statements, and the alarm they create, for a 50 per cent drop in the amount of foreign investment recorded in the first four months of 1996. This provoked an immediate angry reaction from government officials in Hanoi, who attacked the western media for creating a dark image of Vietnam and damaging its economic prospects. Vietnam was still on line to fulfil all its foreign investment targets, they insisted.

But it does seem to be the case that the Vietnamese are damaging their own image, not only with statements like those quoted — although they should be put into context as coming from a sector that would naturally be more suspicious of foreigners, namely the army, given Vietnam's recent history — but also through the actions of short-sighted businessmen, seemingly supported by corrupt bureaucrats, who cannot see further than the end of their nose.

Australian businessman Raymond Eaton, chairman of the Bangkok-based Integra Group,[4] had been in Vietnam several years engaged in trade and clothing manufacturing. For most of that time he was one of the most vocal supporters of the efforts from the American business community in Southeast Asia to persuade the U.S. Government to lift its trade embargo on Vietnam. He has spoken well of Vietnam and its leaders at many international conferences and urged other businessman to look to the prospective market there for their future investments.

And yet, he eventually closed down an office in Hanoi and walked away from a manufacturing joint venture there, losing $600,000 in the process. 'The reason is that the Vietnamese partner had no genuine intention to make the business a success but merely look for every opportunity to cheat and steal from me. I made numerous requests to the Vietnamese authorities for something to be done, but nothing happened.

'As a result, I consider that Vietnam has what could be described as an unfriendly foreign investor climate — unlike, for example, Thailand. I am genuinely concerned that the Vietnamese could make everything so difficult for foreign investors that they either cancel existing investment plans, withdraw from current joint ventures, or don't bother giving investment in Vietnam serious consideration, preferring to place their money into countries of a more attractive nature. The warning signs are there.'

I have perused many of Mr Eaton's speeches to various international forums in recent years and feel that there is someone who genuinely wants to see Vietnam do well. he wants to do business there and he wants others to follow his example. The government in Hanoi surely can ill afford to alienate such people. It certainly cannot turn round and say this is just an anti-Vietnamese fabrication of the Western media — although this is what tends to happen when criticisms are voiced.

IS A U-TURN POSSIBLE?

Despite the hard-line Marxist-Leninist rhetoric of continued class struggle and the eventual victory of socialism over capitalism, which one continues to see expressed by some conservative leaders or by certain official newspapers and journals, it seems most unlikely that the process of economic reform and transformation of the country is going to be reversed.

I return to a point made earlier: Vietnam is still a very poor country. The government and the party say so over and over again. I do not think there is a single Vietnamese with any desire to remain poor. As in China, the survival in power of the Communist Party rests heavily on its ability to bring about a significant level of prosperity for the vast majority of people — particularly, if the insistence that it is the true representative of the will of the people is to have any meaning at all.

There is a great debate going on at all levels in Vietnam about the country's future direction. There are some who want to see the reform process speeded up — abandon all the dogma and go for broke. There are some who want to see the process slowed down and brought under tighter party control. There are even a few who would like to see it stopped altogether, regarding *Doi Moi* as leading the country down the road to destruction and domination by the very forces defeated in 1975.

'The country has entered the stage of industrialization and modernization,' observes the *Quan Doi Nhan Dan*. 'This is a great opportunity for the revolution. However, current and future danger and challenges are still creating pressure and difficulties for us.' These dangers, the army newspaper observed, could be condensed into two issues: the danger of economic backwardness and the danger of 'deviation' due to the degeneration of the of the ruling party (especially the greed and corruption that now permeates the structure from the national to the local level through the unprecedented money-making opportunities offered by the 'open door' policies).

The last point cannot be ignored. The party has faced many dangers in the past, but the present ones are of a different kind than before. Vietnam is not at war any more. There is no one at present that seems to be considering, or to have the capability, to invade Vietnam. The problems are now those of adjusting to peace and they are all internal. Like Communist parties around the world, the Vietnamese party is having to redefine its role or face extinction. As the masses benefit from the reforms, enjoy a better life and become more educated, they will ask more and more questions about their rulers.

The party is certainly responding. In a tough speech to a Ho Chi Minh City party congress, Secretary General Do Muoi described the old southern capital as a 'prime ground' for political sabotage. 'Hostile forces' were working for the 'collapse of the revolutionary administration of Vietnam', he said, warning of attempts to create political and economic instability and cultural 'pollution'.[5] The comments come after several years of relative tolerance during which Ho Chi Minh City has been allowed to become the centre for foreign investment and to establish links with overseas Vietnamese communities. The city has proportionately fewer party members than most parts of the country, and many of these are veterans who fear the links with the outside world are changing Vietnam too fast and thus threatening party control.

There is little doubt that in advance of the Eighth Party Congress – the first in five years, during which so much has changed in Vietnam – there was a strong upsurge in conservative sentiment. This led some observers to see a struggle for control between liberal and conservative elements in the party leadership which the latter appeared to have won, thus threatening the future of foreign investment. The evidence for this is scanty, based on a few speeches and the campaign against spiritual pollution, including Western product advertising, described in the last chapter.

On the one side we have statements like this from Do Muoi: 'Though the collapse of socialism in the former Soviet Union and Eastern Europe caused a temporary recession for socialism, the common trend is to continue striving in many ways and by different methods for a better, more civilized society – that is socialism. Since its establishment, our Party has always been loyal to the goals of national independence and socialism. The development of Vietnam's revolution bears out that socialism is the only right choice that accords with evolutionary law and gains popular consensus.' Vietnam cannot survive or prosper, he insists, unless the Communist Party is in full control, and that means keeping its hands firmly on the economic reins.[6]

But he also agrees that Vietnam has to industrialize. The main draft document for the party congress insisted on the need to transform agrarian Vietnam into a prosperous industrialized society within 25 years. This will require discipline at the administrative level; the development of science and technology; better education; a deeper renovation of the economic system, especially the banking, financial and monetary aspects, the encouragement of individual creativity; and an opening up not only to the capital and technology of the outside world but also to at least some of its ideas.

Prime Minister Vo Van Kiet recognizes this need. 'We are not doing industrialization in a closed centrally planned economy. Highlighting sovereignty and independence, industrialization should help exploit all comparative advantages of the country to integrate more into the global and regional economic development to gain optimal economic effectiveness and better meet the needs of national development.'[7]

Vietnam has to be integrated into ASEAN for a start. Then it faces further integration into wider regional and global structures. This cannot be done successfully by clinging to old dogma. These are the best reasons of all for thinking that only a leadership which can deliver all these things is likely to be able to hold onto power with widespread public acceptance in the years ahead. There may still be some twists and turns on the road, but a U-turn does not seem possible.

PROBLEM AREAS IDENTIFIED – AND SOLVED

There can be no argument, however, that Vietnam is gaining negative international media coverage for some of the obvious pitfalls which are lurking foreign investors at present. These have already been discussed elsewhere in this book, but as a reminder the key ones are: excessive bureaucracy, ambiguous business regulations, inadequate infrastructure support, difficulties with the implementation and inter-pretation of the law, the non-convertibility of the Dong, a shortage of hard currency, and the difficulties of obtaining project financing.

The system is not perfect, but what needs to be borne in mind is that senior members of the government clearly recognize this and are intent on doing something about it.

Le Dang Doanh, President of the Central Institute of Economic Management, says: 'Reform has brought about some important initial changes such as the reduction of administrative procedure for business activities like licensing, foreign investment, and import/export. But it is also obvious that the speed of economic and admin-istrative reforms has not yet caught up with the demands of development. We have passed the smooth part of the *Doi Moi* road, which has achieved results only through liberalization and the removal of restrictions. We cannot keep reducing taxes as a means to attract more foreign investment, just as we cannot encourage the farmers by simply contracting more farming land to them.

'The coming period requires new approaches to solve more complicated problems. There is a pressing need to reform public finance, establish a capital market — including a stock market — and increase the domestic savings ratio. We also have to be patient in implementing tasks to help achieve high effectiveness in state businesses, restructuring current business circles, and applying different methods to attract capital for modernizing equipment.

'Progress must be made to increase the power of the state bodies fighting corruption and smuggling, and to create a healthy environ-ment for domestic and foreign investment. We need specific regulations to solve problems concerning land use rights and to decrease property speculation and false property price booms.'

Economist Nguyen Xuan Oanh argues, the first stage of reform is now over and the second stage, which he calls 'deepening finance', must begin with a far more radical approach to problems. The key issue, he argues, is that the present financing system is inadequate to fund the nation's ambitious development plans.

The economy has been spearheaded by real estate and construction industry while manufacturing remains the poor relative. 'But if we want to sustain our growth in the next 10–15 years the so far accumulated capital should be channelled to the manufacturing sector in a massive way.'

In the 'finance deepening' stage, the banking and financial services sector have to achieve a much larger share in the economy. In the absence of an efficient and more business-like banking system, coupled with the elusive path towards corporatization of state-owned enterprises and uncertainty about the establishment of the first securities market, the domestic capital market is unlikely to operate at full swing.

Yet, it would be well to remember that the process of *Doi Moi* was only launched in the mid-1980s and that serious foreign investment only began to flow in from the beginning of the 1990s, Thus, Vietnam has come a remarkably long way in a very short space of time. Even the so-called Four Tigers of Asia did not achieve their economic miracle overnight.

'The speed of development in this country is much faster than it was in Taiwan at a comparable stage in the development process,' insists Taiwanese business executive Y.T.Young. 'They're in a much better position than we were. But to do what we did and what they are trying to do is a difficult and very time-consuming process. They need time and they shouldn't be rushed.'

MPI'S PROMISES

Professor Tran Xuan Gia, who holds a doctorate in finance, formerly lectured in the area of pricing until he was brought into the government as Vice Minister of the Ministry of Planning and Investment. The MPI was created in 1995 by merging the former State Planning Committee, a long-standing body which had drawn up the government's various economic strategic plans, and the State Committee for Cooperation and Investment, set up in the 1980s to handle the approval procedures for foreign direct investments.

The idea behind the merger was to streamline the procedures for integrating foreign investment with the overall economic plan and create a 'one door' mechanism for project approval. It also reflects the government's determination to keep the entire invest project approval process under tight control, not allowing different areas of the country to make their own deals with foreign investors — as has happened in China — to the possible detriment of overall national development.

In an interview in Hanoi,[8] the vice-minister acknowledged many of the investors' complaints already outlined, while also stressing the actions the government was taking to deal with them.

If Vietnam was to achieve its targets of attracting – and equally importantly, absorbing – another $15 billion in FDI in the next three years or so, there were several steps that had to be taken, he said. These were:

- **Continue the open door policy.** 'We want to be friendly to all countries and to welcome their involvement in the Vietnamese economy. The normalization of relations with the United States was a highly significant step in this regard.'
- **Create more favourable conditions for attracting foreign investment.** 'We must incorporate foreign investment more closely into our medium and long-term economic planning. We have to work hard to develop the legal environment to provide security for foreign investors. We have to have to press ahead with administrative reform in order to reduce the complicated approval procedures that deter potential foreign investors and streamline the whole process so that it can be completed in a short time.'
- **Create greater socio-economic stability.** 'There are growing economic differences between various areas that is a great source of concern. We must do all we can to prevent a further widening of the gap between rich and poor. We cannot use administrative order to force foreign companies to invest in any particular sector or part of the country. But we can encourage this by creating a more beneficial regime for investors willing to move into difficult areas or sectors in order to help us achieve our economic equalization goals.'

But with Vietnam facing growing competition for foreign capital from other countries in the region, what did specific advantages did the country have to offer to overcome some of the recent negative publicity? The vice-minister chose a business analogy to answer. Manufacturers hoping to succeed in the marketplace had to ensure two things: (1) that the quality of their goods was relatively high, while (2) the price was competitive.

Vietnam could offer both quality and price. It had a large labour force, with a high level of discipline and skill, readily adaptable to new ideas and new techniques, but at a price in terms of wages that others could not challenge. It was up to the government now to create some more attractive packaging for this product, through clear-cut investment-related policies that benefited Vietnam and the international business community.

Seeking to soothe foreign investors' nerves, Professor Gia said: 'We need to do more to make sure we can attract the best types of investment applications, so we don't have projects being cancelled or withdrawn. We must make sure, too, that we spread development to the regions and the sectors of the economy where this is most needed. We believe this is entirely normal for a country in our position. No potential investor should think there will be any uncertainty. We want to make things better for all types of investors. New policies are being announced all the time. And what foreign investors should always remember is that the doors will remain open.'

THE FIFTH TIGER?

Apart from examining the economic and legal environment in Vietnam for the foreign businessman, this book has also sought to consider the country's recent socio-economic development, and, in particular, its prospects for becoming the next 'Tiger' economy in Pacific Asia.

In every encounter with Vietnamese officials, businessmen and analysts, I have raised this question. What has emerged from all these conversations is a strong sense of optimism. It's not guaranteed, people say, but 'there is a good chance we can do it'.

The Vietnamese have a saying 'Ngheo lau, Gian chong' [various accents omitted] which translates as 'if the fates are against you, poverty will cling for a long time; if you're lucky, you can become rich very quickly'. The vast majority of Vietnamese have been poor for many generations and recent generations have little chance to escape from that poverty. But in the last few years, as policies have been created to release the pent-up money-making skill and ingenuity of the people, genuine success stories have appeared.

According to a Vietnamese official: 'It doesn't take long, sometimes only a couple of years, once the opportunity is created, for some people to grab it with both hands. Look at the rural areas. Farmers had no options for a long time to show any initiative. But once they had, some genuine entrepreneurs quickly emerged. All of a sudden they began looking for commercial opportunities. Some of them are rearing alligators, some snakes, others eels, and making a lot of money.'

Despite the obvious pockets of prosperity, many Vietnamese are still very poor. Life is still very hard. But there is a strong sense of optimism that comes through very strongly. People believe life will get better. If they are not prospering now, then they are in the queue and their turn will come.

I have travelled widely throughout Asia and many other parts of the developing world since the mid-1960s. I have seen a number of countries pulling themselves up by their bootstraps, as well as some unable seemingly to escape from the trough of poverty and despair. I can recall going to South Korea in the late 1960s and seeing a very poor country in the grip of a military dictatorship with only a primitive industrial base. Who would have thought then that within 20 years Korea would be one of Asia's most dynamic economic powerhouses? The key element was that the Koreans showed great resilience. They believed in themselves, were willing to make sacrifices and were optimistic that they would succeed. The Vietnamese show these same characteristics.

So, finally then, is Vietnam a good place in which to invest time and energy to do business? And, if so, is this the right time to be making that effort. Despite the problems I discussed at various times in this book, I believe Vietnam is worth serious consideration right now.

No foreign businessman I have quoted in this book has pretended that Vietnam is an easy place in which to do business. But even that can be a strength. As one astute Hong Kong businessman remarked: 'I don't want it to be easy. If it's a tough market to crack that keeps out my opposition and gives me a free run. But you can do business here. It takes times, patience and a strong sense of commitment no matter what happens. But it can be done.'

Some businessmen suggest that, despite the bad publicity, Vietnam is actually an easier spot in which to invest than neighbouring China. But China is a far bigger potential market, and is further down the road to economic development so that one has to ask whether it is worth making all the effort for a country of 75 million people, few of which have a great deal of money to spend.

But Vietnam can no longer be considered in isolation. Taking a long-term perspective, by the turn of the century it will be a fully-participating member of ASEAN, which by then, with the admission of Cambodia, Laos and Myanmar (Burma), will offer a total market of some 500 million people. Narrowing the focus somewhat, Vietnam will be a leading member of a looser economic cooperative grouping now emerging under the title of the Greater Mekong Subregion (MRS). This comprises a population of some 230 million at present in Cambodia, Laos, Myanmar, Thailand, Vietnam, and Yunnan Province in Southwest China. The common link is the Mekong River which either borders or flows through all six areas. There are common borders, close cultural, historical and linguistic links, and common natural and mineral resources which they can exploit together.

This may be a far more viable grouping than ASEAN for a foreign businessman looking for a regional business base with enough customers to make big investments in manufacturing and distribution worthwhile. With the help of private investment and through aid from such international organizations as the Asian Development Bank, the MRS has begun to explore greater cooperation. Many of the regional road and rail projects discussed in Chapter 5 on infrastructure come under this heading.

Thailand is the natural dominant presence in the MRS at present, but Vietnam has many attributes which will make it a strong competitor in the years ahead.

I would suggest, therefore, that it is from this larger perspective that one has to consider Vietnam's future – its ability to become a new Asian Tiger and also its potential as a base for significant amounts of foreign investment. The arguments for moving in now look fairly strong.

The advanced Asian economies – Korean, Singapore and Taiwan – have already demonstrated their recognition of Vietnam's importance, as have some of the emerging Asean economies, notably Singapore and Thailand. Western businesses need to get their foot in the door now, perhaps enduring some years of frustration and difficulty, in order to avoid being squeezed out in the long run.

One possibility would be to tie up with a regional partner to ease some of the difficulties of breaking into the Vietnamese market. Some European companies have already found it advantageous to sign joint venture agreements with some of the bigger (often government-supported) firms from Singapore, for example.[9] Singaporean investment has grown rapidly in the mid-1990s, with manufacturing accounting for 61 per cent by the end of 1995. Again, there are comparisons between Singapore's early days as an independent country in the 1960s and Vietnam today. Older Singaporeans seem to find Vietnam's current atmosphere of fragile, improvisatory achievement very similar to their own youth. This tends to breed a tolerance for many of the problems facing investors today, summed up by the thought that 'we did it [achieved a strong economy from unpromising beginnings], and you will too'.

This attitude seems to typify many of the Asian investments in Vietnam. Businessmen from the region can remember their own humble national beginnings and that seems to make them more tolerant and willing to wait for Vietnam to 'get its act together'. Western businessmen have no such memory and therefore tend to be more impatient of the seeming 'slow progress' of the Vietnamese in putting together an investor-friendly environment.

In the final analysis, one should look at Vietnam's history in deciding whether it is worth 'taking the plunge' as a business investor. The fact is that every time the Vietnamese have set their sights on achieving some goal — no matter how great the odds against success — they have succeeded. Their military victories in this regard speak for themselves. I believe the economic victory will be just as dramatic — even if it takes as long to achieve. And I also believe that, in the long run, foreign businessmen will have an important share in that victory.

NOTES

1. Vietnam Economic Times, March 1996.
2. 27 March 1996.
3. The technology flow is invariably from the foreign to the Vietnamese side, it should be pointed out.
4. Interviewed in Bangkok 5 May 1996.
5. 'Hostile Forces Threaten Rule', South China Morning Post Weekly Edition, 18 May 1996
6. Interview in Vietnam Economic Times, May 1996.
7. Ibid.
8. 2 May 1996. I don't know whether it was just polite flattery, but ministry officials told me it was extremely rare for Professor Gia to accept interview requests from foreign journalists and writers.
9. See Murray G. and Perera A., *Singapore:The Global City State* (1995, China Library) for a detailed discussion of this strategy.

APPENDIX A:

KEY FACTS ABOUT VIETNAM

[As of January 1 1996]

Area 330,991 sq.km

Population 73.5 million. Estimate for 2000 is 82 million, with population growth rates of 1.6 per cent for urban areas and 2–2.5 per cent for the countryside.

Density 219 people per sq.km.

Ethnic breakdown Vietnamese (86.8 per cent), Minorities (10 per cent), Chinese (1.5 per cent), Khmer (1.4 per cent).

Major cities Hanoi (capital), Ho Chi Minh City, Haiphong, Hue, Can Tho, Nha Trang, Da Nang and Vung Tau.

GDP 22.2 trillion VND ($20.2 billion at 1995 average exchange rate).

Annual Growth Rate 9–10 per cent since 1991.

Exchange rate 10,900/11,000 VND=$1.

Exports $5.5 billion (1995) including crude oil, minerals and coal (30 per cent). rice, rubber, other agricultural products and marine products (50 per cent), manaufactured goods, mainly textiles (20 per cent).

Imports $7.5 billion (1995), including raw materials, fuel, steel, fertilizer (60 per cent), machinery, vehicles and motorcycles, spare parts (24 per cent), consumer goods (16 per cent).

Major trading partners Taiwan, Japan, Singapore, South Korea, Hong Kong, Australia, France and the United States.

Total Foreign Investment (1988–95) by sectors Manufacturing $8,500 million, hotels and tourism $6,300 million, oil & gas $1,130 million, communications $1,060 million, industrial zones $335 million, finance and banking $250 million, export processing zones $202 million, services $155 million, housing development $86 million, fisheries $61 million.

Leading Investors

Country	No. of projects	Investment capital
Taiwan	237	$3,317,777
Hong Kong	185	$2,153,962
Japan	127	$2,035,693
Singapore	114	$1,524,023
South Korea	137	$1,506,523
United States	54	$1,141,721
Malaysia	42	$846,662
Australia	47	$703,243
France	70	$638,591
Sweden	15	$584,819
British Virgin Islands	29	$514,276
United Kingdom	19	$477,097

Investment by Area

Province/city	No. of projects	Investment capital
Ho Chi Minh City	507	$5,822,794
Hanoi	222	$3,674,018
Dong Nai	145	$2,379,655
Haiphong	46	$793,781
Vung Tau/Baria	47	$773,944
Quang Nam/Da Nang	36	$496,769
Song Be	59	$453,117

APPENDIX B:

KEY EVENTS IN VIETNAM'S DEVELOPMENT

22 Dec. 1944	Founding of the first unit of the Vietnam People's Army commanded by General Vo Nguyen Giap.
2 Sept. 1945	An estimated 100,000 people crowd into Hanoi's Ba Dinh Square to hear Ho Chi Minh read the Declaration of Independence creating the Democratic Republic of Vietnam.
Nov. 1946	DRV government elected by the National Assembly, headed by President Ho Chi Minh.
19 Dec. 1945	First Indochina War officially begins.
May 1954	The Vietnamese flag flies over the French bunkers at Dien Bien Phu heralding the end of French colonial rule.
2 Aug. 1964	Gulf of Tonkin incident precipitates full American military involvement in Vietnam.
8 Mar. 1965	Some 3,500 US marines land in Da Nang at the start of major troop build-up to eventual figure of 500,000.
2 Sept. 1969	President Ho Chi Minh dies.
27 Jan. 1973	Signing of Paris peace Agreement ends US involvement in Vietnam but does not bring intended peace.
30 April 1975	Tank #843 of the NVA 2nd Army Division crashes through the iron gates of the presidential palace in Saigon marking the end of the Vietnam War and the unfication of the country.
3 June 1976	Formation of the Socialist Republic of Vietnam.
1979	Vietnam occupies Cambodia to end four years of border clashes with the Khmer Rouge. China invaded northern Vietnam in relatiation but is repulsed with heavy losses.
1986	The Sixth Congress of the Communist Party of Vietnam, known as the 'congress of renovation' launches radical economic reforms under the name of *Doi Moi*.
1987	Foreign investment law passed.
1988	First step in agricultural liberalization.
	Initial reform of the banking system.
	Establishment of two-tier banking system.
1989	Dong revaluation to free market rates.
	Operational autonomy for state-owned enterprises.
	Export subsidies eliminated.
	Tax system revised.
1990	State Bank rules on banks, credit cooperatives and financial companies passed.
	New laws on sales, profit and consumption taxes.
1991	Currency exchange trading centres created.
	State monopoly over international trade dismantled.
	1992 New constitution adopted.
1993	Extensive land use rights for farmers announced.

	Bankruptcy law passed.
	First enterprise privatized.
	Elimination of import quotas begun.
	Full price liberalization.
1994	State conglommerates founded.
	Interbank forex market established.
11 July 1995	Relations finally normalized with the United States.
28 July 1995	Vietnam joins Association of Southeast Asian Nations (ASEAN).

APPENDIX C:

KEY LAWS

Laws are passed by the National Assembly. Ordinances are passed by the Standing Committee of the National Assembly when the assembly is not in session. Decrees are passed by the government and generally implement the laws or ordinances. Decrees are often accompanied by more detailed regulations. Circulars are issued by individual ministries and usually provide guidance as to how a particular ministry ill administer a law, ordinance or decree. Guidelines are not legal instruments. They are policy outlines issued by the Prime Minister indicating that governmental committees should be set up to deal with issues. The recital of each legal instrument normally sets out the other legal instruments to which it is subordinate. If a legal instrument is intended to replace an earlier instrument, this will usually be mentioned towards the end of the legal instrument.

JOINT VENTURES

Decree #215 UB/LXT issued by the SCCI (now the MPI) dated February 8,1995, to streamline procedures associated with direct foreign investment in Vietnam. It sets out the procedures to be followed by JV companies and 100 per cent foreign-owned enterprises following the granting of their investment licence by the SCCI and the time limits within which they must attend to those procedures. It also regulates many other procedures and transactions associated with the operation of Business Cooperation Contracts, JVs and 100 per cent foreign-owned enterprises. The new decree replaces 19 others including several industry specific regulations, streamlining this area into one legal instrument.

Organization and Management of Enterprises

The management boards of JVs
- Each party shall appoint members to the board in a proportion corresponding to their capital contributions, but the Vietnamese party shall appoint at least two members. If the JV is between an existing JV and a foreign company then the existing JV shall appoint at least two members one of whom must be a Vietnamese citizen.
- The board must meet at least once a year. Meetings may be convened by the chairman or by two-thirds of the members of the board. Two thirds of the members of the board must be present to constitute a legal meeting. Members may attend by duly authorized proxy.
- The following matters require a unanimous resolution of the board:
  - annual and long-term production, business projects, budgets and loans to the enterprise;
  - amendment of and addition to the JV charter; and
  - the appointment and dismissal of the chairman of the board, the general; director, the first deputy general director and the chief accountant.

- Other matters require the approval of two thirds majority of the members of the board attending the meeting. If a unanimous resolution on any of the matters requiring a unanimous resolution cannot be reached, then the board may choose the following alternatives:
  - refer the matter to a reconciliation committee made up of an equal number of representatives from the JV parties and chaired by a SCCI representative. The decision of a simple majority of this committee will be final and binding on the parties;
  - request the SCCI to act as arbitrator. Its decision will be final and binding; or
  - dissolution of the enterprise.
- The duties of the chairman of the board will include convening and chairing meetings of the board and playing a key role in supervising the implementation of the decisions of the board. It is not part of the chairman's duties to give direct instructions to the general director or the deputy general director of the enterprise.
- Within six months prior to the end of the term of the board it must hold a meeting to review the activities of the board during the term, arrange for the appointment by the parties of the new members of the board and hand over the management of the enterprise to the newly appointed members.
- When the term of the enterprise expires or is otherwise terminated prior to the expiry of the term, the board must establish a liquidation committee and set out its terms and obligations. Once the liquidation has been completed, the committee must present a report to the board which will resolve outstanding matters in accordance with the relevant laws.
- Board members shall not receive a salary but they may receive emoluments to be determined by the board for their activities as board members. This expense must be included in the enterprise management expenses.

The general director of JVs

- The general director and deputy general director, unanimously appointed by the board, are responsible for the management of the day-to-day activities of the JV.
- Where only one deputy general director has been appointed, that person will act as first deputy general director. The general director or first deputy general director must be a Vietnamese citizen residing in Vietnam. The duties of the general director and hs/her deputy will be determined by the board. They may not concurrently hold positions in other enterprises including those of the JV parties.
- Where the chairman is also the general director, the two roles must be kept separate depending on the nature of the activities carried out and the documents executed by him/her. A document cannot bear his/her signature in both capacities.
- The general director and his deputy are responsible to the board for the operations of the enterprise. The general director has the right to make the final decision on the day-to-day operations of the JV. He must consult the first deputy general director before deciding on issues directly affecting the implementation of the resolutions of the board and the following matters:
  - organizational machinery, personnel, salaries and bonuses;
  - appointment and dismissal of personnel in key positions in the enterprise.
  - periodical and annual financial reports of the enterprise; and
  - signing of economic contracts.

- The opinion of the general director shall prevail in these matters, but the deputy general; director may voice his/her dissent at the next meeting of the board or he/she may request the chairman to convene an extraordinary meeting of the board to resolve the matter.
- It is the responsibility of the general director and the deputy general director to implement the decisions of the board if they are not contrary to the laws of Vietnam, the JV charter or the JV contract. If a resolution of the board is not suitable in practice then they may request the chairman to convene an extraordinary meeting of the board to re-examine the matter and resolve the problem.
- The general director and the first deputy general director are entitled to refuse the direct personal directives of the chairman or other members of the board where a directive of the board is unlawful.
- The general director and deputy general directors shall sign labour contracts with the chairman pursuant to the relevant provisions of the Labour Code.

Enterprise Management Company
- A foreign investment enterprise may hire a management company to manage the operation of the enterprise. The decision to hire a management company must be approved by the unanimous resolution of the board.
- The contract of hire of a management company must be approved by the SCCI, which may not approve a contract which does not result in the efficient operation of the enterprise.
- The management company must be registered in its field of operation. When in Vietnam it must register with the people's committee in the city or province where the head office of the enterprise is located and comply with all Vietnamese laws including the payment of taxes.
- The management company shall operate under the name, seal and bank account of the enterprise.
- The performance of the management company must not have any negative impact on the objectives of the investment project or the interests of the state of Vietnam was prescribed in the investment license.
- The foreign investment enterprise will be responsible for the operations of the management company in accordance with the management contract. The management company will be directly responsible for activities beyond the scope of the management contract.
- Any disputes between the management company and the foreign investment enterprise shall be solved by amicable negotiation and failing that by the Vietnam Economic Court in accordance with the laws of Vietnam.

Capital contributions

- The price of equipment, materials and technology used as capital contribution will be agreed between the parties.
- Once the contribution has been certified by the board of management the enterprise must submit a report to the SCCI within 30 days.
- An enterprise may only increase its capital for the following reasons:

- to expand the scale of production or to add in accordance with list of investments encouraged by the Vietnamese Government.
- to maintain business production in the case of natural disaster or other difficulties.

• The capital of a foreign investment enterprise may not be increased for the following reasons:

- to raise the quota for duty-free import of machinery, equipment, materials, transport which is not necessary for the capital construction of the enterprise;
- for the sake of operational objectives which are not in accordance with the government's investment policy;
- where there are not adequate conditions for expansion of production.

Increase in the equity of a Vietnamese party to a JV and the acquisition of part of the capital of a 100 per cent foreign-owned enterprise.
• For important economic joint ventures, the parties must provide in the JV contract for the gradual increase in equity of the enterprise owned by the Vietnamese party.
• For important 100 per cent foreign-owned enterprises, the SCCI will guide the application for the investment licence by the foreign investor to include the possibility for a Vietnamese enterprise to acquire part of the capital to convert it into a JV.

Reinvestment

Foreign investors using their share of profits from the foreign investment enterprise to re-invest in the enterprise or to invest in another project in Vietnam will be entitled to a refund of taxes paid on these profits.

Transfer of assets

• The voluntary transfer of assets from the foreign party to the Vietnamese party without payment will be provided for in the JV contract and the investment license.
• The assets to be transferred when the project is finished must be guaranteed operational.
• The SCCI will grant favourable financial treatment under the current regulations to the projects where the foreign party transfers its assets to the Vietnamese party at the completion of operations.

Taxation

• The transfer of a interest in an enterprise must be approved by the SCCI.
• The transferor will be required to pay tax at the rate of 25 per cent on any capital gains made on the transfer.
• All equipment, machinery, spare parts, production materials, production and business mean and facilities including transportation means imported for investment in capital construction and formation of a foreign investment enterprise or the creation of fixed assets to implement a BCC will be exempt from import tax in accordance with Article 76 of decree #18 CP, dated April 16,1993.

Formation, appraisal and implementation of an investment project

Article 9.1 sets out the documents which need to be submitted with an application for a foreign investment license.

- The applicant must submit 12 copies of the application, including one original. Each copy should be bound in a cover to protect the documents.
- Within five days of receiving the application, the SCCI must send a copy to all concerned ministries who in turn must submit their respective opinions to the SCCI within a further 20 days.
- Within 50 days of receipt of the application in the Group A the SCCI must submit its opinion to the prime minister, and must notify the applicant of the latter's decision within seven days. The chairman of the SCCI will make decisions on applications in the Group B category, and shall advise investors within 45 days.

Implementation of a project

- The contents of the investment licence must be published in a local or central newspaper within 30 days of the date of issue.
- The first board meeting must be held within 90 days of the issue of the investment license. The principal objectives of the first board meeting are:
  - to approve the composition of the board;
  - to elect a chairman and a deputy chairman;
  - to appoint a general director, deputy general directors and chief accountant;
  - to determine the working relationship between the board and the executive officers of the enterprise, the chairman and the general director and first deputy director;
  - to determine a plan for the contribution of capital by the parties;
  - to determine a production and business plan;
- Immediately following their appointment, the general director and the deputy general directors must:
  - arrange to have a seal of the enterprise made and registered;
  - register the office of the enterprise with the local people's committee;
  - open an account of the enterprise at a bank. If the enterprise is required to open an account for foreign loans, this must be approved by the State Bank of Vietnam.
  - register the plan for labour recruitment;
  - draw up an inventory of materials and equipment required to be imported;
  - complete procedures for obtaining permits to carry out construction work;
  - complete procedures for opening a representative office or branch office of the enterprise in another location (if necessary). This must be approved by the SCCI.
- Each of the above tasks must be completed within six months of receiving the investment licence.
- The time limits and obligations set out above apply equally where practicable to a 100 per cent foreign-owned enterprise as they do to a JV.

Liquidation of an enterprise

- An enterprise may be liquidated in the following circumstances:
  - the term of the JV has expired;
  - the enterprise is terminated prior to the expiry of the term for any of the following reasons: (a) force majeure, (b) one or both joint venture parties fail to perform their obligations, (c) other causes in the contract.
  - the enterprise is terminated by the SCCI for a breach of the objectives.
- A liquidation committee will be formed in accordance with Article 39 of decree #18/CP under the direction of the board.
- All activities of the enterprise must cease once the decision to form a liquidation committee has been made.
- Within 30 days after the liquidation, the liquidation committee must advertise the results and return the seal of the enterprise.

Opening branches and representative offices

- If a foreign enterprise wishes to open a branch or representative office it must submit, with its application for its investment licence, justification to open such an office and an opinion from the local people's committee.
- The same procedure must be followed after the investment licence has been obtained.

Allocation of responsibilities of state management

Ministries, ministerial agencies, government agencies and people's committees are responsible for guiding and inspecting the operations and activities of foreign investment enterprises.

Inspecting the activities of the enterprise

- Inspections of the implementation of the provisions of the investment licence will be undertaken by the SCCI with assistance of related branches and localities.
- They will be conducted not more than once a year. If necessary, inspections will be carried out by the ministries and people's committees also not more than once a year.
- An extraordinary inspection will be held when there is evidence of a breach of the terms of the investment licence or the laws of Vietnam.
- Any organization conducting an unauthorized inspection or taking advantage of an inspection to cause inconvenience to the operations of the enterprise will be responsible for damage caused by the inspection.

APPENDIX D:

TAXATION

CORPORATE INCOME TAX

Enterprises with foreign owned capital and business cooperation foreign partners pay corporate income tax at 25 per cent of the profit made except in privileged cases which enjoy lower tax rates in order to encourage investment. In respct of projects for exploitation of oil and gas and some rare and precious natural resources, the rate may be higher than 25 per cent of the profit made depending on the nature and characteristics of each project. Projects liable to the 25 per cent of profits tax, however, may be considered for exemption in the first profit-making year and reduction of 50 per cent in the following two years.

1 Investment incentives in privileged cases are:

- Twenty per cent for projects having at least two of the following requirements:

  - Employing 500 or more workers;
  - Using advanced technology;
  - exporting at least 80 per cent of its products;
  - having prescribed capital or contributed capital in business cooperation of $10 million or more.

Projects in this category may be considered for tax exemption in the first two profit-making years and for reduction of 50 per cent in the following three.

- Fifteen per cent for projects of:

  - infrastructure construction;
  - exploitation of natural resources, except oil and gas and rare, precious resources;
  - heavy industry (metallurgy, basic chemicals, mechanical manufacture, cement etc.);
  - investment in the mountains and regions of harsh natural and socio-economic conditions (including hotel projects but not rare or precious resources exploration);
  - non-compensatory transfer of properties to Vietnam.

Projects in this category may be considered for income tax excemption for the first two profit-making years and a reduction of 50 per of cent for the following four years.

- Ten per cent for enterprises with foreign capital carrying out projects of:

  - building infrastructures on mountains and in regions of harsh natural and socieconomic conditions.
  - afforestation;
  - designated 'special importance'.

Projects in this category may be considered for tax exemption for the first four profit-making years and reduction of up to 50 per cent in the following four.

2 Foreign organizations and individuals that reinvest their share of profits for a period of three or more years are entitled to a refund of tax paid on the amounts involved.

3 In industrial zones, foreign invested enterprises and foreign partners pay profit tax as follows:

- Manufacturing enterprises — 18 per cent.
- Enterprises exporting at least 80 per cent of their products — 12 per cent.

In both cases, exemptions are allowed for two years from the first profit-making year.

- Services — 22 per cent, with an exemption in the first profit-making year.

4 Enterprises in export processing zones pay tax as follows:

- Manufacturing — 10 per cent, with exemption in the first four profit-making years;
- Services — 15 per cent, with exemption for two years.

5 BOT companies will only face a 10 per cent tax rate with exemption in the first four years of profit, and a reduction for another four years.

WITHHOLDING TAX

Foreign organizations and individuals shall be subject to a withholding tax on overseas remittance of profits at the following rates:

1 Five per cent where the contributed prescribed capital or business cooperation capital is $10 million or more. This rate also applies to all foreign investors in BOT projects.

2 Seven per cent where the invested capital is $5 million or more.

3 10 per cent in all other cases.

IMPORT TAX

Enterprises with foreign capital and parties to a business cooperation, including BOT companies and sub-contractors in BOT projects, are entitled to exemption from import tax in the following cases:

- Machinery, equipment, spare parts and production-business facilities (including transport means) and other materials imported into Vietnam for investment in the capital construction of the enterprise or to be used as fixed assets of the contractual business cooperation;
- Raw materials, spare parts, accessories and other materials imported for the production of export goods. These articles, when imported, are subject to a temporary import duty payment but a tax repayment proportional to the export volume will be made;
- Patents, technical know-how, technological processes, technical assistance, etc. contributed by the foreign partners as part of the prescribed capital or to a business cooperation shall be exempt from all taxes in relation to the transfer of technology.

APPENDIX E:

USEFUL ADDRESSES AND TELEPHONE NUMBERS

GOVERNMENT OFFICES

Hanoi

IDD Code 84–4
Ministry of Planning and Investment, 2 Hoang Van Thu Street, Tel. 8458261, Fax. 8232494.
Ministry of Industry, Tel. 8267870. Fax. 8269033.
Ministry of Construction, 37 Le Dai Hanh Street, Tel. 8268271 Fax. 8215591.
Ministry of Education and Training, 17 Dai Co Viet Street, Tel. 8264795.
Ministry of Aquatic Products, 57 Ngoc Khanh Street, Tel. 8325620/8.
Ministry of Trade and Tourism, 31 Trang Tien Street, Tel. 8264693, Fax. 8264696.
Ministry of Labour, Invalids & Social Affairs, 12 Ngo Quyen Street, 8246137, Fax.
　8248036.
Ministry of Energy, 18 Tran Nguyen Han Street, 8255786.
Ministry of Foreign Affairs, 1 Ton That Dam Street, Tel. 8458201.
Ministry of Food Industry and Agriculture, Bach Thao Street, Tel. 8468160.
Ministry of Interior Affairs, 15 Tran Binh Trong Street, Tel. 8268131.
Ministry of Science, Technhology & Environment, 39 Tran Hung Dao Street, Tel. 8252731.
Ministry of Finance, 8 Phan Huy Chu Street, Tel. 8262991, Fax. 8262266.
Ministry of Defence, 28 Dien Bien Phu Street, Tel. 8468101.
Ministry of Culture & Information, 51 Ngo Quyen Street, Tel. 8253231.
Ministry of Water Resources, 164 Tran Quang Khai Street, Tel. 8268141.
Ministry of Justice, 25A Cat Linh street, Tel. 825339.
Civil Aviation Administration of Vietnam, Gia Lam Airport, 8271513.
PetroVietnam, 22 Ngo Quyen Street, Tel. 8252526.
General Post Office, 75 Dinh Tien Hoang Street, Tel. 8262707.
Entry-Exit Permit Department, 40A Hang Bai Street, Tel. 8266200.
The State Bank of Vietnam, 7 Le Lai Street, Tel. 8258388, Fax. 8244662.
Chamber of Commerce & Industry, 33 Ba Trieu Street, Tel. 8262894.

Ho Chi Minh City

IDD Code 84–8
Chamber of Commerce & Industry, 171 Vo Thi Sau, District 3, Tel. 8230339.
City Customs Office, 2 Ham Nghi, Tel. 8297449.
City Planning Committee, 30–32 Le Thanh Ton street, District 1, Tel. 8290904.
City Post Office, 125 Hai Ba Trung, District 1, Tel. 8293310.
Department of External Relations, 6 Thai Van Lung Street, District 1, 8224128.
Tax Bureau, 140 Nguyen Thi Minh Khai Street, District 3, Tel. 8292141.
Foreign Investment Services Co., 12 Nam Ky Khoi Nghia Street, District 1, Tel. 8293616.
Department of Labour, 159 Pasteur Street, District 3, Tel. 8291302.
People's Committee, 86 Le Thanh Ton Street, District 1, Tel. 8291054.

Department of Foreign Economic Relations, 1 Nam Ky Khoi Nghia Street, Tel. 8298116.
Trade Department, 45–7 Ben Chuong Duong, Tel. 8299876.

FOREIGN BANKS

Hanoi

ANZ Bank, 14 Le Thai To Street, Tel. 8258190, Fax. 8258188/9.
Bank of America, 27 Ly Thuong Kiet Street, Tel. 8249316, Fax. 8249322.
Barclays Grooup, Room H22, 33A Pham Ngu Lao Street, Tel. 8250907, Fax. 8250789.
Citibank 51 Ly Thai To, Tel. 251950, Fax. 243960.
Credit Lyonnais, 10 Trang Thi Street, Tel. 8258101, Fax. 8260080.
Hong Kong and Shanghai Corp., Suite 502, 5th Floor, 8 Tran Hung Dao Street, Tel.
    8269994, Fax. 8269941.
Indovina Bank, 88 Hai Ba Trung, Tel. 8265516, Fax. 8266320.
Standard Chartered, 1st Floor, 27 Ly Thai To, Tel. 8258970, Fax. 825880.
VID Public Bank, 194 Tran Quang Khai Street, Tel. 8268307, Fax. 8266965.
Vietcombank, 47–9 Le Thai To Street, Tel. 8265501, Fax. 8269067.
Banque Francais du Commerce Exterieur, 26 Nguyen Huy Tu Street, Tel. 8259813, Fax.
    8265874.

Ho Chi Minh City

ANZ Bank, 11 Me Linh Square, Tel. 8299319, Fax.8299316.
Banque Francais du Commerce Exterieur, 11 Me Linh Square, Tel. 8222830, Fax.
    8229126.
Bank National de Paris, 2Fl.1 Ton Duc Thang, District 1, Tel. 8299504, Fax. 8299486.
Citibank, 7th Floor, 8 Nguyen Hue, Tel. 242118, Fax. 242267.
Credit Lyonnais, 17 Ton Duc Thang, Tel. 8299226, Fax. 8296456.
Firstvina Bank, 3–5 Ho Tung Mau, Tel. 8291566, Fax. 8296465.
Hong Kong & Shanghai Corp., 75 Pham Hong Tai, District 1, Tel. 8292288, Fax.
    8230530.
Indovina Bank, 36 Ton That Dam, District 1, Tel. 8224995, Fax. 8230131.
Standard Chartered, 3rd Floor, 203 Dong Koi, Tel. 8288383, Fax. 8298426.
Thai Military Bank, 11 Ben Chuong Duong, District 1, Tel. 8222218, Fax. 8230045.
VID Public Bank, 15A Ben Chuong Dong, Tel. 8223583, Fax. 8223612.
Vietcombank, 29 Chuong Duong, District 1, Tel. 8297245, Fax. 8257228.

ACCOUNTANTS

Price Waterhouse, 88 Nguyen Du Street, District 1, Ho Chi Minh City, Tel. 8230796, Fax.
    8251947; 38A Trieu Viet Vung Street, Hanoi, 8228985/6, Fax. 8228992.
Coopers & Lybrand, 142 Nguyen Thi Minh Khai Street, District 3, Ho Chi Minh City, Tel.
    8292389, Fax.8292392; Unit #02, 3rd Floor, International Centre, 17 Ngo Quiyen
    Street, Hanoi, Tel. 8251215, Fax. 8251737.
KPMG Peat Marwick, 64 Pham Ngoc Thach, District 1, Ho Chi Minh City, Tel. 8200159,
    Fax. 8200158; 2A Nguyen Dinh Chieu, Hanoi, Tel. 8228128, Fax. 8226355.

Bibliography

BOOKS

Anh, V.T. *Development in Vietnam. Policy Reforms and Economic Growth.* 1993, Singapore, Institute of Southeast Asian Studies.

Citibank. *Vietnam: An Investment Guide.* 1995, Hanoi, Citibank N.A.

Field, M. *The Prevailing Wind: Witness in Indochina.* 1965, London, Methuen.

Lonely Planet. *Vietnam: A Travel Survival Kit.*

McAlister, J.T. *Vietnam. The Origins of Revolution.* 1969, New York, Alfred A. Knopf.

Ministry of Planning and Investment. *Guidelines for Foreign Direct Investments in Vietnam.* 1995, Hanoi.*

Ministry of Planning and Investment. *Guidebook for Foreign Investors in Vietnam,* 1995, Hanoi.*

Ngoc Huu, *Sketches for a Portrait of Vietnamese Culture.* 1995, Hanoi, The Gioi Publishers.

Than, M and Tan, J. (eds.) *Vietnam's Dilemmas and Options.* 1993, Singapore, Institute of Southeast Asian Studies.

Vien, N.K. *Contemporary Vietnam,* 1981, Hanoi, Red River Foreign Language Publishing House.

West, R. *Sketches from Vietnam.* 1968, London, Jonathan Cape.

OTHER SOURCES

Bangkok Post.
Business Day, Bangkok.
Economist.
Financial Times.
London Times.
South China Morning Post Weekly, Hong Kong
Straits Times, Singapore.
The Investors Bulletin, Investment Transaction Centre, Hanoi.
The Saigon Times Daily.
Vietnam Business Journal.
Vietnam Commerce & Industry.
Vietnam Economic Times.
Vietnam Investment Review.
Vietnam Law & Legal Forum.
Vietnam Times.
Vietnam Today.

*These two books were actually published by the State Committee for Cooperation and Investment, one of the predecessors of the MPI.

Index

258